# PSYCHE AND TEXT

SUNY Series in Psychoanalysis and Culture
Henry Sussman, Editor

# PSYCHE AND TEXT

## The Sublime and the Grandiose in Literature, Psychopathology, and Culture

Henry Sussman

State University
of New York
Press

Published by
State University of New York Press, Albany

Production by Susan Geraghty
Marketing by Lynne Lekakis

Printed in the United States of America

For information, address State University of New York Press,
State University Plaza, Albany, N.Y., 12246

Library of Congress Cataloging-in-Publication Data

Sussman, Henry.
    Psyche and text : the sublime and the grandiose in literature,
psychopathology, and culture / Henry Sussman.
        p.    cm. — (SUNY series in psychoanalysis and culture)
    Includes bibliographical references and index.
    ISBN 0-7914-1569-4. — ISBN 0-7914-1570-8 (pbk.)
    1. Psychoanalysis and literature.   2. Sublime, The, in literature.
3. Characters and characteristics in literature.   4. Subjectivity in
literature.   5. Critical theory.   6. Object relations
(Psychoanalysis) in literature.   I. Title.   II. Series.
    PN56.P92S87     1993                                    92-30927
    801'.92—dc20                                            CIP

10   9   8   7   6   5   4   3   2   1

# CONTENTS

# ACKNOWLEDGMENTS

This book would not exist were it not for a sabbatical leave in Spring, 1990, provided by the State University of New York at Buffalo and a residential fellowship at the Camargo Foundation, Cassis, France. The work conditions that resulted in a first draft of this book were sustained and enhanced by the Foundation's Director, Michael Pretina, and its Associate Director, Jean-François Gagneux. M. Gagneux passed away during the Winter of 1990–1991. As I prepare this manuscript for publication, I think of his uncommon generosity and support for intellectual deliberation.

Permission to cite passages from Heinz Kohut's *The Analysis of the Self* and to reproduce diagrams both in my text and as part of the cover design has been kindly granted by the International Universities Press of Madison, Connecticut. I am most grateful to Dean Kerry Grant of the Faculty of Arts and Letters at the State University of New York at Buffalo for his general support of Comparative Literature and for establishing a research support fund whose function is in part to defray the at times considerable costs of obtaining publishers' rights and permissions. This book has benefited from Dean Grant's recently established fund.

When I think of the intellectual mentors whose presentations, articles, books, and classes make the following experiment possible, I realize that I have assembled quite a cast of characters. One including, on the literary side, Jacques Derrida, Hillis Miller, Richard Macksey, Earl Wasserman, Allen Grossman, Neil Hertz, Eugenio Donato, Carol Jacobs, Gerald Hamm, and Werner Hamacher; in terms of my psychological education, Joseph Masling, Joan Copjec, Michael Raulin, Murray Levine, William Hirst, Shlomo Breznitz, J. David Smith, Joan Lucariello, Emily Ets-Hoken, Stuart Keill, and Cathleen A. Carter. Professor Richard Feldstein of Rhode Island College has played a particularly constructive role as a collaborator in earlier psychoanalytical projects and as someone who has demonstrated to me the interplay among Lacanian theory, Cultural Studies, and the field of object relations. Ms. Gloria Aniebo of the Department of Psychology, State University of New York at Buffalo, furnished invaluable assistance with the preparation and editing of the manuscript. Jan Plug provided outstanding assistance in copy editing and preparation of the index.

Carola Sautter, my editor at SUNY Press, has been exemplary in her support, responsiveness, and advocacy of psychoanalytical thinking and scholarship. Her suggestion that SUNY Press might well serve as home to an integrative series on Psychoanalysis and Culture, which this book has the honor of initiating, came after the present study's formal editorial review. In initiating such a series, Ms. Sautter has demonstrated creativity, generosity, and unusual sensitivity to the actual conditions under which writing is produced at the current historical moment. The overall support that SUNY Press has provided has been excellent. Much of the innovative thinking that makes a Psychoanalysis and Culture series possible was furnished by Professor Feldstein.

Regardless of budgetary conditions, the support furnished by the Lockwood Library at the State University of New York at Buffalo is invariably unstinting and forthright.

# PREFACE

## THE POET, THE CRITIC, AND THE JOURNALIST

The subtle influence of the moment impinges upon us as we write. This is what both the scribe of fantastic fictions and the austere critic have in common with the journalist: regardless of how implausible the story or rigorous the interpretation, there is a level at which the moment of writing, with its socioeconomic and psychopolitical dimensions, itself conditioned by its predecessors, enters the process and outcome of the composition itself. It is in this sense that there is a journalistic dimension to every fiction and every critical treatise.

I place before you a little volume on the question of character in literary and psychological terms. It takes off slowly, softly, and generally, so there is little in the way of substance a Preface can add. Before I present some of the influences and supports that facilitated the whole process, I would like to speculate, briefly, on how I arrived here, in private and journalistic terms.

It has been about fourteen years since I produced my first critical book. Three or four overriding files or interests have organized my work since then: (1) literary experimentation as it became a distinctive fingerprint of twentieth-century culture and art; (2) the philosophical and systematic backgrounds against which this elaboration was set. This included both nineteenth and twentieth-century Continental and British philosophy, and it was made accessible and generative to the intellectual public through the extraordinary efforts of a group of writers including Jacques Derrida, Roland Barthes, Michel Foucault, Claude Lévi-Strauss, Jean-François Lyotard, Paul de Man, J. Hillis Miller, Jean-Luc Nancy, and Philippe Lacoue-Labarthe; (3) the tradition of psychoanalysis both as an artifact of Romantico-Modernism and as an inquiry holding much in common with the literature of the period; and

(4) the sociopolitical dimensions and implications of the literature we read and teach and the criticism we write.

This is a justification as to why I would write a book on character combining current literatures in critical theory, modernism and postmodernism, psychoanalysis, and clinical psychology. But it does not fully account for my particular performance. In pressing a bit further in this effort, I confront the tangible influence of the moment that is the ultimate subject of journalism.

I have dwelt, intellectually and pedagogically, for some time with a bevy of twentieth-century characters whose resemblance to what we normally associate with human subjectivity is tenuous at best. It was Kafka, my first extended literary interest, who summoned some of the most memorable of these creatures to the page: Odradek, Gregor Samsa, the subterranean rodent of "The Burrow." I read the texts in which these characters and their relatives played most carefully at the same time that, in the literatures of psychoanalysis and critical theory, I explored the conditions of subjectivity as they evolved over the course of the nineteenth and twentieth centuries. The discovery that in the literatures of psychoanalysis and psychology an attempt had become necessary to postulate and explore a model of subjectivity no longer within the confines of the Freudian model, itself a construction of the "Hegelian aftermath," became an extremely important occasion for testing what I had previously studied.

Walter Benjamin and the Frankfurt School have perhaps best and with most persistence explored the ideological, phenomenological, and psychological implications of modernity. It is within the purview of their type of analysis that some of the developments I have myself witnessed during the stretch of the twentieth century to which I have been privy become most meaningful: the obfuscation of the mechanisms and sources of technology, economics, and communications; the critical state of the stable family; in American society, the polarization between classes with and without access to economic life; the disappearance of forms and levels of production and manufacture; the burgeoning of urban areas at the expense of rural ones; the orientation of political decisions toward transnational organizations and interests rather than local ones; and substance abuse and other debilitating behaviors resulting from the poverty of experience and the paucity of social settings.

These factors, at work at least since the dawn of the urbanization that Benjamin chronicled, have exerted a profound impact on those bizarre literary surrogates that have fascinated me for so many years. They are also at play in the very possibilities for subjectivity and interpersonal relationships, in and beyond academia, during our current historical situation. One of the thinkers of greatest moment for the present extended hypothesis, Otto Kernberg, has described this psychosocial condition as the "subjective experience of emptiness." To locate a set of literary works, literary critics, and psychological thinkers that address the "subjective experience of emptiness" both clinically and esthetically has been a most intriguing occasion for me. Those who read these pages will have to determine if I have risen to it. I do not presume that psychological and psychoanalytical writers have approached the subjective, phenomenological, and esthetic conditions sketched out above in exactly the same way as critics and literary scholars. But the fact alone that a set of texts could be assembled that would allow for a dual-sided exploration of the pressing epistemological limits of our moment, its technology, and its sociopolitical stresses, is itself suggestive and hopefully generative.

A second parallelism that has energized and hopefully justified this project is the importance of language both to contemporary critical theory and the literature of cognitive psychology. These two academic subdisciplines are asking many of the same questions, but in very different ways. Where critical theory and literary studies in general eschew the empirical dimension of experimental research, empirical studies have accepted the multiplicity and limited validity of conceptual models and the ephemerality of (often hard-won) results in a way that the "humanities" can only admire and emulate. Current cognitive scientists are asking, in a rigorous and painstaking way, how much perception and cognition take place in some irreducibly imagistic form, or whether in fact all mental experience is not somehow reducible to propositional networks. "Propositionalists" are operating with assumptions not at all alien to Heidegger or Derrida; they believe, for example, that all mental codes are ultimately verbal. Yet the methods of research and means of proof are so different on both sides of the watershed separating the "humanities" from the "social sciences" that any set of issues, for example, the question of character, capable of coordinating the literatures is an occasion for curiosity and ardent exploration.

The following project poses a question far more than it volunteers any definitive solution. What has literature had to say regarding the evolution of subjectivity since the Romantic age, and how has this been paralleled in the disciplines of psychology and psychoanalysis? What is the connection between the productive margin from which deliberate writing emanates, the margin that differentiates the literate sensibility from the ideological doxa prevailing in any society, and the borderline that has become an important fingerprint and possibility for subjectivity in our world? The question of character and literary surrogates has offered a location at which the psychological and esthetic ways of dealing with the world could enter some telling discourse with each other.

My task has been made far easier by a number of scholarly contributions that have either cleared a path for this project or confirmed it in its quite openly pronounced direction. I think above all of the groundbreaking work Neil Hertz has done in linking the "internal" transaction of psychoanalysis to the vertiguous experience of the sublime that enabled the Romantics to initiate the current modernity in an experience of ironic, sometimes terrifying awe. Through his notion of surrogation, Hertz has also made it possible to discuss subjective and characterological representation in literature in a responsible way. J. Brooks Bouson, in *The Empathic Reader,* has published the first full length account of which I am aware of the connection between psychoanalytical empathy, as it has evolved in the tradition that began with Sullivan, and enlightened critical reading. Hans-Rudolf Schärer, in his *Narzissmus und Utopismus,* has made the by no means obvious connection between Kohut's version of psychoanalysis and Musil's *The Man without Qualities.* And along with Hertz, Geoffrey Hartman has explored psychoanalysis in a way that is, on one flank, rhetorically and theoretically rigorous, while on another, open to clinical issues and concerns.

My own bearing, in this investigation, has been as much that of a journalist, an intellectual *flâneur,* as of an academician. It is important to keep in mind that deliberate scholarship and journalistic chronicle do not cancel each other out. Cognitive scientists would say that the primary difference between them is one of "grain," the finitude of their articulation. It is possible for journalists, in the relatively large grain of their writing, to violate distinctions that have been worked out in the academy on a small scale. Academicians, on the other hand, in "the narcissism of small differences," the overvaluation of the small variations necessary for precision, are perfectly capable of leaving the "big picture," the wider context for their discourse, behind. It is not necessarily productive for critics and scholars to block out too effectively the public and private motives for their interventions. It is this connectedness, as articulated in different ways by Kernberg and Kohut, for which I am militating in my acknowledgment of my own journalistic bent.

My own written secretions have followed the series of artifacts, intellectual schools, and socioeconomic conditions that I have confronted with some engagement. I close this Preface with the sense that disciplinary and institutional affiliations are counterproductive in innoculating us from the conditions under which we write. These conditions may engender blindness, stupefaction, or even breathtaking lucidity. I embrace the journalistic dimension of my work in an effort to incorporate the epistemological conditions that limit me in my own writing.

My investigation has unearthed nothing more decisive than a web: one that would presume, in some way, to combine Freud, Sullivan, Kernberg, Kohut, Lacan, Derrida, *Antigone*, *Othello*, *The Man without Qualities*, *The Silence of the Lambs*—and a variety of related artifacts, models, and productions—in a meditation on the possibilities of subjectivity and its representation. Cybernetically viewed, a linguistic artifact may be conceptualized as a network of pathways eventuating at a matrix of possibilities. My profoundest hope for this project as I complete it is that it opens a number of pathways, even if far short of the quantity comprising the simplest microprocessor.

# CHAPTER 1

# *Introduction*

The question of character has surely been with us as long as writing. Now as always its discussion is already impeded at the outset with an impasse likely never to be resolved: what we ask of our characters in literature we would never dream of imposing on ourselves. The indirections and promiscuities selected, even demanded by our language in order for its most characteristic qualities to be realized would be, acted out, disastrous to the social and psychological fabrics of our lives. We ask, and have always asked, our literary characters as figments of language to dramatize, intensify, subject themselves to, triumph over, or be destroyed by the very qualities and actions that empower the dynamics of language. Literary characters may be construed as embodying the very power and success of language as a signifying system and a medium of transference.

Can we not situate the scene of tragedy as a genre at the place where the very success of language as a medium of distribution and absenting verges upon the disaster that these qualities wreak within the domain of sociopsychological experience? The moment at which the fate of the characters achieves the certainty of a machine that will not be impeded is exactly the moment at which the script reaches a certain level of cohesion, self-reference, and efficiency as a system of meaning. The power and exemplarity of the tragic character is precisely tantamount to his or her centrality to a language system and to achieving conditions of absolute impossibility within the existential sphere.

Literary characters are, then, culture's Sirens, who both teach us the music of music and the poetry of poetry, and who sing us toward the verge of moral and psychological dissolution. They characterize an impasse; an impasse is their essence and nature. It is not we who, after all the time in which characters have been crystallized and forgotten, are about to resolve this tension, this ambivalence, about language and about ourselves.

1

# CHAPTER 2

# On Character

If the Marxian contour of Walter Benjamin's discourse would bemoan in modernity the loss of the aura that is the signature of a worker's personal, individualized rapport to his or her own work—by a similar logic the psychologists of the self advise us that having a personality in the contemporary world, as a last vestige of individuation or personal difference, has become a liability.[1] This is an historical argument, limited by the progressions and developments that tend to be read from history, but this dimension of the observation does not categorically disqualify its veracity.

The entities of psychopathology have evolved from psychoses and neuroses themselves endowed with distinct characteristics into personality disorders whose telling quality seem to be their inconsistency, a bewildering range of densities of purpose, cohesion, and rectitude. The Freudian psychotic and neurotic hail from an age of stifling interpersonal initmacy. Moral strictures, behavioral structures, and well-meaning relatives, are hanging all over them. The classical diseases of psychoanalysis are conditions of repression.[2] Once contact between aware (self-conscious?) consciousness and the incompatible instinct or its ideational form has been made (or reestablished), the reason for the symptomatic condition has been destroyed. The Freudian psychopathology is of the shooting gallery or pinball variety. Once conscious mind has met its target, the disease dies, in a blaze of flashing lights and sirens.[3]

If instincts are not the driving force of existence and if the submerged facet of mental life known as the unconscious is not its ultimate truth—interrogations almost coterminous with the history of psycholanalysis—then it is not necessary to presuppose that every individual owns? carries? manifests? contains? a discrete personality. The literary sensibility bristles at the thought that an envelope or a container as closed and recognizable as a personality could represent a consciousness. Lemuel Gulliver and Alice's

3

changing dimensions, Poe and Dostoyevsky's doubles, the chasm between Lord Jim and Nostromo's mythical and existential attributes and Gregor Samsa's carapace are very different manifestations of literature's discomfort with cohesive subjectivities or personifications. In the wake of the New Criticism and under the influence of the Sciences Humaines, a certain literary audience was already primed for the radical questioning of subjectivity undertaken by Derrida, one organizing in no schematic way earlier interrogations in this direction by Nietzsche and Heidegger among others.[4] The idea that a single identity, character, or set of traits could encompass or exhaust a consciousness, as rich, say and as questioning as Joyce's Stephen Dedalus and Leopold Bloom, is intolerable—but then so too is the posturing that must be maintained constantly in order to resist this type of reduction. Post-Freudian psychology, in response to the alienation, depersonalization, and unstable lifestyles chronicled by Benjamin, Marcuse, and other members of the Frankfurt school, had to reformulate its object, the subject, and to address it, at least in part, morally. The child of the contemporary age suffers from the inconsistency and instabilities of personality disorders; dwells in a borderline domain where polarized values reverse themselves unpredictably and in which the good is compartmentalized and sundered from its others.

As psychology revises its Freudian heritage in redefining its subjects of inquiry, aspirations, and methods—critical thought, in resisting its own obligations to ideation, systematicity, and thematism, assumes the attitudes and postures relegated by psychology to the borderline. Astonishingly, there is a high correlation between critical-theoretical descriptions of undermining conceptual fixity and certain characteristics of personality disorders as described by psychoanalysts and clinical psychologists. In both cases, there is a pronounced indifference to substance or affect and a disqualification of structure. The primary *difference* between these two characterizations of attitudes that have become endemic to the late-capitalist, postmodern, and post-structuralist words, is that the psychological model is relentlessly normative, disparaging the revised subject it has in part created;[5] while the literary-critical version is utopian in the tradition of Romantic revolutionism. Both agree, however, on the indifference, self-absorption (whether textual or narcissistic), and decentering that have taken over contemporary mental and intellectual life.

This agreement in sense but not in reference is the taking off point for the present study of character. How could attitudes so essential to intellectual integrity and vitality be so pathogenic within the sociopsychological sphere? The issue in which this aporia most significantly dwells is, for this writer, the question of character. Over the same period during which fiction records the transformation of literary characters whose preeminent quality seems to be their *unmistakeability* such as Sterne's Uncle Toby and Dickens's Mr. Wemmick, into noncharacters of the sort summoned by Beckett, psychology has introduced an axis of personality disorders into its prevalent diagnostic instrument alongside its battery of classical and well-formed psychoses and neuroses, suggesting that vacuums, the vacancies of character are every bit as telling as its path or substance.

Can we indulge ourselves in the luxury of a historical argument positing a more or less parallel development of clear character into vapid or noncharacter in literature and "classical" conditions into the vagueness of personality disorders in psychology? This kind of thesis is tempting because it is demonstrable and in part true. After all, however much classical authors such as Balzac, Goncharov, and Conrad[6] playfully or angrily resist the inherited tradition of characterization, these authors have not yet arrived at the ruminating nonentities that predominate in the late Kafka, Beckett, and Calvino.[7] *Something* happens over time, both in the possibilities open for literary surrogation[8] and in the scenarios of psychological activity and interpretation rehearsed with such uncanny comprehensiveness by Freud.

But does this *something* that takes place in the domains of literary possibility and psychological understanding carry the force of historical destiny? Not if the Platonic dialogues already interpolate allegories of gods and idealized qualities into their drama, as if argument and conflict were insufficient in themselves; not if Oblomov's optimal state is his *withdrawal* from the activity that would define his social status and his character; not if Conrad, anticipating Proust, sunders the significant surrogates populating his highly conventional novels and characterization between their self-serving myths and their self-revealing actions.

As the *mark* of something, stamped on its face, the idea of character is stifling, arbitrary, intolerable. Yet it is also the location where literary pretension and psychological wisdom fold upon themselves and reverse positions, where the existential implications of esthetic play, transgression, and excess are registered, and where compensation is forthcoming for the excessive clarity in which the first generations of psychoanalytic deliberation sketched the field's categories.

# CHAPTER 3

# *Characterization in* Antigone *and* Othello

The question of character has never been a simple matter.

The term, deriving from the Greek Χαρακτήρ, has always been intimately linked to the ambiguities and artificiality of writing. In ancient Greek, the OED informs us, the word signified an "instrument for marking or graving; impress; stamp, distinctive mark, distinctive nature, f. Χαράττ-ειν, to make sharp, cut furrows in, engrave." In its verbal form, character means "1. *trans.* To engrave imprint; to inscribe, write. 2. To represent, symbolize, portray. 3. To describe the qualities of; to delineate, describe." Both in terms of our wider discussion of characterology and the formulations of Musil's *The Man without Qualities,* one of the derivatives of the substantive form will be particularly significant: "16. A person regarded in the abstract as the possessor of specified qualities; a personage, a personality."

In its etymological grounding, character has never been party to a simple, transparent, or naturalistic transposition of subjectivity, or its traits, from the domain of human interaction to that of cultivated codes, whether narrative, poetic, or dramatic in nature. Character, in other words, has always been alien to mimesis, even when deployed in works or media with certain other mimetic strata.

One might hope to locate "pure" characters, ones that represent subjectivity in its most accurate, compelling form—like so many other things—at the "roots" of Western culture, in the literary productions of the Greeks. This hypothetical quest is, however, tragically flawed.

The Greek tragedians engaged in a particularly artificial, one might say characteristic, deployment of their characters. The characters in Sophokles's *Antigone* do not "represent" subjects or sub-

7

jectivity nearly as much as they dramatize and fill *functions*: of a conceptual, representational, and metacritical nature.

Even the most perfunctory review of literary history suggests that the main problem posed by the question of character is that the term is spread out on so many levels. We ask literary characters to do and be many things at the same time. By virtue of several factors, most notoriously the linear progression and arrangement, respectively, of speech and writing, characters are capable of slipping in and out of their defining roles and functions easily, imperceptibly. They base their effectiveness and power on a certain Freudian overdetermination.

Literary characters are protean (Kernberg might say "polymorphous") in the dimensions of their representation, the rhetorical orders on which their play impacts, and in the factors that impinge upon their effectiveness. One and the same character (say Sophokles's Antigone, Shakespeare's Iago, or Joyce's Bloom) can perform a surrogate's actions; think a surrogate's thoughts; dramatize a surrogate's sexual behavior and desire; engage in a surrogate's (societal, familial, legal, commercial, marital) functions; dramatize a surrogate's idealogical points of view (e.g., loyalty to, opposition to the State); and meet the internal representational requirements of the medium (e.g., serve as sources of information regarding off-stage action and the past).

We may think of this striking multiplicity of roles that we have assigned to our literary characters as a splaying out on different rhetorical levels:

1. the *allegorical,* in which characters dramatize functions of rhetoric and textuality (as when Iago, whatever his moral values may be, serves as the dramatic *copula* of *Othello*, the internalized playwright, whose personal schemes nonetheless furnish the tragedy with whatever motive and coherence it possesses).

2. the representational, in which characters maintain the recognizability of their psychosocial traits and in which their actions carry discernible "meanings," at least within the framework of the artifact.

3. the metacritical, in which actions and traits furnish a critical commentary on the surrogates who perform them, the situa-

tions into which they have been inserted, or the text in which they have been inscribed.

4. the functional, exemplified by Creon's role in the *Antigone,* in which characters act out a function not bound to the metaphysics of identity or subjectivity; and,

5. the *nonrepresentational,* in which characters play a role whose functionality is not immediately or directly evident in the dramatic or representational design.

Literary characters are not only elusive in the manner of their representation, and in the unavoidable conflict of interest between their multiple functions and rhetorical levels; a broad range of historical and local factors impacts on any particular instance of characterization. Every significant, "weight-bearing" character arises, is born at a node of intersection joining multiple parameters: A moment of history, at which a particular model of subjectivity and a certain characterological typology prevails; an epoch of archeology, in Michel Foucault's terms, in which knowledge is determined by certain epistemological constraints.[1] There is a greater expectation of subjective rationality, for example, during Foucault's "Classical Age" (the seventeenth and eighteenth centuries in Europe) than during the epochs that preceded and succeeded it (the Renaissance and Romantico-Modernism). The work of Louis Marin, other scholars of the French Classical period, and American New Historicists has been particularly astute in tracing out the implications of political ideology for dramatic characterization.[2] Needless to say, there is an important sense in which a work's psychological context, the prevailing theory of the mind and how it works, impacts profoundly upon the composition and action of characters; as do factors of demographics, technology, and the media of political control and domination.

No literary construct is subject to profounder antimonies than the notion of character. One way of expressing the fundamental paradox that sunders all efforts at characterization is as follows: literary surrogation demands some psychological element in order to make recognition possible; yet the psychological element of characterization always falls under the constraints of textual principles and functions. This summarizes the excruciating but never dispensible interplay between Psyche and Text. Fiction and drama *work* only because on some levels they are analogous to human thought processes. The analogy is itself a major theoretical assertion and problem. At the same time, characters, as is evident even in the earliest mimetic artifacts, are subject to the linguistic schemata of the text. In the text they behave as signfiers, copulas, shifters, synonyms, antonyms, and even homonyms—but not as psychological simulacra. This is a fundamental antimony, making the psychological study of literature a "natural" topos, but also severely restricting the assumptions regarding the mutual transference between Psyche and Text that can be posited.

> The dead individual, by having liberated his *being* from his *action* or his negative unity, is an empty singular, merely a passive being-for-another, at the mercy of every lower irrational individuality and the forces of abstract material elements, all of which are more powerful than himself: the former on account of the life they possess, the latter on account of their negative nature. The Family keeps away from the dead this dishonouring of him by unconscious appetites and abstract entities, and puts its own action in their place, and weds the blood-relation to the bosom of the earth, to the elemental imperishable individuality. The Family thereby makes him a member of a community which prevails over and holds under control the forces of particular material elements and the lower forms of life, which sought to unloose themselves against him and destroy him.
>
> This last duty thus constitutes the perfect *divine* law, or the positive *ethical* action towards the individual. (Hegel, "The Ethical Order" in *The Phenomenology of Spirit*)[3]

With bemused hindsight, we can enjoy the manner in which Hegel fits his subject matter to his conceptual argument; how, under the guise of a certain innocence, he introduces certain material knowing full well how it fits into his strategy. Conceptually, in the above lines, Hegel is setting up a situation in which the Family enforces certain Laws independently of the State. The rites surrounding the protection and burial of human corpses are under the care and responsibility of the Family. It would be possible for a situation to arise in which the State, through the stipulations of its Civil or Martial codes, would oppose the Familial fulfillment of its Natural Law, of a pedigree even higher than State decree.

Such a situation would of course be interesting to Hegel because it would illustrate the dialectic of the individual and the universal within the conceptual domain of an opposition between two legal codes, pertaining to the Family and the State, each compelling and not easily abridged or emended. And this situation is precisely the one that Sophokles elaborates in *Antigone*. At the same time that Hegel innocently sets the "stage" in his own philosophical argument for *Antigone's* dramatic situation and conflict, he is also appropriating the venerable play as an anticipation and justification for his own thinking.

The irony here is that while *we* might think that Hegel is putting a fast one over on Sophokles, whose expectations for his play were somehow different, in fact Sophokles has articulated the interests and concerns of his text in ways that anticipate Hegel. Instead of wondering at Hegel's ingenious use for this classical workhorse, the attentive reader of the tragedy asks Hegel, "so what? What else is new?"

Sophokles is perfectly aware that the characters in this drama are performing functions, in relation to the State, the Family, philosophical concepts, and the text's representational and semantic networks, far more than they are expressing or reproducing any truths or essences of themselves as surrogate human subjects. At the very outset of the tradition of Western drama, the playwright knows that characters are simulacra of functions rather than of subjects and subjectives. Within the play's thoroughly artificial situation and setting, Creon, "the Great One," will enforce the Civil Law uniformly and unfeelingly. Antigone, whose name means "contrary to proper genetics," will oppose a baser form of universality, the civil code, with a higher emanation, the Law of Nature.[4]

From the outset of the drama, Antigone demonstrates awareness that her position is against the Law; or rather, that she opposes Law such as it is with an even higher principle.

Antigone:
But Polynices' corpse, cast out in shame,
No man in Thebes—so hath he made proclaim—

> Shall give him tomb nor tear; there he shall lie
> Unwept, unburied, lovely to the eye
> Of staring vultures, hungry for their prey.
> Such law on thee doth our good Creon lay,
> Aye, and on me, on me! . . .
>   Whoso disobeys ere night
> Shall die the death . . . by stones without the wall.
> So runs his order. (A, 18)[5]

Already in her third speech in the play, Antigone is aware that her conflict is not with a man but with the law he enforces. She has already become a legal critic, opposing contrived strictures with Nature, or rather with the image of an uncouth Nature ravaging the remains of a human being. She stresses the moral imperative upon a civilized community to protect its members after the fact of death. Her rectitude explains in part the ready-madeness of this artifact for a schema such as Hegel's, in which culture surpasses the givens of physical and natural universes by means of the self-generated concepts and inventions of human consciousness. The medium through which Sophokles schematizes this set of issues and conflicts is the drama; and the talent for which the tragedian is revered still today consists partly in drawing out the personal implications of the choices underscored by the dramatic situation.

> Antigone:
>   My brother's burial I
>   Will make, and if for making it I die
>   'Tis well. I shall but sleep with one I love,
>   One who loves me, and my offence shall prove
>   Blessed. I need the love of Them Below
>   More than of earthly rulers, for, I know,
>   There I shall lie for ever. (A, 20)

From the outset of the tragedy, preempting any dramatic surprises, Antigone is aware that in having chosen to advance Nature's interest (that is to say, her interpretation of a set of natural constraints more compelling than the civil code), she has opted for certain interruptions in the otherwise naturalized course of her life: she has chosen the grave instead of the marriage bed with Haemon; the denizens of Hades instead of the human paradise of Eros. Creon, by the same token, through a pig-headedness for which Tiresias will chide him (1015–30), has thus set himself on a collision course with the wedding plans in his own family and with the interests of virtually every other character.

> Creon:
>> Elders of Thebes, the vessel of our state,
>> Though shaken in wild storms, by God's good fate
>> Stands upright once again , and from you all
>> The folk of Thebes are here by separate call
>> Summoned to council. For I know full well
>> The reverence constant and unshakeable
>> Ye bore toward Laius' crown; and later, when
>> King Oedipus first saved the land and then
>> Perished, ye still upheld in fealty true,
>> The children of your kings. But since they too,
>> By twofold visitation in one day,
>> Each stained with brother's blood, have passed away,
>> Slaying and slain, it falleth now to me
>> To hold their powers and seat of royalty
>> By right of nearest kindred to the throne. (*A, 25*)

It is appropriate for Creon to invoke the barely-terminated tragedy of Oedipus. Creon is in effect shifting a Lacanian tragedy of the belatedness of knowledge and the elusiveness of the Other to its sociopolitical, communal setting. *Oedipus the King* transpires at the levels of personal desire and the psychological law. *Antigone* is not without its implications in terms of desire and familial consummation; but it takes place more at the levels of communal mores and statutory law. When Hegel designates "Woman kind—the everlasting irony [in the life] of the community,"[6] he is in part reflecting on the fact that in the Sophoklean division of labor, the task of embodying tragic conflict with society has been entrusted to a woman; while post-Freudian discourse evaluates Oedipus's burden primarily in psychosexual terms. Antigone the character bears the onus of a tresspass of the communal law that can only be articulated publically as madness. She demonstrates the genesis of psychological categories out of the situation of an individual's conflict with society, or more precisely, out of the situation of an individual's posing a seemingly higher or more natural code against an established one. It is for this reason that Lacan would devote his seminar on Ethics to a study of *Antigone*.[7]

Antigone:
>I deemed it not the voice of Zeus that spake
>That herald's word, not yet did justice, she
>Whose throne is beyond death, give such decree
>To hold among mankind, I did not rate
>Thy proclamations for a thing so great
>As by their human strength to have overtrod
>The unwritten and undying laws of God:
>Not of to-day nor yesterday, the same
>Throughout all time they live; and whence they came
>None knoweth. How should I through any fear
>Of proud men dare to break them and then bear
>God's judgement?—As for death, some day no doubt
>I am sure to die. I knew that even without
>Thy laws; and if I now shall die before
>My time, that grace shall I be thankful for. . . .
>I tell thee, 'tis a trifling hurt or none
>To die thus. Had I left my mother's son
>Dead and unburied in that field to rot,
>That would have hurt me. These things hurt me not,
>Ye call this madness? Madness let it be,
>For surely 'tis a madman judgeth me. (A, 38)

The lines immediately above harbor the crux of two tragedies, Antigone's and the play's. In terms of the wider dramatic structure as we have seen, Antigone poses a higher code and necessity against a better-established, more utilitarian modus operandi. In exposing the hypocrisy underlying an established civil order (not very long-lived at that), she polarizes public attitudes toward that social system. We commend her for this polarization; this rhetorical as well as political act becomes the basis for her moral superiority and the reason why Western culture elaborates her position and names and remembers her. Passages such as the one immediately above demonstrate her internal conflict. On the basis of, or in collusion with an opposition experienced "internally," Antigone polarizes the social milieu around her. A long tradition of moral and dramatic values commends her for this social activism, which has as its origin and end polarity. Yet as we shall see below, for psychoanalytical theorists such as Kernberg and Kohut, bipolarity carries with it its own set of sociopsychological problems. This becomes the crux of *our* problem: how can attitudes and ways of dealing with the world that seem so right from moral and esthetic points of view be so difficult to live with? For this brings us to Antigone's personal tragedy: the choice of death, on the basis of principle, over Eros and pleasure in general. As the above passage indicates, Antigone is well-aware of her deeds' consequences.

> Creon:
>> Know this. It is the proudest hearts that fall
>> The deepest, and the hardest iron withal,
>> Stark-tempered in the furnace, that ye see
>> Most broken and shivered. . . .
>> This girl showed insolence before, to brave
>> The ordained law; and now, new insolence,
>> She mocks us and hath pride in her offence.
>> No man were I, more of a man were she,
>> Should she now triumph and be gone scot-free.
>> Be she my sister's child, be she by birth
>> Closest of all who worship at my hearth,
>> I vow that shall not save her, nay, nor yet
>> Her sister from full payment of their debt.
>> I know she is guilty too. She had a share
>> In plotting for this burial. . . . Call her there!
>> (*A*, 38–39)

Creon, in his analysis of the situation, reduces Antigone's position to a problem of attitude. Not unlike certain major elements in the tradition of psychoanalysis, he ponders moral rectitude less intensely than he considers a certain psychological amiability. Antigone is too uppity. Creon articulates and enforces the tragic tradition of *hubris*. Antigone's pretense makes her culpable in spite of her royal lineage and connections. It also commits the sin of placing her on an equal plane with a man; of presuming to dissolve gender differences. While Antigone gives us heed because she questions the foundations of the civil order, we pause over Creon as well, because certain aspects of his position, although obviously much more vulnerable than Antigone's, are not without their following in the history of psychological throught.

The tragedy would not work were Antigone's loss not tangible. Our title character is not above invoking metaphysical traditions of her own when the time comes for her to pay.

Antigone:

> O grave, O bridal chamber; O thou deep
> Eternal prison house, wherein I keep
> Tryst with my people, the great multitude
> Below to Queen Persephone subdued.
> To them I take my way, of all the last
> And lowliest, ere my term of life is past. . . .
> For thee too
> Dead Polynices, the same office I
> Sought to fulfil; and 'tis for this I die.
> What law of heaven have I offended? Yet
> How dare I look to Heaven and hope to get
> Pity or help from there? I have sought to ensure
> Our purity, and lo, I am found impure!
> If these things be God's pleasure, before long
> By pain I shall be taught mine was the wrong.
> (A, 60–61)

Antigone has chosen death over Haemon (or it is the hymen)? She has indeed achieved a parity with men by arranging for a dehumanized man's burial, and by receiving the same desserts meted out to the man she honors.[8] The bond of the family has proven stronger than the the civil tie of marriage, just as the value of Nature has outshown the obligations of civil and martial codes. *Antigone* persists as a tragedy because its terms have remained with us, at least within the parameters of Western values. The Law is indeed obtuse, insensitive, overgeneral. Its opposition and resistance indeed *shine,* with undiminished intellectual brilliance and esthetic beauty. Yet as the psychologists of character have pointed out, living with such ideality is not easy. Sophokles' tragedy makes the point explicitly: Antigone ends up marrying a corpse and a rock. The enunciator of the ideal position in this play is a woman who has not broken with her family. As persistent as this tragedy is, the roles that define its characters are expressed in terms of functions and philosophical positions. The play of characters is less a play of literary human surrogates than of sociopolitical, sexual, and representational functions.

Only about half the text of *Antigone* represents the issues concerning the characters we have discussed so far: Antigone's resolve to bury Polynices, her brother; Creon's law-and-order position and its implications for Haemon, his son. The rest of the text, it must be said, is even less devoted to characterization and more to functional and representational elements: the chorus, Tiresias, the guard, a messenger. With the possible exception of Tiresias, these elements have nothing at stake in the drama: yet it could not take place without them. They comprise the drama's internal communicative system, its way of communicating with itself. From a dramaturgical point of view, the conflict of *Antigone* is not overly complex. One purpose of the chorus is to function as a spacer during scene-changes, such as between Antigone and Ismene's introduction and Creon's first declaration (*A*, 22–24, 61); yet of course the chorus is also free to introduce themes and metacritical comments unavailable within the "drama proper." Both here and in *Oedipus the King*, Tiresias functions as the village gossip who alone makes public the terrible truth that would otherwise remain at the level of immanent, personal knowledge. It is Tiresias who transforms first Oedipus's, then Creon's insights, or personal knowledge of themselves, into items on the public docket of concern. He declares, for example, in *Antigone* that Creon's "stubborn, cleaving fast to [his] own mood" (11.1025–26) "hast brought this sickness on the land (1.1015).

The chorus functions as the play's internal narrative or introjective voice. This voice is not *of* the action but constitutes a metacritical commentary upon it. Its importance is not in terms of the plot or character development but epistemologically, in terms of levels of knowledge. It corresponds to the internal language of subjectivity that, according to a tradition of object-relations thought extending from Klein to Kohut and Kernberg,[9] is absorbed at a very early age. The language of introjections, in Derridean terms, is a "language before language," demonstrating the futility of assigning any absolute origin in language development.[10] Children are born into language as much as they are into a biological environment. If the linguistic inheritance of infancy is highly emotionally charged or contradictory, so runs the theory of object-relations, negative, disruptive introjections will persist throughout life and interfere with the process of intellectual and emotional integration. One way of approaching lyric poetry, aphorisms, and chorus-speeches in Greek and other tragedies is as introjections embodied in literary form.

Object-relations theorists are not necessarily aware of the full linguistic and theoretical radicality of the conceptual field they have developed. Otto Kernberg is still trying to ground the notion of the introjection in the domain of instincts when he defines it as

> the earliest, most primitive level in the organization of internal-
> ization processes. It is the reproduction and fixation of an inter-
> action with the environment by means of an organized cluster of
> memory traces implying at least three components: (i) the image
> of an object, (ii) the image of the self in interaction with that ob-
> ject, (iii) the affective coloring of both the object-image and the
> self-image under the influence of the drive representative present
> at the time of the interaction. (*EPOOR, 360*)[11]

By making the introjection form under the aegis of the "drive representative," Kernberg is merely adding affect (mostly rage or desire)
to a fundamentally imagistic, linguistic process. Of primary importance for the psychoanalytical deployment of object-relations theory in diagnosis and treatment is the impact of such a highly
charged language of images, memories, and affects upon such
defensive strategies as polarization and splitting. Parental neglect
and a highly emotionally charged infantile setting endow the language of introjection with what Kernberg terms valences with
important consequences for later life. The emotional messages (or
double messages) contained in the introjective "language before
language" predicate in important ways the subject's self-
conception, conception of others, and her milieu for interpersonal
interactions.

> The affective colouring of the introjection is an essential aspect
> of it and represents the *active valence* of the introjection, which
> determines the fusion and organization of introjections of similar
> valences. Thus, introjections taking place under the *positive val-
> ence* of libidinal instinctual gratification, as in loving mother-
> child contact, tend to fuse and become organized in which has
> been called somewhat loosely but pregnantly 'the good internal
> object.' Introjections taking place under the *negative valence* of
> aggressive drive derivatives tend to fuse with similar negative
> valence introjections and become organized in the 'bad internal
> objects.' (*EPOOR, 360–61*)

Kernberg is assigning the internal mental "voice" of implicit
and long-lasting values an important place in the structure and sub-

stance of the psyche. But introjective language is not limited to living subjects. The interventions of the chorus in tragdies such as *Antigone* are introjective in nature. They are metacritical of autonomous characters and emanate from a location "internal" to the dramatic machinery. In the play under discussion, the chorus's interventions recapitulate the historical background on an epic level (11.100–161); they speculate on the metaphysical conditions and prospects of Man (11.316–72); and, they note the futility of repression (11.944–86). The Sophoklean chorus is an internal interpreter within the drama.

Greek tragedy transpired in an open-air theatre. Means for depicting offstage and past actions were few. One of the reasons that so much responsibility is entrusted to the chorus in *Antigone* and to such characters as Tiresias, the Guard, and the Messenger is that they open up and account for the dimensions of the past, the future, and elsewhere. Yet there is another reason as well for the investment of so many dramatic resources outside the story involving the main characters and their conflicts. The stage-machinery of the drama is to some extent an analogon to the structure and workings of the mind. As we have seen, *Antigone* is a drama of polarization replete with an introjective voice of valuation and meta-commentary. Characters, in this scenario, are as much *about* subjectivity—its structure, workings, and modes of representation—as a reflection *of* subjectivity. If Sophokles writes somewhere near the *origin* of theatrical notation, he places the endeavor on an extremely high theoretical plane, from the very start.

*The Tragedy of Othello* is not without its own similar paradoxes. We are reaching toward a notion of tragedy as a genre juxtaposing the existential and linguistic natures of its characters in an impossible, but for this reason esthetically interesting way. In Shakespeare's drama, the character who creates the action, moves it along, and is directly responsible for anything interesting that transpires throughout its duration is the villain, not the hero. We ourselves must live with this consequence: that the only surrogate of interest, whose interest is the only justification for the other, more just characters, is Iago, whose characteristics, were we to extrapolate them to the psychological sphere, would qualify him as a severe borderline personality. Shakespeare warns us against such persons and their characteristics in real life; at the same time that he demonstrates their indispensability to literary, esthetic, and theoretical interest. The term I am applying to Iago's virtue here is "interest," a term that occurred to Romantic theorists including Kant, Schlegel, and Kierkegaard, in explaining the particular power of esthetics and the sublime.[12] There will be more in chapter 4 on Romantic accounts of the collusion between psychological grandiosity, exemplified by Othello's blindness and Iago's plotting, and the sublime. The difference between my own concern with characters such as Iago and the Romantics' is that they would locate the compelling qualities of sublimity and interest in the external world. The Romantics were not without a psychology of their own, but its trials and tribulations (as in associationism) were always rooted in externality. The psychoanalytical tradition linking Freud to Sullivan, Kohut, and Kernberg, on the other hand, the one I am exploring, treats the sublime as a psychological rather than an "objective" perceptual or esthetic quality. While the Romantics have situated sublimity or grandiosity in scientific experimentation or at the North Pole (Mary Wollenstonecraft Shelley), in the Alps (Wordsworth; P.B. Shelley), or in the splendor of St. Peter's, Rome (Kant),[13] the tradition of object-relations theory and other psychoanalytical approaches have opted to explore the psychological implications of grandiose representations, such as the system of rays through which Daniel Paul Schreber, in a famous Freudian meditation, communicated with God.[14] Surely the Romantics demonstrated some psychological understanding of the grandiosity that makes Iago both so horrifying and interesting: Coleridge's Ancient Mariner, who learns to revere the creations of Nature, is a case in point. The Romantics were also obsessed with Shakespeare.[15] But although they tend to situate grandiosity, and its sublime qualities, in the external world, where it becomes an objective problem, the tradition of psychoanalysis tends to locate it in the mind, where it becomes an individual phenomenon and responsibility.

Perhaps the most exasperating irony pervading the *Antigone* is that the sociopolitical system that could be so odious in denying Polynices a decent burial is close to the programmatic nature of the drama. Creon functions in the drama as a lawgiver. He takes it upon himself to interpret and instrument the Law. He enjoins Antigone to "be brief and clear" (1.445), a direction anticipating one Karl Rossman will give the Stoker in the inaugural chapter of Kafka's *Amerika*.[16] As Aristotle knew, the resolution of tragedies also adheres to a specific set of laws. The figure of a lawgiver such as Creon in a play mediates between two Laws: the statute at stake on the thematic level, in the drama proper, and the law of dramatic development and dénouement, a code subsuming the play in its entirety.

We condemn Creon, yet it is Creon's quality as a lawgiver that extends itself in the dramatic playing out of the dénouement. This ambivalence is closely akin to the one we feel toward Iago. This latter character is the source of dissimulation, evil, and plotting in the play; yet he is its most dramatic character and agent. We depend upon him dramatically—as a manufacturer and executor of devices—precisely for the same reason we question his morals. From an esthetic point of view, he is precisely what makes the play possible, yet existentially, when our defenses are in good order, we avoid his *semblambles* in the "real world" vigorously. Late in *Othello,* the title character steps into Creon's shoes, wishing, belatedly, that he could resolve a woman with the Law:

> *He kisses her.*
> O balmy breath that dost almost persuade
> Justice to break her sword! One more! one more!
> (V.ii.16–17)[17]

On a wider level this classical drama creates a dissociation between existential and esthetic levels in which what is deplorable on the conscious, existential plane is at the very crux of dramatic design. Classical drama then becomes a script fundamentally ambivalent about its scriptoral nature.

It may not be entirely accidental that *DSM III-R,* the current diagnostic handbook in clinical psychology and psychiatry structures each diagnosis according to two axes:[18] one corresponding to the disorder as it would be evaluated in terms of the "classical" psychoses and neuroses as they have been elaborated in the tradition beginning with Kraepelin and Bleuler, passing through Freud, and refined by such clinicians as Fenichel and Arieti. Yet each instance of a disorder is also qualified, in this edition of the *Manual,* by its definition in terms of the psychopathology of personality disorders, those elusive occasions and subjects of object-relations theory. The very format of the *Manual* suggests that as we now understand psychopathology, a psychological disorder is to be understood as the *intersection* between a dysfunction in the order of instinct and desire and a disfiguration or structural deformity in the self.

Literature is filled with striking dramatizations of the interactions between surrogates with classical psychoses and neuroses[19] and those with personality disorders. This interaction is one of the most colorful that literature has to depict. It is invariably intense and memorable. This is one way in which we can characterize the relationship between Othello and Iago. The title character corresponds to a neurotic subject saddled with a good deal of social and sexual insecurity whose possessiveness often results in obsessive and escalating ruminations. Iago, the borderline "personality" in the duo exploits this preexisting instability through a fatal mastery in anaclitic manipulativeness and inconsistency.

Yet *Othello* is far from the single title in what we might term "the literature of the fatal dialectic between the neuroses and the personality disorders," the subject of a *livre à venir* I would much like to write or see written. One immediately thinks, in this regard, of Madame Verdurin's predatory control over the unfortunate Swann in Proust's monumental *Recherche* on her way to a dominant position in Parisian society; of the reserved Marlowe's fascination and contempt for the narcissistic Lord Jim; of Karl Rossmann's imprisonment at the hands of the slovenly diva, Brunelda, in *Amerika.*[21] Within this scenario, the neurotic, whose instincts occasion conflict and inefficiency, serves as dupe and prey to surrogates of far more questionable character, structuration, and consistency. In the example from Proust, the patient and ascendant Madame Verdurin dominates, torments, and excludes Swann, a generous and sympathetic character. His psychosomatic eczema, a classical conversion symptom, is merely the superficial mark of his neurotic disposition. His chief vulnerability consists in his obsessive possessiveness toward his beloved Odette, a characteristic he shares with the "Marcel" of *The Prisoner* and the ill-fated Othello. Swann's defeat at Madame Verdurin's hands may well constitute

Proust's paradigmatic allegory of societal interaction. The struggles of Ulrich, by the same token, hero of the encyclopedic Musil novel we will discuss in detail below, his conflicts with his quasi-friends and superficial associates may also be situated within the framework of this psychosocial drama.

In Shakespeare's rendition of the eternal, possibly cosmic drama in which the psychopath destroys the neurotic, often with the neurotic's full collusion, Othello, an excessively simple and direct surrogate with strategically placed blindspots, loses his marital equanimity, his professional effectiveness, and ultimately his life to an Iago characterized by a weak identity, a persistent bubbling jealousy and rage, callous manipulative relationships, and a joy in destructive polarization for its own sake. Many of the traits making Iago most memorable have configured themselves around the personality disorder axis of the diagnostic manual. There is much to say about the character Othello and his role in the tragedy, but since Joel Fineman, in his "The Sound of O in *Othello: The Real of the Tragedy of Desire*" has said this so definitively and eloquently,[21] I will focus in my discussion on the surrogate, or character, or non-character, of Iago, who, in a crucial early passage, defines himself as follows:

*Iago:*

> For, sir,
> Were I the Moor, I would not be Iago.
> In following him, I follow but myself.
> Heaven is my judge, not I for love and duty,
> But seeming so, for my particular end;
> For when my outward action doth demonstrate
> The native act and figure of my heart
> In complement extern, 'tis not long after
> But I will wear my heart upon my sleeve
> For daws to peck at. I am not what I am.

*Rodrigo:*

> What a full fortune does the thick-lips owe
> If he can carry't thus!

*Iago:*

> Call up her father:
> Rouse him, make after him, poison his delight,
> Proclaim him in the streets, incense her kinsmen,
> And though he in a fertile climate dwell,
> Plague him with flies; though that his joy be joy
> Yet throw such changes as vexation on't
> As it may lose some color. (1.1.71–78)

Iago explicitly states here that had he his druthers, he would be someone else, namely Othello. He has so projected his own sense of power and well-being upon Othello that there is an intertwining of "identities" and interest. His fixation upon Othello's actions and vicissitudes is an obsessive one. Yet he holds a multifaceted contempt for his target, whose agonistic elements include racism and envy. The means by which he will precipitate Othello's downfall at this juncture in the drama will be a campaign of negative public relations directed toward Brabantio, Desdemona's father. As the above speech indicates, the campaign proceeds through a reversal or negation of Othello's public value. It is crucial to note that at this point of the play Othello is a powerful figure; an outsider to the society in which he resides, Othello has made it "on his own." Iago's will to power asserts itself in the reversal of fortunes of a surrogate, who, although internally flawed, possesses his own distinctive character.

Iago seems incapable of accomplishing very much on his own. Not only his relations of hatred are characterized by a surface of anaclitic closeness resting atop a substratum of contempt. There is even an aspect of inter"subjective" intertwining between Iago and Rodrigo, his primary cohort in plotting. Yet as the outcome reveals, their alliance rests only on the shakiest grounds of self-aggrandizement.

Iago manages to sublimate a good portion of his aggression through his designs and manipulation of public opinion regarding his target. Yet his bubbling rage seldom disappears far beneath the surface. In the following passage, the major element of Iago's plot is "hatched." A dissimulator through and through, Iago will disguise a political and economic plot in the form of a domestic travesty, a contrived melodrama of adultery. Crucial to Iago's description of his scheme is a rhetoric of monstrosity parading as a legitimate and healthy birth:

*Iago:*

I hate the Moor;
And it is thought abroad that 'twixt my sheets
'Has done my office. . . .
Let me see now:
To get his place, and to plume up my will
In double knavery—How, how? Let's see.
After some time, to abuse Othello's ear
That he is too familiar with his wife.
He hath a person and smooth dispose
To be suspected—framed to make women false.
The Moor is of a free and open nature
That thinks men honest that but seem to be so,
And will as tenderly be led by the nose
As asses are.
I have't! It is engend'red! Hell and night
Must bring this monstrous birth to the world's light.
(1.3.404–22)

Iago knows full well that the Moor's Achilles's heel is his "free and open nature," which we may think of as an inability to curb his appetite for direct and frank collaboration. Iago will instigate a situation in which Othello publically abdicates the position of esteem in which he is held through acts of domestic stupidity and blindness. Iago has at his disposal his own brand of psychology, one not dedicated to altruistic uses. Within its code, a "free and open nature" contains a hint of passivity, a hesitation in the Will to Power, the ability to "be led by the nose." It is on the basis of this flaw that Iago, a demonic psychologist, will hatch his plot, which according to his own description will dawn upon the world as a deformed monstrosity.

For all his personal repulsiveness, however, there is the "touch of an artist" about Iago. His scheming and use of others are nothing if not artful. We cannot assess his character without according full credit to the fact that in terms of artistry and dramatic direction, Iago is Shakespeare's "man in the text," the character coming closest to an internal playwright and director in the play. In this paradox we observe the fullest culmination of the dialectic in which what is good for the text may not be good for one's health, in which the most memorable creatures of the text may not make the most salutary helpmates.

*Iago:*

> And what's he then that says I play the villain,
> When this advice is free I give and honest,
> Probal to thinking. . . .
> How am I then a villain
> To counsel Cassio to this parallel course,
> Directly to his good? Divinity of hell!
> When devils will the blackest sins put on,
> They do suggest at first with heavenly shows,
> As I do now. For whiles this honest fool
> Plies Desdemona to repair his fortune,
> And she for him pleads strongly to the Moor,
> I'll pour this pestilence into his ear—
> That she repeals him for her body's lust;
> And by how much she strives to do him good,
> She shall undo her credit with the Moor.
> So will I turn virtue into pitch,
> And out of her own goodness make the net
> That shall enmesh them all. (2.3.338–64)

This is as close as we come to a "crisis of conscience" in the artful Iago. Yet even as he rhetorically dimishes the value of the damage he has done, Iago describes his actions in terms that make perfect esthetic and dramatic sense. This is the fundamental ground of paradox in which we inscribe our most memorable and beloved literary characters. This is why literary production transpires under the dual illuminations of rhetoric and psychology. The remainder of this study will be devoted to the interplay between the psychology and esthetics of writing, whose interaction reaches a climax in the construct of character.

# CHAPTER 4

# Grandiosity and the Romantic Sublime

An argument has begun, already, in these pages, and like all arguments, it possesses its own machinal, autonomous qualities. It behooves us to step back from it a moment, as Victor Frankenstein would have been well-advised to do from his own creation, lest this conceptual framework begin to predetermine the meaning of the details falling under its purview.

There is nothing new about the concept of the grandiose to Western thought. Already the "action exciting terror and pity" which, in the Aristotelian *Poetics*,[1] is the imitative base or source of tragedy, possesses a distinctive grandeur. Our discussion thus far has noted that characterization, from the outset of Western drama, includes functional and allegorical as well as representational elements; also, that the representation of subjectivity has, since its origins, struggled with the vacillation between modesty and grandiosity in subjective "self-awareness." My argument, to the degree I comply with the conventions of pedagogically-oriented literary criticism (thus assuring myself of a certain modesty), thus already leads in a certain direction. It underscores a commonality of interest between the psychoanalytical approach known as object-relations theory and subjective issues at the heart of classical drama and ethics. It suggests implicitly as well that Freudian theory, in its fascination with dialectical models and in its urgency to establish itself clinically and socially, may have lost some of its focus in apprehending the influence and workings of the grandiose (even where such constructs as the unconscious and the id clearly are possessed of sublime, grandiose qualities).

I am arguing, then, that the object-relations theory some of whose literary implications will be outlined below, reaffirms, for better and worse, a concern with magnificence and grandiosity, particularly when these attitudes spill over into personal attitudes and behavior that has been virtually coterminous with the tradition of Western thought (and has surely tempered non-Western artifacts). This unease, or disease, of grandiosity surely constitutes a major lietmotif of Western ethics. The order of the esthetic, from Plato through Kant and beyond, hovers on the cusp of this discomfort with the magnificent. Magnificence is both the content and the mode of art and creativity at the same time that it signifies, when translated into attitude and behavior, moral and existential disaster. In terms of the psychohistory compressed into this volume, object-relations theory recuperates and rejoins this moral preoccupation, which became marginal in terms of certain Freudian concepts and concerns.

At the endpoint of my argument (or the period it covers) we will find characters that have all but abdicated any imperatives to surrogation that literature might have once entertained. These are the Kafkan creatures of the text; the Beckettian listless narrators. Surely object-relations theory, with its sensitivity to psychological death and "the subjective experience of emptiness" speaks to such characterization in a particularly compelling way. By the end of this study, we will have encountered Moosbrugger, a psychopathic murderer, whose sudden and volatile shifts between affability and dramatized rage serve as an emblem for the transition away from the petty vices of neurosis and toward a state of consciousness divided from itself in an irrevocable and dangerous way. Characters from the cinema such as Max Cady in both versions of "Cape Fear" (1961 and 1991) and Hannibal Lecter and Jame Gumb in the recent "The Silence of the Lambs," are, in terms of psychopathology, close relatives to Musil's Moosbrugger.

The struggles of Hamlet and the machinations of Iago are symptoms of an age of traumatic tension and redefinition for the Cartesian subject. It is a long way from *Othello* to *Molloy*, and it is surely beyond the scope of this study to furnish a comprehensive history of the freedoms and stumbling blocks encountered by the Subject during this period. Among a plethora of attempts to formulate and dramatize the dynamics of subjectivity and representation along the course of the Cartesian subject, surely the systematic and literary productions of German Idealism and Romanticism warrant special notice. Such endeavors as Kant's *Critiques*, Hegel's

*Phenomenology of Spirit,* Goethe's *Faust,* and Wordsworth's *Prelude* become arenas in which post-Cartesian subjectivity confronts its competence and enfranchisement in the absence of certain predetermined constraints; in the absence of the a priori limits furnished by divine authority, absolute political power, and their institutions. The scope of the Kantian and Hegelian systems can hardly be taken for its modesty. A certain mood of moral crisis and natural upheaval, housed in settings of vast extension, colors a wide range of artifacts from the Romantic era.

I would argue that the sublime, both as a philosophical term and as the keyword at the basis of an esthetic, constitutes a cultural attempt at negotiating grandiosity, even if it is not entirely clear where the sublime is situated, whether in nature, the empirical world, or the individual mind. Romantic efforts to formulate the motives and effects of sublimity in turn constituted a significant cultural legacy underlying Freud's own speculations.

Kant was explicit about his being a psychologist, and he was right. For Kant, the sublime is a borderline phenomenon. The sublime, or the phenomena belonging to its order, constitutes a quantitative outrage. It begs description. It is bigger and more monumental than it has any right to be, at least from the perspectives of proportion and propriety. Yet it is there. Its unmediated Being-there anticipates the Lacanian Real. It must be acknowledged.

Creative genius is the mode through which human beings apprehend, represent, and transfer the Transcendental to each other. Genius is a unique human faculty that finds itself at home with the sublime. Genius both apprehends the sublime and is itself possessed of sublime dimensions, pretensions, and deviance. If I am right in asserting that a major part of Kant's cultural legacy consisted in his formulating a secular art religion founded on Enlightenment principles, within this religion geniuses play the role of nature's appointed priests. While the sublime is the dimensionality that allows esthetics to break away from the measurements specified by the social contract of art, the sublime relies on genius as the mode of its apprehension and transmission. If as a result of Enlightenment and Romantic political theory, every (male) citizen of advanced Western societies could dream of becoming President, as a result of the Kantian esthetics, every artistically inclined citizen could aspire toward the status of genius. (This is a paradox that Kant opened up but did not resolve: Nature chooses its geniuses, but in such a discreet way that free individuals can still hope to assist Nature in his/her choice.)

The role of genius, and pretensions toward genius, in the psychology of the grandiose can hardly be overestimated. In a passage I will have occasion to cite again, Kernberg writes:

> Their histories reveal that each patient possessed some inherent quality which could have objectively aroused the admiration or envy of others. For example, unusual physical attractiveness or some special talent became a refuge against the basic feelings of being unloved and of being the objects of revengeful hatred. Sometimes it was rather the cold hostile mother's narcissistic use of the child which made him "special," set him off on the road in the search for compensatory admiration and greatness.[2]

While the thrust of Kant's endeavor is to articulate a secular metaphysics in which philosophy can continue its formal tradition in accordance with Enlightenment ideals, Kant contributed significantly to the conceptual baggage according to which human value, talent, and striving in the Modern (post-Cartesian) world are articulated. He achieved this in his formulations on genius, the modality in which the sublime is apprehended.

The sublime has been anticipated in its position within the Kantian system by the beautiful. In the *Critique of Judgment*, the Analytic of the Beautiful precedes that of the Sublime and endows it with its form and its deductive thrust. The sublime borrows much from the beautiful, particularly its paradoxical nature and its status as the exception that becomes systematically exemplary; yet the purpose of the sublime is to violate, in the sense of rape, the beautiful as well.

The overall *telos* of the Kantian philosophy is to serve as the conceptual instrument by means of which Judeo-Christian ontotheology is supplanted with a secular religion. Whereas Judeo-Christianity is deity-centered and presupposes the predetermination of human faculties and choices, the Kantian religion is secular in nature and implemented by purely intellectual (i.e., logical) processes. It is in keeping with an anthropocentric ideology that all transcendental or supersensible entities and processes for which the Kantian speculations make provisions must be *deducible,* on the basis of human brain-power. The Christian critique of Judaism was directed from the outset at the absoluteness of the Judaic deity, its nonnegotiable nature, the absence of mediations between this deity and its human subjects. The Christian deity is to a large extent *defined* by its mediatorial qualities and actions. This deity is at once human and divine, corporeal and incorporeal, mutable and transcendental. In the Kantian speculative systems, the comprehensively mediatorial quality of the Christian deity is displaced to a series of shifters that mediate between the empirical and the transcendental, but in a strictly secular way. In different ways, the Kantian Beautiful, Sublime, and Genius occupy an analogous position and effect similar linkages. They can all be deployed in an intellectual deduction whose result is to reveal to human consciousness more about the transcendental than it can know purely from the empirical phenomena themselves.

The entire Kantian speculation marshalls itself toward a deduction; its trajectory is deductive. The thrust of the First Critique, *The Critique of Pure Reason*, is toward a logically structured and sanctioned deduction of the transcendental from within the framework of the empirical. *The Critique of Judgment* substantiates the transcendental deduction by deploying beauty, the sublime, and genius all as instances of something awesome and miraculous that humans can experience without recourse to theological entities or superstitions. The Kantian speculations affirm their allegiance to Enlightenment ideals through their repudiation of nondeducible, that is, nonintellectual constructs of knowledge. What is so irresistible about art and esthetics to Kant is that their appreciation establishes a transcendental deduction, and apprehension of meta-human faculties and institutions, at the level of what we would today call "hard wiring" (or what Noam Chomsky, extrapolating Descartes's linguistic implications, would call "deep structures").[3] If art displays something of a world beyond, then normal human beings are fitted out to apprehend it. Ostensibly eschewing organized religion, Kantian speculation is irreducibly Christian in its bias, for indeed, the categories upon which Kant calls in deducing the transcendental on the basis of human capacities and in an empirical mode share the very categories that Christ claimed in his dethroning of Judaism. Art, awe (the affective correlative of the sublime), and genius all inhere to human beings. With the exception of genius, they are common experiences: we regularly see things that are beautiful or awesome. The Kantian system shares a fundamental Christian placement of transcendental power in human capabilities.

The intensity of Kantian thought in no small measure derives from Kant's patience, by his willingness to work out with precision the conditions arising from the placement of the human intellect between the world of experience and vast "designs"—of life, of matter, of theory—that it will never fully master. Indeed, despite the systematic scope of his enterprise, its encompassing parameters are only two: that the source of authority be ultimately human or internal to human capacities; and, that the transcendental overview of the interrelation between different levels of knowledge and intellectual functions be systematic and philosophically rigorous. Philosophical rigor epitomizes or becomes the ultimate model for an authority with transcendental scope emanating from a human source.

Romantic artworks including Mary Wollstonecraft Shelley's *Frankenstein* and Percy Bysshe Shelley's "Mont Blanc," "The Cloud," and "Prometheus Unbound," incorporate the double-sided ambivalence that pervades the Kantian enterprise. On the one hand, authority must be immanent; it must proceed from inside, yet it must be possessed of transcendental detachment. This is why "pure *a priori* principles are indispensable for the possibility of experience. . . . For whence would experience derive its certainty, if all the rules, according to which it proceeds, were always themselves empirical, and therefore contingent? Such rules could hardly be regarded as first principles. At present, however, we may be content to have established the fact that our faculty of knowledge does have a pure employment" (*CPR,* 45).[4] Building upon the Cartesian tradition of duality, Kant argues the necessity for pure, that is, detached and rigorous, intellectual principles in a culture aware of its own history and potential. Yet the scene and locus for intellection are, ultimately, human ones. In order to account for a "pure" intellectual order nonetheless human in nature, Kant, opposing himself to Hume, allows "that the understanding might itself, perhaps, through these (*a priori*) concepts, be the author of the experience in which its objects are found" (*CPR,* 127). As opposed to more rigid and naive dualists, Kant provides for a dialectical process in which the "operating system" of understanding, its capacity for a priori synthetic (or integrative) thinking to some extent authors the experiences that are then evaluated critically through intellectual structures and processes.

At the same time that intellectual authority must to some extent be immanent, "hard wired," always already there, pure reason entirely severed from experience is uncanny, potentially monstrous. Our fear of such an unmoored reason, operating according to its own principles or interests, is akin to the deep-seated suspicion toward writing (as opposed to voice) that Jacques Derrida traces over the span of classical Western culture.[5]

> Space has three dimensions; between two points there can be only one straight line, etc. Although these principles, and the representation of the object with which science occupies itself, are generated in the mind completely *a priori,* they would mean nothing, were we not always able to present their meaning in appearances, that is, in empirical objects. We therefore demand that a bare concept be *made sensible,* that is, an object corresponding to it be presented in intuition. Otherwise the concept would, as we say, be without *sense,* that is, without meaning. (CPR, 259–60)

At the same time that intellection needs to rise above the "mire and complexity" of an empirical, experiential world, excessive intellectual detachment or purity presents us with a complementary threat: of concepts finding no representation. Kant articulates this facet of a certain crisis for Romantic subjectivity as a certain emptiness, a void in meaning, a subjective experience of emptiness. At the level of narrative or dramatic representation, this situation of a purely ideational play devoid of substance surely contains inbuilt potentials for a monstrosity for which Romantic literature provided in its gothic tales and horror stories.

In his philosophical investigations, Kant provides for a spatially-centered, carefully perspectival account of the interaction between materials and thoughts, between intellectual faculties and levels of knowledge. Hegel, on the other hand, furnishes an evolutionary, historical account of the transition between the same steps. Kant's systematic operation is situated in the fissures between levels of knowledge defining irony, although he seldom takes advantage of irony's rhetorical potentials. Because of the persistence with which Kant accounts for the transition from sense-experience to intellection, he is often explicitly struggling with language, with the manner in which thought *represents* its own data or findings to itself. While Hegel, following Kant, readily admits that language is an all-pervasive medium of reflection, throughout the main part of his writings (and the exceptions here are of decisive importance), the issue of language and its theoretical implications is subordinated to the needs of schematic, progressive and multi-perspectival elaboration. Ironically, then, while Hegel was more crucial a background for the experiments of modernism, Kant was more consistently forthright in confronting the necessities and distortions of representation.[6] Kant devotes considerable resources to a determination of the major stations, levels, and "characters" in the complex interplay between experience and intellection, materiality and spirituality, and the esthetic and its disfigured extension, the sublime. Hegel's speculative machinery is the dynamic, narrationally-constituted counter-text to the Kantian perspectivism.

Kant evolves a tropology or rhetoric of the relationship between experience and intellection. He inscribes the relations comprising his rhetorical softwear on the "Table of Categories" to his *Critique of Pure Reason*: Inherence, Subsistence; Causality Dependence; Reciprocity (*CPR,* 113). In any given phase or level of knowledge, one shifter subsumes or generalizes the manifold: judgments do this as do the Categories of Understanding. There is always a shifter to bridge the invisible and the visible, the a priori to the a posteriori.

Kant's voyage out to the horizon of knowledge, or toward the North Pole, involves a repetition of structures—Kant calls them schemata—in increasingly wider arenas of generality. But when he reaches the Transcendental, quantity merges into quality. A qualitative transformation occurs. The Transcendental casts an eerie and bewildering illumination back on a reasonably self-evolved world. In this twilight, directions are lost; mistakes are made; people, collectively or individually, suffer serious delusions. This is the illumination that infiltrates the sublime canvases of Friedrich, Turner, and Courbet. The dénouement of the *Critique of Pure Reason* is as important as the hopeful leave-taking. The terminus of this grand project is beset by uncertainty. What Kant calls the "transcendental illusion" is the preparatory ground for the disruption in scale he will later characterize as the sublime.

Over a long tradition of philosophical speculation, systematic thought has undergone a number of tests or challenges linking the most unlikely philosophers to each other. There is a certain Joyous Seduction of the Rational by the Irrational outlined by Plato in *Phaedrus*;[7] joined by Kant in his accounts of the beautiful, the awesome, and the sublime as instances of the *necessity* of a constitutive role in understanding by irrational concepts and processes; dramatized by Wittgenstein in his resignation to metaphors and other poetic devices in a philosophical discourse striving for logical rigor at every turn.[8] Surely the Extension toward the Indeterminate out of the Determinate by Means of Mediation is a tradition achieving a certain apex in Kant and Hegel but joined by empiricists as well. A third such transepochal philosophical tradition to apply here, even when it shakes the very foundations of systematic thought, is the Dissolution of Oppositions Previously Necessary for the System. One thinks here of the formal, substantial emptiness of the Hegelian Absolute Knowing; of the heuristic ladder that Wittgenstein retracts at the end of his *Tractatus Logico-Philosophicus.*[9]

By virtue of a certain inbuilt, almost "natural" momentum, systematic philosophy strives for the farthest application and extension of its principles. Thus in Kant's Third Critique, the *Critique of Judgment*, philosophy would account for phenomena or abberations of the type *most inimical* to orderly, rational thought. At the same time, precisely by virtue of this practical application of conceptual procedures to the irrational, systematic thought, at certain moments among which I would include Kant's, peers over into its disintegration or death, contemplates its own suicide, its foundering on what it cannot assimilate. In the will to extend, to perpetuate through application, there is a fascination with systematic death, the death of systems. Where death becomes impractical, systematic thought describes the unassimilable as a stomach sickness, a vomiting (*CJ*, 126–27, 154–55),[10] in the same sense in which *Moby Dick,* in its myth of a comprehensive cetology, incorporates ambergris.[11]

In the case of Kant's *Critique of Judgment*, the beautiful, an esthetic category, is already situated in a no man's or no woman's land with respect to pure reason. And the sublime, a quantitative extension of the beautiful, exists all the more so at an extreme: one at which it is possible for philosophy to transform itself into something unprecedented and monstrous even while having made conceptual, philosophical provision for its deviance. It is questionable whether Hegel, even with the vertigo of Absolute Knowing, has made so much allowance for systematic foundering as has Kant in the notion of the sublime.

Beauty is an intermediary category, a way-station *between* pure reason and the sublime. Measured, proportional, seductive in its own right, beauty is a stepping-stone toward the monstrosity that both violates the system and enables it to work. Kant's widest pronouncements on beauty assume the form of inevitable paradoxes or antinomies reminiscent of how the glimmerings of the Transcendental filter through to an understanding engulfed in experience: in the form of antinomies, the paralogisms and antinomies of Pure Reason. According to the Third Antimony of Pure Reason, for example, a causality beyond the "laws of nature" is necessary to explain "the appearances of the world. . . . To explain these appearances it is necessary to assume another causality, that of freedom" (*CPR,* 409). Within the parameters of the Third Antimony, however, this assertion of free will is immediately opposed by its antithesis, "There is no freedom; everything in the world takes place solely in accordance with laws of nature" (ibid.). Kant refers ultimate questions regarding free will and determination to an antinomial structure; only between the thesis and the antithesis will some synthetic understanding of this impasse arise. Beauty both relies upon and severs its connection to certain megaconcepts, such as freedom (*CJ,* 75, 80–81), necessity (*CJ,* 77), and the law (*CJ,* 73–74). Beauty is utterly paradoxical to its very core; it empties itself. Yet from a systematic point of view, it is only the first step in the direction of the sublime. A preexisting battery of concepts, deriving from the conceptual softwear of philosophy, is available for Kant to deploy in his analysis of beauty. This he does in pairs. The analysis of beauty proceeds according to antinomian conceptual pairs, among them particularity and generality (*CJ,* 46–47); subjectivity and objectivity (*CJ,* 48–49); determination and freedom (*CJ,* 52–54); "purity" and complexity or ornament (*CJ,* 60–62), interiority and exteriority (*CJ,* 65–67); ideality and normality (*CJ,* 68, 72–73); and necessary and unnecessary satisfaction (*CJ,* 73–77). Throughout these discussions, beauty worships its internal laws by violating them; it submits to binary logic only to synthesize, in an interesting way, both poles of whatever oppositions predicate and inform it. This is the context in which Kant can categorize the beautiful according to the following postulates, beautiful, by the way, in themselves. Beauty involves "a conformity to a law without a law" (*CJ,* 78); "All stiff regularity . . . has something in it repugnant to taste. . . . On the other hand, that with which imagination can play in an unstudied and purposive manner is always new to us, and one does not get tired of looking at it" (*CJ,* 80).

Beauty, in its self-negating quality, or more properly, self-emptying gravitation to form at the expense of content, betrays a certain fickleness, ascribed in patriarchal metaphysics to the beautiful woman. The beautiful woman is omitted from virtually every one of Kant's abstract parameters for beauty, yet is figuratively "present" in the *form* of beauty's hovering. Kant admits desire into his speculative system as one of the faculties of the mind or soul (along with knowledge and pleasure/pain; *CJ,* 13, 34). But sexuality, while a pervasive force in his writing, no more evident than in the post-orgasmic relaxation that for Kant succeeds a significant expenditure of energy, is, like beauty, intellectualized to the highest degree.

As tantalizingly ambiguous as the beautiful may be, the sublime comprises an even more disruptive halt or emptying to the philosophical enterprise. Its disruption to continuity, scale, and coherence is irrevocable. We have already begun to discuss its role and placement in several contexts: it *is,* in a sense, the uncanny light reflected back into the empirical world from the radical alterity of the transcendental. It is a possibly self-inflicted form of systematic death; the death a system must undergo before experiencing a certain apotheosis. The sublime opens a disruptive abyss. It is the context for the mock deaths, which, according to John Irwin, abound in nineteenth-century American literature and inscribe its relation to posterity.[12] The rebirth or renaissance that Kant would celebrate on the far side of the abysmal sublime is an account of human intellectual, cultural, and sociopolitical activity both subjectively based and in keeping with the Western tradition of philosophical rigor.

"We call that *sublime* which is *absolutely great*" (*CJ,* 86). The sublime is a dimensionality of quantitative greatness whose existence alone arouses uncertainty and tension and whose apprehension brings with it (post-orgasmic) relief. The sublime *mounts up* in its size and its tensions, like a "hysterical attack" (like the governess's projections in James's "The Turn of the Screw"). In its quantitative dimension, the sublime has a constructed quality about it. This is why Kant's initial examples of it are architectural, the Egyptian pyramids and the dome of St. Peter's in Rome. The sublime builds up, unit by unit, until units of measurement are no longer of any use or hope. "For there is here [St.Peter's] a feeling of the inadequacy of his imagination for presenting the ideas of a whole, wherein the imagination reaches its maximum, and, in striving to surpass it, sinks back into itself, by which, however, a kind of emotional satisfaction is produced" (*CJ*, 91). Sublimity engenders a certain envy on a human, rather than personal scale. The relief of this envy is tantamount to a (figurative, of course) coupling with the source of envy and discomfort.

Constructing, in an architectural sense, the analytic of the sublime directly upon that of beauty, Kant nonetheless goes to considerable effort to distinguish these two modalities. "Therefore, just as the aesthetical judgment in judging the beautiful refers the imagination in its free play to the *understanding,* in order to harmonize it with the *concepts* of the latter in general . . . so too does the same faculty, when judging a thing as sublime, refer itself to the *reason*" (*CJ*, 94). Beauty belongs to the understanding; sublimity to reason. The construction of sublimity poses a threat to reason. Its threat consists as much in this progressive thrust, this elaborated modality, as much as in any objective scale or loss of scale.

> We hence see also that true sublimity must be sought only in the mind of the [subject] judging, not in the natural object the judgment upon which occasions this state. Who would call sublime, e.g., shapeless mountain masses piled in wild disorder upon one another with their pyramids of ice, or the gloomy, raging sea? But the mind feels itself raised in its own judgment if, while contemplating them without any reference to their form, and abandoning itself to the imagination and to the reason—which, although placed in combination with the imagination without any purpose, merely extends it—it yet finds the whole power of the imagination inadequate to its ideas. (*CJ*, 95)

Kant, an asexual thinker if there ever was one, not only depicts the allure of imagination's "extending" itself and reaching a limit, here, he is also calling the shots in the mood and setting of some of the most memorable (Romantic) sublime art to emerge from his philosophy. Percy Bysshe Shelley, for example, couches his descriptions of the flanks of Mont Blanc, one of British Romanticism's most persistent literary scenes of the crime, in terms that could come directly from Kant's philosophical formulations:

> Far, far above, piercing the infinite sky,
> Mont Blanc appears,—still, snowy, and serene—
> Its subject mountains their earthly forms
> Pile around it, ice and rock; broad vales between
> Of frozen floods, unfathomable deeps. . . .
> A desert peopled by the storms alone,
> Save when the eagle brings some hunter's bone,
> And the wolf tracks her there—how hideously
> Its shapes are heaped around! (60–70)

> The glaciers creep
> Like snakes that watch their prey, from their far fountains,
> Slow rolling on; there, many a precipice,
> Frost and Sun in scorn of mortal power
> Have piled: dome, pyramid, and pinnacle,
> A city of death, distinct with many a tower
> And wall impregnable of beaming ice
> Yet not a city, but a flood of ruin
> Is there . . . (100–108)[13]

Astonishingly, the landscape of Mont Blanc could derive from Kant's musings on the sublime! And Mary Wollstonecraft Shelley could situate her own commentary on Romantic genius amid polar ice floes and on the slopes of Mont Blanc. These are the preferred settings in which Victor Frankenstein, scientific genius extraordinaire, and his monstrous (that is, sublime) creation hold their rendezvous. Victor Frankenstein, whether knowingly or not, establishes a plot development followed by a vast swathe of modern horror literature when he pursues the wider trajectory of the Kantian speculations. This literature describes a large cat-and-mouse game in which the investigator (the scientist, the genius) proceeds outward toward the limits of the Kantian empirical world, only to return in terror, in search of shelter (*CJ,* 101–2) when the Transcendental (the monster, e.g., "The Thing") reciprocates in its interest, and returns the pursuit.

So vast and momentous is the sublime that it leaves useless units of measurement in its wake, like the abandoned weaponry that is always inadequate, at least at the start, to contain the monster of horror-literature:

> A tree, [the height of] which we estimate with reference to the height of a man, at all events gives a standard for a mountain; and if this were a mile high, it would serve as unit for the number expressive of the earth's diameter, so that the latter might be made intuitable. The earth's diameter . . . for the known planetary system; this again for the Milky Way; and the immeasurable number of Milky Way systems called nebulae. . . . Now the sublime in the aesthetical judging of an immeasurable whole like this lies, not so much in the greatness of the number [of units], as in the fact that in our progress we arrive at yet greater units. (*CJ,* 95)

The sublime not only surpasses all measurement; it initiates a vertiginous, progressive movement of the removal of scale. It is both pleasurable and frightening to arrive, by progress, "at yet greater units." These reactions anticipate another kind of ambivalance, the one situated by Margaret Mahler in what she calls the "separation-individuation subphase"[14] of childhood personality development, the odd mixture of diffidence and insecurity experienced by the two to three year old child as it first asserts its autonomy from its mothering parent.

In keeping with a distinctive Kantian legislative diplomacy, the sublime assures the humanity of certain powers and freedoms at the same time that it imposes certain severe restrictions in scale. Humanity, within the framework furnished by the sublime, is situated somewhere between humiliation and solicitous patronage:

> Now, in the immensity of nature and in the insufficiency of our faculties to take in a standard proportionate to the aesthetical estimation to the magnitude of its *realm*, we find our own limitation, although at the same time in our rational faculty we find a different, nonsensuous standard, which has that infinity itself under it as a unity, in comparison with which everything in nature is small, and thus in our mind we find a superiority to

nature even in its immensity. . . . Thus humanity in our person remains unhumiliated, though the individual might have to submit to this dominion. In this way nature is not judged to be sublime in our aesthetical judgments in so far as it excites fear, but because it calls up that power in us . . . of regarding as small the things about which we are solicitous . . . and of regarding its might . . . as nevertheless without any dominion over us and our personality to which we must bow where our fundamental propositions, and their assertion or abandonment, are concerned. (*CJ,* 101)

Such is the human condition, according to Kant. The sublime begs representation, "is an object (of nature) *the representation of which determines the mind to think the unattainability of nature regarded as the presentation of ideas"* (*CJ,* 108). Its "stormy motions of the mind" (*CJ,* 114) may be set off by natural (*CJ,* 110) or manmade phenomena, the latter including wars (*CJ,* 100, 102) or religion (*CJ,* 103, 114–15). In its affective range, the sublime encompasses astonishment (*CJ,* 109), enthusiasm (*CJ,* 112), and grief (*CJ,* 113). Through its progressive abandonment of scale and measure, sublimity pushes representation to the very brink or limit of nonrepresentability. The Kantian sublime thus articulates the esthetic ideology underlying the landscapes of Caspar David Friedrich, in which dwarfed human figures furnish a measure of scale as they peer over abysses of far vaster dimensions; at work in the seascapes of Turner, from whose far horizons a bizarre light radiates toward the viewer, illuminating a scene in which, anticipating Proust's composite painter Elstir, air, water, and land merge into each other, abandoning their boundaries, exchanging their habitual gradations of clarity and substantiality.[15] This illumination is the light of human intelligence gazing back from the Transcendental in the deductive schema set out in the *Critique of Pure Reason.* Kant, in his discussion of the sublime describes it "as a clear mirror of water only bounded by the heaven" (*CJ,* 111).

This is the same light that issues from the eyes of Caspar David Friedrich in his self-portraits.[16] To gaze upon these canvasses (or even a reproduction) is to confront the image of genius. Original genius is the lightning rod of sublimity, the inborn capacity by which the magnificence of the universe is transferred to human beings. By means of genius, a certain knowledge that would otherwise be lost is transmitted from the One to the Many, from the individual who is both exceptional and exemplary to his fellow creatures. Genius is itself a natural phenomenon; it is distributed with natural paucity to the human community. The institutions of art are to genius what organized religion is to the fiction of a divinity: a system of dissemination and distribution.

"Genius is the innate mental disposition *(ingenium) through which* nature gives the rule to art" (*CJ*, 150). "Genius is a *talent* for producing that for which no rule can be given; it is not a mere aptitude for what can be learned by a rule" (*CJ*, 150). "Its products must be models, i.e. *exemplary,* and they consequently ought not to spring from imitation" (*CJ*, 150–151). "Genius is entirely opposed to the *spirit of imitation.* Now since learning is nothing but imitation, it follows that the greatest ability and teachableness (capacity) regarded *qua* teachableness cannot avail for genius" (*CJ*, 151). "Again, artistic skill cannot be communicated; it is imparted to every artist immediately by the hand of nature; and so it dies with him, until nature endows another in the same way" (*CJ*, 152). "Now since the originality of the talent constitutes an essential (though not the only) element in the character of genius, shallow heads believe that they cannot better show themselves to be full-blown geniuses than by throwing off the constraints of all rules; they believe, in effect, that one could make a braver show on the back of a wild horse than on the back of a trained animal. Genius can only furnish rich *material* for products of beautiful art; its execution and its *form* require talent cultivated in the schools" (*CJ*, 153). "Thus genius properly consists in the happy relation [between these faculties], which no science can teach and no industry can learn, by which ideas are found for a given concept; and on the other hand, we thus find for these ideas the expression by means of which the subjective state of mind brought about by them . . . can be communicated to others" (*CJ*, 160). "It shows itself, not so much in the accomplishment of the proposed purpose in a presentment of a definite concept, as in the enunciation or expression of aesthetical ideas which contain abundant material for that very design; and consequently it represents the imagination as free from all guidance of rules and yet as purposive" (*CJ*, 161). "Genius is the exemplary originality of the natural gift of a subject in the *free* employment of his cognitive faculties" (*CJ*, 161).

Originality, exemplarity, proportion, freedom, the utility and communication of the otherwise unattainable: these are the terms in which Kant couches his definitions and discussions of genius. Genius constitutes the intersection between transcendental knowledge, human capability, and systematic, legislative thought. Genius bears with it certain distinct responsibilities and obligations; yet it opens up enormous opportunities as well. Its opportunity corresponds to the facet of interest, a pivotal facilitator in the economy of esthetics that also signifies financial accretion.

*Frankenstein* may be interpreted as a tale of Kantian genius gone awry. The genial scientist achieves his aim. Through his unique insight into the nature of things, he creates, or at least recreates human life, thus usurping the function reserved throughout all prior history for divinity. In this respect, he truly is, as the novel's subtitle specifies, "The Modern Prometheus." Yet Victor Frankenstein abdicates the moral, legislative responsibilities that accrue with genius. He rejects his creation; he denies his creation the resources that would provide comfort even for a despised and rejected subspecies. Having journeyed outward toward the limits of knowledge in his scientific quest, symbolized in such settings as the North Pole and in such images as lightning, he engineers a situation in which his creation pursues *him* from the isolation of those very marginal domains. Whether by virtue of his unnatural talents or his childhood wounds (he has been the son of a loving, if aged and absent father), Victor belongs to the narcissistic walking wounded. In a nurturing role, as an artificial father or scientific step-parent, Victor displays crass indifference characteristic of the "schizophrenogenic mother." Mary Wollstonecraft Shelley's novel, *Frankenstein*, arises from the very nexus of Romantic ideology and the esthetics of the sublime, yet it dramatizes a narcissistic predicament whose comprehensive understanding is still very much in development. In its own limited and fragmentary way, the present study dedicates itself to pursuing precisely this transition.

CHAPTER 5

# Object-Relations Theory: Otto Kernberg

The history of psychoanalysis may be regarded as a series of revisions undertaken in order to correct, modify, and supplement (the latter in quantitative and textual terms) the biases operative in the various sub-bodies of Freud's writings. In its exegetical dimension, this dynamics of revision and supplementarity is not different from the endless mutual correction of interpretations that takes place in literary or philosophical criticism. As in the case of Saussure's differential notion of the sign, new approaches and positions arise as much in the lacunae within and between existing ones as because of any "inherent" or "essential" need or value.[1]

Freud's thought is itself highly complex, and passes through an at times nonlinear sequence of stages. For all its internal articulation, however, Freud's intellectual operations are marked by a certain fingerprint that furnishes alternative psychoanalytical approaches with a point of departure. Although Freud's writing is itself fraught with ambivalences, above all between structural and evolutionary, spatial and temporal modes of articulation, it has indeed left room for and even necessitated a vast body of corrections and improvements, primarily from interpersonal, semiological, feminist, and object-relations points of view.[2]

The period between *Studies on Hysteria* (1893–95) and *Three Essays on the Theory of Sexuality* (1905) has occupied a position of strategic importance in my literary understanding of Freud because within it Freud entertains a rather full range of the theoretical and methodological bearings between which he had to select. As I have elsewhere suggested, Freud, in the concluding remarks to *Studies on Hysteria*, major sections of *The Interpretation of Dreams* (1900), and *Jokes and their Relation to the Unconscious* (1905) takes a curious holiday,[3] a "strange interlude" from the enterprises of founding a new branch of medicine and establishing

45

scientific means of verification and transmission. In these works, his emphasis is linguistic rather than neurological; his field is spatial, rather than developmental; and his bearing, the quality of the intellectual operations he employs, is structuralist in nature. During this period, which intervenes between a rigorous scientific and philosophic training and the founding of a classical and intellectual school, Freud is establishing, for his purposes, the basic whats and wherewithals of mental life. He is elaborating, among other things, the psychological parameters of rational thought, the mechanisms of its distortions in such phenomena as jokes, dreams, and parataxes, and the dynamics of memory. Given Freud's ambition and his historical sense of his own destiny, it is remarkable how much time and effort he was willing to devote to this basically phenomenological exploration, which nonetheless proved a wise investment. The notions of primary and secondary process, defense, condensation, displacement, repression, projection, the unconscious, and resistance, among others that he developed during this pivotal transitional period were to comprise the very stuff, the ideational material, that he would later be able to arrange according to evolutionary schemata, whether related to psychosexual development or therapeutic transference.

The motivations underlying Freud's work during this period of unbounded speculation are often unstated, effaced; as are the uses to which it will ultimately be put. The same stage of intellectual work nonetheless results in the 1905 *Three Essays in the Theory of Sexuality*, in which much of the evolutionary schematization and normative thinking that will infuse psychoanalytic theory are already present. The instinct, in this work and afterwards, runs a gauntlet of expressions and repressions, attractions and repulsions, whose structure ultimately derives from Hegelian speculation and nineteenth-century thermodynamics.[4] The stages of the instinct can be known in advance. Some outcomes of instinctual drive and object-choice will be favorable. Psychological disorders and dysfunctions may be interpreted as deviations from the dialectical norms.

Freudian thinking, in the aftermath of this first rehearsal of its full range, hangs in the balance between the open-ended interpretation set into play among other places in *The Interpretation of Dreams*, and the normative-evolutionary schematization first fully mobilized in *Three Essays on the Theory of Sexuality*. The intellectual power of the full-blown case histories, such as the 1909 "Notes Upon a Case of Obsessional Neurosis" ("Rat Man"), the 1911 "Psycho-Analytical Notes on an Autobiographical Account of Paranoia (Dementia Paranoides)" (Schreber), and the 1918 "From the History of an Infantile Neurosis" ("Wolf Man")[5] may be described as the *coordination* that Freud achieves within them between a highly receptive, at times almost playful exegesis and the closure furnished by an evolutionary, dialectical (in both operational and progressive senses), and normative schemata. Subsequent readers and clinicians, I am suggesting, will find the *interface* between his often sensitive and receptive readings and the schemata (of consciousness, development, transference) to which he affixes them a primary site of the distinctly Freudian repression.

For indeed, both the thinking and feeling subject and the therapeutic process arrive at a certain *character*, in Freud and in each of the major subsequent analytical schools. It is the *character* of the psychoanalytic deliberation and partnership that must be stressed as we pursue the development from Freudian thinking, and the very specific neuroses and psychoses for which it allows, toward the domain of personality disorders, documented early, among other places in Musil's *The Man without Qualities*.

The neuroses by which the Freudian subject may be beset, and Freud was far more eloquent and articulate at the level of neurosis than psychosis, are themselves endowed with character, if with nothing else. And their specific quality results from the calculi of expression-represssion, appropriate or inappropriate object-choice, developmental phase-appropriateness, and heterosexual or homosexual orientations. Thus, the hysteric, the founding citizen of the neurotic world suffers from repressed sexual wishes; the obsessive-compulsive expands the energy generated by such incompatible ideas in ritualized thinking or behavior; the paranoid transforms homosexual love into hate, projects it from the self onto a malevolent other.[6]

It was not by accident that Freud maintained a collection of ancient figurines in the apartment at Berggasse 19 where he also kept his office. The work of Freudian psychoanalysis is above all an archeological excavation to submerged states of consciousness undergone by the patient in partnership with the analyst. This interaction is itself subject to dialectical laws of projection and reciprocity. The purpose of the partnership is to reestablish contact with something that has been lost, something of an exceptional or subliminal order. The establishment of the contact is itself tantamount to the dissolution of the disease and its symptoms, the disqualification of their raison d'être.

It is precisely the identifications produced by the Freudian system, its own greatest simulation of character, that imitate the broadest overall resistance to it. In different ways, Sullivanians and cognitive therapists will reject Freud's essentializing the unconscious and the subliminal at the expense of, respectively, interpersonal relationships and conscious thinking. Lacan and certain feminist critics will focus on the *substantiality* of certain of the Freudian identifications. As Lacan himself admits, he is always a Freudian, respectful of the Freudian field's boundaries. Yet his bearing to Freud is that of the passive and meditative partner in an endless dance, the partner with the greatest fidelity to the dynamics of language.[7] Lacan is the belated therapist who would push Freud toward a fuller engagement with his own unconscious, even when that unconscious consists of his own earlier work, for example, the linguistic topography at the end of *Studies on Hysteria*. Lacan supplies the unconscious, the semiological linkages that Freud glosses over, even though he has already accounted for them, in fulfilling his clinical and historical imperatives—but at the expense of a certain closeness to Freud, the familiarity of a permanant dancing partner. The focus of Lacanian analysis shifts from the genital sites of sexual identification and the way stations of psychosexual evolution to the linguistic medium in which the analytical narrative and the commentary upon it take place.[8] This is a subtle but crucial modification, because as the implicit theater of psychodrama moves from the individual and his milieu to the vast and more impersonal system of language, so too do the nature of selfhood, responsibility, and opportunity change in fundamental, often less pathetic ways.

There is a mythical quality to the phantasmatic drama implicit in Freudian psychoanalysis, in which the subject "guided" by the analyst, undertakes a discovery-voyage of the unknown within himself, and in this fashion plumbs the depths. The symbols in its repository, although not specifically archetypal, are of an enduring, universal quality. In this process of psychological refinement, an enormous weight is placed on the individual and the concept of concepts, the value of ideation itself. Lacanian theory somewhat alleviates this burden by shifting it to a system of codes and signs independent of the subject who experiences symptoms and resistant to abstract generalizations. One thing common to virtually all of the approaches beyond the Freudian "drive/structure" model, as Mitchell and Greenberg term it,[9] and its Lacanian reiteration, is a view of the analytical process as an outgrowth of interactions that people have with objects: whether these latter be regarded as other people (Sullivan),[10] things as substitutes for people (Winnicott),[11] the body and its parts as synecdochical/metonymic reductions of people (Klein),[12] or introjections as internalized voices of people (Kernberg).[13] The de-literalization of Freudian metaphors, the incorporation of the pre-Oedipal into the standard range of psychosexual development (common in different ways to Lacan, Klein, and Mahler),[14] and the de-essentialization of gender differences coincide with a reinscription of concerns related to the object and its qualities of otherness and interpersonality. It is not enough, for several of these post-Freudians, that object relations "surface" in the therapeutic narrative as part of the subject matter. They must enter into the therapeutic dynamics itself, be "acted out" and "worked through" as a focal element of the process. The individualized quest of Freudian psychoanalysis imposes a narcissistic isolation on the patient and the process. While Freud was himself quite aware of narcissism and its role in idealization, desire, depression, and art, it is extremely curious that various post-Freudian efforts to restore psychoanalysis to its grounding in interpersonal experience end up setting narcissistic disturbances in even greater relief. In effect, the unspoken narcissistic dimension of Freudian psychoanalysis masks a certain degree of the self-cathexis by the self that we now associate with the personality disorders. The economy of narcissism has become a paradigm for contemporary mental disorders somewhat in the way that the repression of hysteria may be regarded as the ultimate model for many if not all of the Freudian dysfunctions.

The real players in psychoanalysis as it is theorized by contemporary psychologists of narcissism are no longer the ego and the analyst but the self and its internalized others in itself: its prior versions, its effaced earlier editions. A self is already somewhat broader than an ego; it incorporates a social dimension, for one. The analyst sits on the sidelines and very delicately mediates the interplay between an injured self and its fragmentary counterversions. The horizon of the analyst's role has been diminished; the requirements of her diplomacy, at times starting with a microscopic fragment of self-esteem to build upon, have been exponentially increased. The drama has metamorphosed itself from a revelation of the incommensurable through the agency of the analyst to a labor mediation, the reestablishment of a working relationship between the self and its images arbitrated by a partner whose function is defined as much by exclusion as inclusion; whose empathy is maintained in the face of a careful understanding of the pitfalls of preaching, moralism, and countertransferential acting out. Contemporary psychoanalysis needs to make do with a vastly reduced sphere of intervention, whose terrain and attributes must be known in excruciating detail. The work of Kernberg, Kohut, and Modell in particular, is as much about the assumptions and tacks that analysts should avoid as it is about therapeutic power.

The voice and bearing of psychoanalytical discourse changes as it becomes less oracular, normative, and judgmental, and as it opens itself up to incorporate the role and dynamics of the other (or the object). As theoreticians of psychoanalysis respond to the needs to hold fire on their assumptions and to rigorously contextualize their evaluations, the language of psychoanalytical discourse becomes relentlessly descriptive. Its style, as I have suggested elsewhere,[15] begins to take on the stark ruminative quality of certain of the postmodern fiction with which it is intellectually contemporary: I think above all of Beckett; also, the late Kafka and the *nouvau roman*; Calvino and Bernhardt among more recent authors. Where this discourse is less historical in its perspective and more focused in its object, as in the case of Kernberg, it can at times sound ominous, of the mood that Beckett and Bernhardt share. This discursive voice, however, which goes hand in hand with the reinscription of the constitutive role of the object (or the other) in the primal scene of psychoanalysis: when deployed as a corrective to historical errors of generalization, literalization, and valuation can also verge on the "upbeat," as it is in the writing of Heinz Kohut, a careful observer and annotater of intrapsychic processes in his own right.

In Kernberg's writings on narcissistic phenomena, there is a certain unflinching quality to the analytical gaze.[16] Its steadiness is a foil or counter to the inconsistencies in psychic cohesion and in behavior that it observes. Kernberg is not antipathetic to making judgments: so rooted are these, however, in his clinical stance that they take on a certain transparency. This clinical detachment and distance are, in the end, the result of a certain analytical pain, one that Kernberg, in full cognizance of his own vulnerability, shares with us. This overview of the personality disorders is far-reaching. He examines them both where they intertwine with the conventional neuroses of everyday life and where they approach psychotic distortion and deviance. As characterized by Kernberg, pathological narcissists and borderline personalities emerge as the unique psychological children of our times. They have been born into a moment of accelerated lifestyle, increased impersonality in education and other social institutions, and severe instability in the nuclear and extended family. At the risk of sounding abstract and impersonal in his own right, Kernberg assembles, from a wide conceptual and social terrain, the structural, cognitive and behavioral characteristics of his favored subjects. Among his great contributions is precisely that of *assembly*, of gathering a large number of often extreme and self-contradictory behaviors into a coherent, and increasingly recognizable profile or profiles. Kernberg is somewhat of a pure theorist. He combines the clinical traits of these conditions and his observations in the most cogent narrative he can manage, and leaves the conclusions, and many of the therapeutic inferences, to be drawn by the individual practitioner.

In his 1975 *Borderline Conditions and Pathological Narcissism*, Kernberg formulates the "ego weakness" common to both these pathologies.

> These patients present an unusual degree of self-reference in their interactions with other people, a great need to be loved and admired by others, and a curious apparent contradiction between a very inflated concept of themselves and an inordinate need for tribute from others. Their emotional life is shallow. They experience little empathy for the feelings of others, they experience little enjoyment from life other than from the tribute they receive from others or from their own grandiose fantasies, and they feel restless and bored when external glitter wears off and no new sources feed their self-regard. They envy others, tend to idealize some

people from whom they expect narcissistic supplies, and to depreciate and treat with contempt those from whom they do not expect anything (often their former idols). In general, their relationships with other people are clearly exploitative and often parasitic. (*BCPN*, 17)

We gain from this remarkable descriptive passage of the borderline syndrome a curious sense of indefiniteness and inconsistency. The borderline personality is very much on the scene, conspicuously present, yet underlying the "glitter" is vacuousness, an impoverished sense of self, what Kernberg describes as an emotional superficiality.

Kernberg goes on to catalogue the defensive operations underlying and maintaining this style of personality. Among these he includes splitting, primitive idealization ("the tendency to see external objects as totally good, in order to make sure that they can protect one against 'bad' objects," *BCPN*, 30), "early forms of projections, and especially projective identification" (*BCPN*, 30), denial, and omnipotence and devaluation. With regard to splitting and one of its variants, omnipotence and devaluation, Kernberg writes:

Splitting, then, is a fundamental cause of ego weakness. . . . The direct clinical manifestation of splitting may be the alternative expression of complementary sides of a conflict in certain personality disorders, combined with bland denial and lack of concern over the contradiction in his behavior. . . . Probably the best known manifestation of splitting is the division of external objects into "all good" ones and "all bad" ones, with the concomitant possibility of complete, abrupt shifts of an object from one extreme compartment to the other; that is, sudden and complete reversals of all feelings and conceptualizations about a particular person. (*BCPN*, 29)

On a superficial level, the splitting that Kernberg associates with his area of interest would seem to have much in common with the inversion of values that Aaron Beck, for one, ascribes to depression.[17] But if we read more carefully, borderline and serious narcissistic splitting is not an ambivalent fluctuation between idealization and denigration in a centered ("classical") personality, but rather the belated and hence exaggerated effort to interject values in a relatively unformed personality, one that has suffered some major absence in its structuration, a vacuousness achieving phantasmatic proportions in the figure of Moosbrugger, the affable psychopathic murderer in *The Man without Qualities*. We will encounter the notion of splitting again, in Kohut's survey of roughly the same territory. But there, the coexistence of primitive alternate selves to the one that must ultimately achieve for itself a certain cohesion is regarded not only as a source of tension but also as a challenge and a motivation. The anaclitic tendency mentioned above by Kernberg is the manifestation of a self that depends on others for contents and values, a debt so staggering that a unilateral cancellation and a devaluation of its source to nothing are the only ways of coping with it.

Kernberg's term for the context in which such defensive operations arise is "the subjective experience of emptiness." His characterization of this condition in the interchapter between the work on borderline conditions and its more everyday-seeming correlatives in the domain of narcissism is a major cultural statement on our age, with philosophical and literary as well as psychological importance. "There are patients who describe a painful and disturbing subjective experience which they frequently refer to as a feeling of emptiness," Kernberg begins his analysis of this condition (*BCPN*, 213).

> These depressed patients' feelings of emptiness come close to the feeling of loneliness, except that the feeling of loneliness implies elements of longing and the sense that there are others who are needed, and whose love is needed, who seem unavailable now. Psychoanalytical exploration regularly reveals that these patients suffer from an unconscious sense of guilt and that the "emptying" of their subjective experience reflects their superego's attack, as it were, on the self. The harsh internal punishment inflicted by the superego consists in the implicit dictum that they do not deserve to be loved and appreciated and that they are condemned to be alone. On a deeper level, and in severe cases, internal fantasies. . . . are that because of their badness they have destroyed their inner objects and are therefore left alone in a world now devoid of love. (*BCPN*, 214–15)

The loneliness that Kernberg tells us at the beginning of the passage these patients are incapable of feeling corresponds to the loss of an ideal state that seems to run through the literature of depression and other conditions, implicitly or explicitly, from Freud through cognitive approaches into behaviorism.[18] The metaphors that Kernberg evokes to describe its equivalent in the narcissistic personality disorders are reminiscent of cancer and the immunological breakdown that it often involves. The subjective experience of emptiness arises in the context of an obliteration of the structures, values, and even emotions that would allow loss and error to be felt before the coherence and integration of a self has ever been established. The agent of this erasure is a malignant superego that has gone unchecked and unbalanced by a firm, securely founded ego. The somewhat exhibitionistic self-presentation based on this emptiness is a false self, the simulacrum of a personality.[19] The historically fluctuating values dramatized by such a subject are counterfelt values, all the more vivid to simulate real ones.

Were I to integrate two terms characterizing the climate for analytical work in Kernberg's universe, they would be "editorial" and "reconstructive." The first of these refers to the analyst's confinement of her commentary to the object-relations dimensions and implications of the evolving interaction, which is in turn reconstructive as a realistic relationship in which the pronounced idealization, devaluation, and splitting carried over from "real life" are eventually, and through many reversals, neutralized. (On this latter point, Kernberg, for all the subdued timbre of his tone, is quite close to Kohut).

The disappointments with which Kernberg's pathological narcissists have had to contend are very real ones, suffered at developmental stages of great vulnerability.

> Chronically cold parental figures with intense aggression are a very frequent feature of the background of these patients. A composite picture of a number of cases that I have been able to examine or to treat shows consistently a parental figure, usually the mother or a mother surrogate, who functions well on the surface in a superficially well-organized home, but with a degree of callousness, indifference, and nonverbalized, spiteful aggression. . . . In addition, those parents present some quite specific features that distinguish them from other borderline patients. Their histories reveal that each patient possessed some inherent quality which could have objectively aroused the envy or admiration of

others. . . . Sometimes it was the rather cold hostile mother's narcissistic use of the child which made him "special," set him off on the road in a search for compensatory admiration and greatness, and fostered the characterological defense of spiteful devaluation of others. For example, two patients were used by their mothers as a kind of "object of art" . . . These patients often occupy a pivotal point in their family structure, such as being the only child, or the only "brilliant" child, or the one who is supposed to fulfill the family aspirations. (*BPCN,* 234–35)

Kernberg's "pathological" narcissists have evidently borne quite a cross during their early lives. Their martyrdom is reminiscent of that characterizing the figure of the son throughout Kafka's fiction, whose human or animal fate combines an exquisite esthetic sensibility with equally poignant suffering. Thus, Kafka's Hunger Artist is an exhibitionist of his *métier,* but delights in self-consciously "constrained" gestures, and Gregor Samsa, at the moment of the "tragic" transformation into a gigantic insect that will relieve him of his human interactions and obligations, is working frenetically as a sales representative to support a family that, as "The Metamorphosis" goes on to demonstrate, could manage just as well without him.

Kernberg's portraits of pathologically narcissistic and borderline patients are as vivid as the most striking characterizations to have emerged in the history of the novel, whether by Balzac, Flaubert or Proust, Dickens, Eliot, or Melville. He writes with a definite literary flair. His forte is a mixture of description, assembly, and correlation, that is, diagnosis. There is a distinct diagnostic thrust to his writing, countered in Kohut's work by a therapeutic emphasis, an attempt to establish a dynamics and interplay between the nature of the illness and its productive encounter, between the way in and the way out of the disorder. There will be more on this below. When Kernberg does address the matter of therapeutics, the analytic milieu we enter remains distinct from the Freudian mixture of excavation and revelation. It is characterized by a reconstruction based on the establishment of a working relationship between the salutary nucleus of the self, however reduced and battered, and a paradigmatic object (or other). The initially frail therapeutic lien must bear the burden of all dysfunctions and the past history of injury. The primary hope for improvement resides the productive revision of the necessarily damaged rapport. This is typical of theorists whose structural schematizations have, according to Mitchell and Greenberg, evolved into relational emphases.[20]

For all the starkness of Kernberg's "diagnostic realism," (or "educationalism"), his therapeutic work transpires in an increasingly familiar environment of object-relations theory. One clinical vignette must suffice, within the constraints of the present thumbnail sketch. It would not be surprising if a close examination of it made us ambivalent toward Kernberg, for in it he places himself in a position of extreme vulnerability, especially for a figure whose public profile is already invested with such power and misgivings: he reveals some of his own negative countertransference toward a patient. The reciprocal interaction charging the psychoanalytic field makes it fraught with frustration and pain for both players, for the provider of care as well as the patient. We are not necessarily as well prepared to address the analyst's wound as the patient's.

> A patient with narcissistic character structure spent hour after hour over many months of treatment telling me how monotonous and boring analysis had become, that in his associations the same contents kept coming up again and again, and that treatment was definitely a hopeless enterprise. At the same time, he felt rather good in his life outside the analytic hours, with some relief from his feelings of insufficiency and insecurity, but he was unable to understand why this had happened. I pointed out to him, that implicit in his description of his psychoanalysis, was a description of me as the provider of useless and silly treatment. The patient denied this at first, stressing that it was only his problem, not mine, that analysis could not work. I then pointed out to him that, at the beginning of his treatment, he had considerably envied my other patients, who had already received so much more from me than he had, and that it was strange now that he should feel no envy at all of the other patients, especially in view of his statement that it was his problem only that he could not benefit from analysis. I also pointed out to him that his previous, strong envy of me had completely disappeared, for reasons which had remained obscure to him. (BCPN, 244)

Kernberg makes two major moves in this passage demanding our careful attention: in response to "data" regarding the tedium and hopelessness of the sessions presented by the patient, he redirects or displaces this affective content into a consideration of its significance to the very current and specific state of the therapeutic alliance; and, he confronts the patient with a possible discrepancy between two distinct levels of his own narrative: concerning the affect arising within the confines (and possible artificiality) of the analytical milieu, over and against condition-reports from the "outside world." More briefly put, affective content is redirected toward awareness of the relationship; and "intra-alliance" material is opposed to empirical data from the outside world. The first of these moves is the bread and butter of work done from an object-relations point of view. Its motivation has been a major consideration to contend with at least since Sullivan's insistence upon the inevitability and essentiality of the interpersonal dimensions and themes of psychiatry. The second, "comparative" operation capitalizes on the fictionality of the analytical setting. Rather than obfuscate this artificiality, Kernberg's practice openly admits and exploits it. The experience of and affective response to the "real" world can be tested against the augmented rigor of the analytical setting; but by the same token, therapeutic realignments of awareness will produce tangible (and "testable") results in the "real" world. As a measurable measure of propositions, cognitions, and affects, the therapeutic alliance acquires the dimensions of a model, a reduced-scale replica of interpersonal and intrapsychic interactions, or, in Wittgenstein's terms, of a complex language game.

In the case at hand, the analyst feels free to range over what the patient may *overlook*. It is fair game for the analyst to point out that condition reports concerning "his life outside the analytical hours" have been positive, that envy of other patients and the analyst has subsided, and that, on a metarelational level, the dismissal of psychoanalysis as "silly and useless" extends to the analyst. While these comments concern *omissions*, they don't purport to reveal anything beyond the patient's or the situation's reach. The above comments are justifiable either at the substantive level of the analysand's narrative or through the strategic operation of applying narrative data to the state of the therapeutic rapport. As Kernberg reveals himself in this passage, not necessarily in the most self-aggrandizing way, he feels quite free to furnish a pointed and not

necessarily anaesthetizing commentary, whose parameters, however, are rigorously confined: to the relationship at hand, to the
patient's experiences and evaluations, and to the logical implications linking the experiential sphere to the therapeutic model-
relationship. Although there is little way for Kernberg's discourse
to indicate this, his power and authority, and the range of his commentary, have been considerably tempered by a strong skepticism
toward analytical self-idealization, messianism, and preaching
(articulated by Kohut, for example, near the end of *The Analysis
of the Self*).

Kernberg places his range of interpretation and intervention
under severe constraint, but he knows it intensely. It is the intensity
of his purview that is virtually his only defense as the narcissistic
patient assaults him with a series of identity symbiosis, disfigura-
tions, and out-and-out exchanges of identity.

> At this point the patient became aware that he really thought that
> it was entirely my fault that his analysis was, according to him,
> a failure. He now felt surprised that he was so satisfied to con-
> tinue his treatment while considering me so inefficient. I pointed
> out to him how much satisfaction it gave him for me to be a
> failure while he was a success in his life. I also pointed out that
> it was as if I had become the worthless self of him, while he had
> taken over the admired self of me. At that point he became very
> anxious and developed the fear that I hated him and that I would
> take revenge. Fantasies came up in which he thought that I was
> telling his superiors and the police about activities of which he
> was very much ashamed. I pointed out to him that his fear of at-
> tack from me was one reason which prevented him from really
> considering himself in analysis and that he reassured himself that
> he was not really a patient by asserting that nothing was going
> on in the sessions. At that point the patient experienced feelings
> of admiration toward me because I had not become confused and
> discouraged by his constant repetition that analysis was a failure.
> At the next moment, however, he thought that I was very clever,
> and that I knew how to use "typical analytic tricks" to keep "one
> up" over patients. He then thought that he himself would try to
> use a similar technique with people who might try to depreciate
> him. I then pointed out that as soon as he received a "good" inter-
> pretation, and found himself helped, he also felt guilty over his
> attacks on me, and then again envious of my "goodness." There-

fore, he had to "steal" my interpretations for his own use with others, devaluating me in the process, in order to avoid acknowledging that I had anything good left as well as to avoid the obligation of feeling grateful. The patient became quite anxious for a moment and then went completely "blank." He came in the next session with a bland denial of the emotional relevance of what had developed in the session before, and once again the same cycle started all over, with repetitive declarations of his boredom and the ineffectiveness of analysis.

At times it is difficult to imagine how frequent and how repetitive such interactions are, extending as they do over two or three years of analysis; this resistance to treatment illustrates the intensity of the narcissistic patient's need to deny any dependent relationship. (*BCPN*, 244–45)

So intense, draining, and threatening to the self's sense of its own integrity are the experiences that the analyst is relating in this extended passage that by its end he is asking the reader's sympathy for the demands exacted by this type of work over extended periods of time. (This passage can also be used to explain why the needs for intensive psychotherapy—if not psychoanalysis—in spite of current, often remarkable attempts to develop accessible, multifaceted, and time-bound therapeutic programs, are not likely to be eliminated, at least in the near future.) Note that the patient's ability to regard the therapist as a separate and flawed (although sympathetic) individual is a major waystation along the route of successful psychotherapy, an important goal to be reached. This recognition acknowledges a certain distance and limit in the rapport that constitutes, at the same time, the opening of a horizon of independence and realism. Much of Kernberg's effort, in this passage and elsewhere, is toward a "declaration" to the analysand of the therapist's "independence." This turn of events, in object-relations terms, comprises an important and desired, but not in itself definitive upping of the level of transaction.

The second above extract from Kernberg's clinical illustration is notable for the intensity and range of psychological manifestations that can be evoked in the patient by a series of analytical observations confining themselves to the patient's narrative and the framework of the relationship. These extend from simple emotional reactions of anxiety and fear to paranoid fantasies ("I was telling his superiors and the police") and mental lapses ("then went completely 'blank' "). The emotions themselves inhabit a vast scope, largely along the continuum of "omnipotence" and "devaluation." Logically, the patient inscribes the analyst within a claustrophobic domain of double-binds. He first admires Kernberg for his clear-headed response to his disparaging criticisms of the process and then dismisses the ability as cleverness. The analyst's supportive observations, instead of relieving the patient, give rise to guilt over past feelings of aggression and envy at the analyst's moral integrity.

I situate both Kernberg and Kohut in a common model despite their ongoing debate over the matter of educationalism. Kernberg, in characterizing treatment of cases in which there is a severe effacement of psychological structure, whatever that might be, provides for a subtle and delicate, but very important element of education in the psychoanalytical process itself. According to him, in certain cases of personality disorders and extreme narcissism, psychoanalysis rebuilds or establishes for the first time structures or awarenesses that were, by virtue of a polarized, neglectful, or in other ways inhuman environment, lacking. Kohut finds this intervention too harsh, this mission too explicit and evocative of resistance. He would substitute empathic support for such a directive intervention.[21]

If Kernberg's characterizations of the analytical process verge on descriptions of prolonged warfare, or at best an uneasy stalemate, the fullest extent of this battle is an assault on the analyst's own self. The implicit battleground of psychoanalysis, in Kernberg's narrative, is nothing less than the analyst's self. This is the context for the analyst's observation (both *for us* and directed at the patient) that the patient, in applying analytical interpretations "to others," is stealing not only the ideas but the analyst's own self. This gesture of plagiarism both acknowledges the analyst's importance and nullifies it; it also relieves the analysand of gratitude. At the dramatic core of Kernberg's clinical experience, the analyst is offering his self to fill in the void indicative of the patient's subjective experience of emptiness. The analyst's self is at the same time being used as a heuristic ladder for the formation of the patient's missing intrapsychic structure and it is under siege. The patient is denigrating it, devaluing it, devouring it, and draining it, while clinging to it in a symbiotic way. Small wonder that Kernberg will warn: "After many months and years of being treated as an 'appendix' of the patient (a process which may be subtle enough to remain unnoticed for a long time) the analyst may begin to feel really 'worthless' in his work with such a case" (*BCPN*, 246) Or: "One should probably not treat many of these patients at the same time, because they put a great stress and many demands on the analyst" (*BCPN*, 247).

Kernberg's work is not advisable reading for individuals with casual or wholly intellectualized interests in psychoanalytical discourse. This is because people with less than a professional interest have a hard time in drawing the line between what we might call "the pathological narcissism of everyday life" and the very serious cases on which Kernberg bases his nosology and therapeutic recommendations. Who among us is not a bit opportunistic in certain of our personal relationships? Who doesn't "feel restless and bored when external glitter wears off"? (*BCPN*, 17). Kernberg directs his work toward a tangible borderline in human thought and behavior and an extreme test to which psychotherapeutic caring may be put. He is unflinchingly honest in his observations and his self-representation in his own writing. This augments the realism and vitality of his descriptions, but it also frustrates his readership's wish to think only with an idealized image of the senior analyst. At the expense of our own long-conditioned desire for happy endings, Kernberg is not above registering his own frustrations, failures, and even destructive fantasies. It is as if, after having confronted disorders of primitive and petrified idealization in a clinical setting for so long, he must preempt their extension in his writing. As a widely familiar artistic illustration of the tension surrounding his work with seriously ill narcissistic and borderline patients he selects Ingmar Bergman's film, *Persona,* a wise and canny choice, and I close this too brief introduction to a literary deployment of his writing with a formulation of analytical ambivalence that he bases on the film.

> A recent motion picture by Ingmar Bergman, *Persona,* illustrates the breakdown of an immature but basically decent young woman, a nurse, charged with the care of a psychologically, severely ill woman presenting what we would describe as a typical narcissistic personality. In the face of the cold, unscrupulous exploitation to which the young nurse is subjected, she gradually breaks down. She cannot face the fact that the other sick woman

returns only hatred for love and is completely unable to acknowledge any loving or human feeling expressed toward her. The sick
woman seems to be able to live only if and when she can destroy
what is valuable in other persons, although in the process she
ends up destroying herself as a human being. In a dramatic development, the nurse develops an intense hatred for the sick woman
and mistreats her cruelly at one point. It is as if all the hatred
within the sick woman had been transferred into the helping one,
destroying the helping person from the inside. (*BCPN,* 245–46)

# CHAPTER 6

# Object-Relations Theory:
# Heinz Kohut

It might appear that any theorist positing a "restoration of the self" would be the ideal antidote to Kernberg's "Swedish" scenario, a sugarcoated pill to chase a bitter one. Heinz Kohut, who wrote a book of that title, would be the optimistic analyst. Because he concentrates his clinical attention and metapsychological meditations on the fashion in which psychoanalysis can constructively address symptoms and phenomena of the sort Kernberg relentlessly describes, he emerges as the more hopeful and empathic object-relations theorist. Yet Kohut is himself a realistic and precise observer, whose theoretical models engage personality disorders by striving for the most accurate description possible of their mechanisms and the conditions under which they arise.

It is not an easy task to extrapolate from psychoanalytic theorization a concrete picture of how the analytical transaction functions; of how different conceptual approaches ultimately impact on the bearing, mood, rhetorical structure, and themes of actual sessions.[1] Yet when we perform this work, when we "read into" Kohut's texts the analytical practice they both record and prescribe, we have ventured into a universe quite distinct from its Freudian counterpart, even though Kohut devotes far more work than Kernberg to identifying the foundations of his concerns and constructs in Freud.

Even when we encounter so basic a passage as Kohut's preliminary definition of psychoanalysis, this process emerges with a quite distinct set of aspirations and mores.

> Psychoanalysis as a form of psychotherapy should, in my opinion, be neither essentially defined by the therapist's application of its theory in the therapeutic situation nor by his providing of insights and explanations—even including genetic ones—which

increase the patient's mastery over himself. While all of these features are part of therapeutic psychoanalysis, something else must be added which produces its essential quality: the pathogenic nucleus of the analysand's personality becomes activated in the treatment situation and itself enters a specific transference with the analyst before it is gradually dissolved in the working-through process which enables the patient's ego to obtain dominance in this specific area. Such a process must, however, not be set in motion if the transference regression would lead to a severe fragmentation of the self. (*AS*, 13)[2]

Two very particular attitudes leap from this passage, demanding to be read: one addressing therapy's implicit scenario, the other the therapist's attitude, which he will later define as a certain empathy. Regarding this latter issue, Kohut tells us early in *The Analysis of the Self* that the therapist should put down all theoretical axes she may have to grind, and should approach what he elsewhere calls educationalism ("providing of insights and explanations") with extreme caution. In his very definition of psychoanalysis, Kohut applies a statute of limitation, not enablement, to the therapist, defining the narrow margin of intervention that becomes, already in this overview, the habitat of the object-relations practitioner. Empathy, the term Kohut applies to a sympathetic but focused therapeutic intervention, will be as much defined by what it excludes as by what it embraces.

Even more pivotal is the approach to psychopathology already emerging in this early passage. As opposed to Freudian psychoanalysis, which strives for the obliteration of symptoms and whole illnesses through the penetration of incompatible ideas and memories from the unconscious, Kohut here and throughout his writing calls for an active partnership between the disease and the salutary state. "The pathogenic nucleus of the analysand's personality becomes activated in the treatment situation and itself enters a specific transference with the analyst before it is gradually dissolved in the working through process" (*AS*, 13). What Kohut would see "dissolved" in the course of treatment is not a disease, an infiltrator, a secret agent once consigned to the unknown, but a prior, grandiose version of the self existing side by side with its present day emanation. Kohut describes an impacted architecture of the self. To "kill" the painful self-fragment, to extrude the source and locus of discomfort, would be literally to throw the baby out with the bath water.

Subjectivity, for Kohut, is not a condition that has become doubled and painfully self-reflexive through the repression of sexuality and an ambivalent exclusion of the incompatible (Freud);[3] nor through a constitutionally belated initiation into the symbolic and social codes that in fact correspond to the structure of desire and consciousness (Lacan).[4] In the universe of Kohutian psychoanalysis, the subject is a palimpsest, a stuck-together agglomeration of more and less recent versions of a draft in progress, the self. Psychological experience for Kohut is a slippage or "snapping in" and "out" of these prose versions of the self in response to a variety of stressors. The figure of Oedipus speaks less to Kohut and other object-relations theorists than he does to Freud or Lacan. It is Oedipus's fate to grope blindly in search of the murderous/incestuous wishes he has felt for his parents (Freud); to congenitally misapprehend the law that his instinctual impulses always already violate (Lacan). But for Kohut, the subterranean Castle Keep of the unthinkable and the unknowable has lost much of its allure and power. Psychological woman and man slip in and out of coexistent versions of emanations of their own selves. They are split, horizontally and vertically, in a sense not alien to some of the polarizations described by Kernberg. Some of these fissures in the self hail from the developmental stage at which the subject stumbled into his own Oedipal surprises, suffered his first irreversible disappointments. The drama of psychoanalysis becomes less to activate the unknown than to facilitate a working relationship between the fragmented versions of the self.

Psychological life is for Kohut a struggle between individuals and the vestiges of the grandiosity that survive, literally, beside them. Under the umbrella term "grandiosity" Kohut groups the overall set of manifestations of narcissistic injuries surfacing in the transferential relationship, which he divides into its "idealizing" and "mirroring" aspects (more on this below). The grandiose behaviors that Kohut witnesses as they are reenacted through the transferential medium correlate well with Kernberg's symptomology: these manifestations include the predictable unrealistic "being taken with one's self"; they also include "Archaic forms of grandiosity: cold, imperious behavior, affected speech and gestures;

unrealistic and grandiose feats; Archaic terms of idealization: ecstatic, trancelike, religious feelings; hypomanic excitement; and Autoerotic body-mind-self; tension state; hypochondria about physical and mental health; self-stimulation; perverse fantasies and activities" (*AS*, 97). Underlying these conditions is a symptomology that Kohut characterizes as "ill-defined, and the patient is in general not able to focus on its essential aspects, but he can describe the secondary complaints (such as work inhibitions or trends toward perverse sexual activities). The vagueness of the patient's complaint may be related to the nearness of the pathologically disturbed structures (the self) to the seat of the self-observing functions in the ego" (*AS*, 16). Kohut distinguishes this "ill-defined" narcissistic symptomology from "central psychopathology" of transference neurosis, which

> concerns structural conflicts over (incestuous) libidinal and aggressive strivings which emanate from a well-delimited cohesive self and are directed toward childhood objects which have in essence become fully differentiated from the self. The central psychopathology of the narcissistic personality disturbances, on the other hand, concerns primarily the self and the archaic narcissistic objects. (*AS*, 19)

Rooted in a poor definition of their personalities reminiscent of the "ego weakness" and "subjective experience of emptiness" invoked by Kernberg, Kohut's narcissistic patients slide back and forth along superimposed continuums of grandiosity and regression. Psychological life, both in its major transitions, and its everyday "slices," is a back-and-forth between primitive and advanced stages of evolution, between child-like overexcitement and relatively calm deliberation and work. Kohut observes these movements in cases of extreme disturbance, but they also define the parameters of normal productive psychological life. In this sense, Kohut's scenario of psychopathology through the agglomeration of more and less primitive fragments of the self destigmatizes certain of the Freudian valuations. The same effect is achieved by Kohut's limiting "anxiety" to its technical sense of dysfunctional hypervigilance and adopting a rhetoric of overexcitement or overstimulation in situations to which Freud might apply a rhetoric of hysteria.

The only way out of the disease, for Kohut, is the way into it, or rather through it, in the sense of "working through." In this attitude, Kohut accords hope and value to the vestiges of grandiosty that give his patients such pain and that create complex difficulties in their lives. The issue for Kohut's patients becomes, then, not to erase the disease; or to master it, or to drive it away or underground, but to "work it through," to integrate it into the self by interrogating the horizontal and vertical axes of splitting. In the reciprocal relationship in which he aligns realistic self-consciousness and grandiosity, insight and regression, optimal conditions and disease, Kohut achieves an atmosphere of yin-yang balance and continuity in which therapeutic work transpires. Since the disease is coterminous with the self, the risk of confronting it is high (one's life). But a certain reassurance is secured for this scenario in the fact that the disease, the narcissistic disturbance, is not merely disruptive, but also militates, under therapeutic conditions, for its own neutralization. The yin-yang dynamic that Kohut discovers to prevail in the narcissistic sphere between the disease and its neutralization, between stability and regression, and between grandiose aspects of the self and its objects is not an isolated phenomenon in the contemporary psychological field. Researchers in the field of anxiety and depression (e.g., David Barlow, Laura Alloy, Lyn Abramson)[5] are finding privileged and subtle reciprocities to prevail between these two conditions, which might seem, superficially, antagonistic to each other.

There is a tendency for Kohut to organize his major conceptual structures reciprocally, lending the processes he describes a certain balance and continuity. This alone does not invalidate the accuracy of his observations. As an interrogator of object relations, his interest in the images of pivotal objects as experienced by children, above all during the pre-oedipal and oedipal stages, is as intense as his interest in primitive senses that children have of themselves. For Kohut, both primitive sense of self and of pivotal objects penetrates into and informs psychoanalytical transference. That element of transference informed largely by persistent vestiges of early images or senses of self he calls the mirroring transference. Its counter-movement, structured by needs to gain self-confirmation in relation to idealized and powerful objects (or others) he terms the idealizing transference. Much of Kohut's account of what transpires during the therapeutic process hinges on the distinction

## Diagram 1

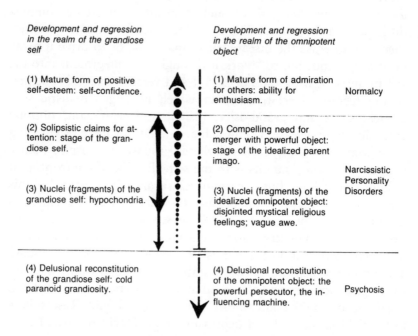

| Development and regression in the realm of the grandiose self | | Development and regression in the realm of the omnipotent object | |
|---|---|---|---|
| (1) Mature form of positive self-esteem: self-confidence. | | (1) Mature form of admiration for others: ability for enthusiasm. | Normalcy |
| (2) Solipsistic claims for attention: stage of the grandiose self. | | (2) Compelling need for merger with powerful object: stage of the idealized parent imago. | |
| (3) Nuclei (fragments) of the grandiose self: hypochondria. | | (3) Nuclei (fragments) of the idealized omnipotent object: disjointed mystical religious feelings; vague awe. | Narcissistic Personality Disorders |
| (4) Delusional reconstitution of the grandiose self: cold paranoid grandiosity. | | (4) Delusional reconstitution of the omnipotent object: the powerful persecutor, the influencing machine. | Psychosis |

The solid arrow indicates the oscillations of the narcisstic configurations in the course of the psychoanalytic treatment of the narcissistic personality disorders; the dotted arrow indicates the direction of the process of cure in the analysis of these disorders. The alternatingly dotted and interrupted part of the long arrow indicates the still reversible depth of the regression toward psychosis; the interrupted part signifies that depth of the regression toward psychosis at which the psychotic regression has become irreversible. (*AS*, 9)

Figure 1

between, and interrelation of, the idealizing and mirroring transferences.

*The Analysis of the Self* derives considerable illumination from three diagrams, corresponding to the beginning, middle, and end of the book, in which Kohut registers either intrapsychic structures or therapeutic processes. Each is remarkable for its ability to represent complicated dynamics and to organize vast bodies of clinical and discursive material.

In the first (Figure 1), reproduced immediately above with Kohut's explanatory caption, it is clear that the development of the self, in lived and clinical experience, is neither linear nor progressive. Both in the column devoted to the status of the grandiose self, whose vicissitudes will later form the mirroring transference, and in that dedicated to the omnipotent object, whose reemergence is registered in the idealizing transference—in both columns there is every opportunity to slip in two directions, ahead toward normality, and regressively toward the extreme of psychosis. The middle range of the chart, where Kohut locates the narcissistic personality disorders, is itself broad and variegated, extended in intensity from a certain inconvenient demandingness to mystified awe. Only on the dotted line is there any hope for progress or full "follow through" or "breakthrough" to the normal, and it corresponds to the course of psychoanalytic treatment (although elsewhere corroborating Kernberg, Kohut will bemoan the gradualness and reversibility of this work). The fluctuation between advancement and regression to which the self is subject is suspended only below the bottom line, at the level of psychosis. The preponderant range of subjective experience is progressive-regressive. Indeed, Kohut's therapeutic scenario, instead of suppressing this capability for regression or "negative" reversal, puts it to full use. In the "mirroring transference" at least, therapy actively initiates regression in the interest of "mobilizing the grandiose self." The diagram's vertical stratification is suggestive of the wide range of "notches" or "stops," from the border of normality to the gateway of psychosis, to which experience, within the narcissistic economy, is susceptible.

Before proceeding to the clinical implications of the scenario, a word about the interplay between the idealizing and mirroring transferences. In Freudian psychoanalysis, a decided emphasis is on the submerged facet of the subject's drives and thoughts. In the spirit of the vast literature of childhood at the turn of the century, extending through Musil, Proust, Joyce, and Kafka, among other examples, Freudian psychoanalysis devotes considerable attention to the subject's early experiences, above all, of itself. Considerations of the other enter Freud's psychoanalytical field primarily in the figure of the analyst through the projective dynamics of the transference. It is the *current* subjectivity of the analyst that must serve as a sounding board or resonator back in the direction of prior emanations of the self or memories of others.

Kohut, on the other hand, would presume to place prior versions or emanations of others internalized within the self on the same plane of importance as early subjective experiences. Even though he reserves the consideration of internalized omnipotent objects for the idealizing transference proper, it is clear that the entire alignment providing both for it and the mirroring transference is largely motivated by the insistence upon giving the experience of others as mediated by the self the same weight as what we may call self-consciousness or self-reflexivity.

In defining the dynamics of the transference in terms of the major activities that articulate its rhythms and progressions (e.g., idealization, mirroring), Kohut is opening up a performative dimension within the psychoanalytical field. He is heeding Roy Schafer's call for a language of action rather than concept in psychoanalysis,[6] and he is pursuing a change of field from the constative to the performative initiated by Wittgenstein and repeated or questioned by writers ranging from Austin and Searle to de Man and Derrida.[7] In the broadest sense, the activities of idealization and mirroring according to which Kohut characterizes transference in the narcissistic personality disorders, are themselves essential factors in salutary social and psychological life. As Freud himself recognizes, ideals function as a horizon toward which individuals work and love.[8] Their maintenance, and the continuity of the striving toward them, is essential for the sublimation that is a hallmark of stable and productive civilization. Mirroring is a basic precondition for the fortifying social interaction between peers. It is a pivotal mechanism in the selection and development of friendships, the units of collaborative activity. While idealization and mirroring may constitute fault lines at which, in the context of the psychoanalysis of narcissistic patients, a certain degree of pain and overexcitement are registered in the transferential process, these terms, in their broader psychosocial senses, describe optimal conditions in the spheres in which they are operative.

Kohutian psychoanalysis is a double-faceted process encompassing both individual and interpersonal fields, aiming (1) to establish communication between the therapeutic self and archaic self-and-object-fragments, from which it has become split, in horizontal and vertical senses (more on this below); and (2) to tame and productively marshall (politically, one might say to coopt) the *intensity* of archaic vestiges of the self and pivotal objects and to redirect this energy, which narcissistic patients experience as threatening, intoxicating, or not at all, to productive uses. This therapeutic ideology carries through both to the idealizing and mirroring transferences:

> The essential working through process, however, aims at the gradual withdrawal of the narcissistic libido from the narcissistically invested, archaic, object; it leads to the acquisition of new psychological structures and functions as the cathexes shift from the representation of the object and its activities to the psychic apparatus and its functions. In the specific case of the idealizing transference the working-through process concerns, of course, specifically the withdrawal of idealizing cathexes from the idealized parent imago and, concomitantly, (a) the building up of drive-regulating structures in the ego, and (b) the increased idealization of the superego. (*AS,* 96)

The idealizing transference, briefly put, mobilizes and addresses primitive images of parenting and authority. It "clears the field" for the ongoing rigors of the therapeutic work through the "withdrawal of idealizing cathexes" from authority figures past and present, the hostility toward whom plays such a prominent role in the continuous stream of psychological "grist for the mill" (also in occupational and sexual object-choices). The territory of the idealizing transference corresponds to what the classical literature of psychoanalysis means by transference in general; the analysis of the rage and resistance encountered in this phase of the work has been well-rehearsed. It is for this reason that Kohut's scrutiny in *The Analysis of the Self* is weighted toward that phase of the work addressing split-off primitive images of the self, the mirror transference.

> The essential aspect of the working-through processes in the mirror transference involves the mobilization of the split-off and/or repressed grandiose self and the formation of preconscious and conscious derivatives which penetrate into the reality ego in the form of exhibitionistic strivings and of grandiose fantasies. Analysts are, in general, familiar with the mobilization of the later stages of the grandiose self when its grandiosity and exhibitionism are amalgamated with firmly established object-directed strivings. Specific environmental situations during the child's

oedipal stage foster this type of grandiosity. . . . If the child has no realistic adult rival, for example, because of the death or absence of the parent of the same sex during the oedipal phase; or if the adult rival is depreciated by the oedipal love object; or if the love object stimulates the child's grandiosity and exhibitionism; or if the child is exposed to various combinations of the preceding constellations, then the phallic narcissism of the child and the grandeur which are appropriate to the early oedipal phase are not exposed to the confrontations with the child's realistic limitations that are phase-appropriately experienced at the end of the oedipal phase and the child remains fixated on his phallic grandiosity. (*AS*, 145–46)

It is in keeping with the yin-yang sensibility informing Kohutian psychoanalysis that the self's grandiose and exhibitionistic features would constitute the most expressive context for penetrating through to the wounds at the basis of the narcissistic economy. The mirror transference involves the excruciating and time-consuming work of recognizing one's own grandiosity, identifying it as such, and entering an active conversation with the self-fragments in which it is expressed and "acted out." Optimally, for Kohut, the bulk of the psychoanalytical work is concentrated amid the relative relaxation and deliberation of the "secondary mirror transference." While the "idealizing transference" is often acutely evident in the early stages of psychoanalysis, it may emerge as a significant factor at virtually any stage of the work, including termination (*AS*, 134).

The disappointments constituting, in the domain of Kohutian psychoanalysis, the breeding ground for narcissistic disturbances are invariably interpersonal in nature. Even where the death and/or departure of primary objects is involved, it is the interpersonal translation of the reversal, not the reversal itself that becomes the pretext for the narcissistic wound. The native land of the personality disorders, as surveyed immediately above by Kohut, is populated more by significant absences than by horrifying presences. A "realistic rival" to mitigate and partially neutralize oedipal excitement and expectations has vanished from the scene; or a parent figure has inadequately served as an audience to the child's phase-appropriate exhibitionism; or a parent figure, by virtue of his own narcissistic wounds, has been unable to satisfy the child's phase-appropriate need for a strong, "ideal" parent figure; or one parent has subverted the child's idealized image of the other. The persistence of archaic images of the self that is such a prominent feature in the psychoanalysis of the personality disorders arises in a context of structural whiteout, which is itself a mark of absenting and the abdication of "presence" in formative interpersonal relationships.

One of Kohut's paradigmatic causes of a narcissistic wound is "the mother who overtly belittles the adult male" (*AS*, 147). The traumas underlying the narcissistic personality disorders are of a somewhat different nature than interloping on the "primal scene" (the "Wolf Man" case) or than the sickness, and death itself of a parent (Fraülein Elizabeth von R.).[9] In the context of such absences and the narcissistic patient's preoccupation with primary-process impulses, "the building up of psychological structure" (*AS*, 186) is not an undesirable outcome of psychoanalysis. Psychoanalytical work restores structures ultimately "derived from the pre-oedipal internalizations of the idealized parent image" (*AS*, 186) at the same time that it reestablishes communication between split-off segments of the self. Such structures ultimately assist the cause of "ego dominance" by establishing through a "scene-in-depth" an "uninterrupted continuum" between "depth and surface" (*AS*, 187). The "split-off and/or repressed self" that preoccupies the mirror transference either went unchecked in its time of origin or was unanswered by love and appreciative admiration. This scenario confirms Kernberg's sense that the personality disorders and the subjective experience of emptiness are above all diseases of absence or effacement of structuration, marked by wide inconsistencies in such areas as maturing, intimacy, and socialization. It has no doubt occurred to the reader already and will be considered in greater detail below that these early and wrenching wounds to one's images of pivotal others and to one's self outlined by Kohut constitute in a very different sphere, a metacritical one, the very traits of writing itself. Among writing's many Derridian attributes, none is more preeminent than its both issuing from and marking a disfiguration of the ideal. In an object-relations sense, writing "marks the spot" of a narcissistic wound so primitive as "always already" to have been there. There is no writing without narcissism; and no undoing of narcissistic splits without the semiological slippage, intertwining, and extension of writing. "A fine wound was all I brought into the world," declares a young patient to Kafka's Country Doctor, in a story of the same title.[10] Not only is the Country Doctor ineffectual in healing the young peasant's wound; he has a bevy of his own insecurities, some sexual, to contend with. The narcissistic wound is both the scene of the crime to which the personality disorders return and the fissure that is the source of writing; the discrepancy between desire and actuality that all literary writing embellishes, disguises, and mourns.

Splitting, along with its performative dimension, a slippage or snapping in and out of states of grandiosity, whether in the sphere of self- or other-image, constitutes the telling feature of Kohut's psychoanalytical landscape. The work of psychoanalysis may direct itself toward mitigating the impact of splitting, but it never fundamentally questions the existence, necessity, or usefulness of intrapsychic splits. Splitting defines, for Kohut, the very atmosphere of contemporary subjectivity. It is also the mechanism providing psychoanalytical treatment with much of its impetus and strategy.

Kohut is nowhere more powerful, conceptually as well as rhetorically, than where he links the existential foreground of splitting to the forensic stance of psychoanalysis. Psychoanalytical intervention is situated at the horizontal and vertical split formed by the persistence of archaic imagery, both of the self and primary objects (others). These figures not only *situate* analytical work; they inform its optimal, in Kohut's terms, empathic bearing.

> The analysand's demands for attention, admiration, and a variety of other forms of mirroring and echoing responses to the mobilized grandiose self, which fill the mirror transference in the narrow sense of the term, do not usually constitute great cognitive problems for the analyst, although much subtlety of understanding may have to be mobilized by the analyst to keep pace with the patient's defensive denials of his demands and with the general retreat from them when an immediate empathic response to them is not forthcoming. If the analyst, however, truly comprehends the phase-appropriateness of the demands of the grandiose self and if he grasps the fact that for a long time it is erroneous to emphasize to the patient that his demands are unrealistic but that, on the contrary, he must demonstrate to the patient that they are appropriate within the context of the total early phase that is being revived in the transference and that they

have to be expressed, then the patient will gradually reveal the urges and fantasies of the grandiose self and the slow process is thus initiated which leads—by almost imperceptible steps, and often without any specific explanations from the side of the analyst—to the integration of the grandiose self into the structure of the reality ego and to an adaptively useful transformation of its energies. (*AS,* 176)

This passage at once paints the analytical manifestations of grandiose fragments of the self and outlines the empathic bearing that Kohut considers the fitting response to them.[11] The mirror transference is that theater of psychoanalysis focusing on the demands and expectations (among them that there is even someone *interested* in the flow of observations, details, and observations) carrying over from a more primitive emanation of the self. Within the parameters of an empathic therapeutics, the therapist aligns himself with the "phase-appropriateness" of the untimely grandiose manifestation, even where it has given rise to considerable trouble and shame (and it often does). At the heart of Kohutian empathy is a certain faith that a rigorous, accepting descriptiveness of object relations in psychotherapy is sufficient to initiate and sustain a productive encounter between the patient and his residual forms of grandiosity. This empathy does not assume the form of (the therapist's) attempt "to replace the patient's narcissistic position with object love" (*AS,* 224). It eschews "the improper intrusion of the altruistic value system of Western civilization" (*AS,* 224). It casts a most skeptical eye on "the messianic or saintly personality of the therapist" (*AS,* 223). Kohutian empathy, in its self-administered constraint, confines itself to explanation where education or preaching might well be more gratifying.

> The analyst addresses himself neither to the part of the psyche where the grandiosity is repressed (i.e., the analyst does not speak to the id) nor to that part of the psyche (including its ego aspect) which is split off. He always addresses himself to the reality ego (or to the remnants of the reality ego). He should no more try to educate the conscious grandiose sector of the psyche than he would try to educate the id—he must concentrate his efforts on the task of explaining the (vertically and horizontally) split-off parts of the psyche to the reality ego (including the reality ego's defensive struggles against them) in order to open the road toward its ultimate dominance. (*AS,* 178)

The empathy of Kohutian psychoanalysis is one of bearing rather than affect. Just as psychoanalysis brings the patient to the salutary but horrifying brink of relinquishing outmoded grandiosities whose attraction consisted in large measure of their making life bearable, so too must the analyst dispense with the "cheaper" (because more direct, quicker) "payoffs" of her own work. From the analyst's eye view, a significant portion of the work consists of repudiating emotional supplies that might otherwise be "perks" of the job: adulation, mirroring, and compliance. It is in this tolerant but restrained sense of empathy, that Kohut would submit any course of therapy to three questions:

> (1) Do we have a systematic theoretical grasp of the processes involved in therapy? (2) Can the treatment method be communicated to others i.e., can it be learned . . . without the presence of its originator? And (3), most importantly: Does the treatment remain successful after the death of its creator? (*AS*, 223)

The hope of Kohutian psychoanalysis resides in its attitude, even within the confines of the methodological specifications outlined above, that cooperation can be achieved between the patient and his chimeras, that shame-evoking grandiosity can be marshaled toward (and has even been motivated by) its own obliteration. In discussing narcissistic patients' unique proclivity for shame, for example, and their tendency to relive powerful situations over and over again, Kohut observes,

> The patient arrives at his session flooded with shame and anxiety because of a *faux pas* that he felt he had committed. . . . When examined in detail, the painfulness of many of these situations can be understood by recognizing that a rejection occurred, suddenly and unexpectedly, just at the moment when the patient was most vulnerable to it, i.e., at the moment when he had expected to shine. . . . These can be very important moments in the analysis of narcissistic persons. They require the analyst's tolerance for the patient's repeated recounting of the painful scene, and for the anguish which the often seemingly trivial event causes him. . . . Childhood grandiosity and exhibitionism, too, must, however, not be condemned. . . . It is only via the slow, systematic analysis of repeated traumatic states of this type that, against strong resistances, the old grandiosity and exhibitionism which lay in the center of these reactions become intelligible and

can now be tolerated by the ego without undue shame and fear of rebuff or ridicule. Only by their gaining access into the ego, however, is the ego capable of building up those specifically appropriate structures which transform the archaic narcissistic drives and ideations into acceptable ambitions, self-esteem, and pleasure in one's functioning. (*AS*, 230–32)

This is among several possible passages from *The Analysis of the Self* indicative of Kohut at his most Kohutian. With an understatement making it easily glossed over, he lends insight to the interdynamics of psychological reward and punishment, narcissistic wounding and narcissistic retribution. In this passage, individuals are most deeply wounded, and learn to wound others most intensely, at those moments when, primed for a reward they suffer bitter disappointment. In psychotherapy, these shame-charged events are relived with a relentlessness that cannot make them morally edifying or esthetically pleasing. It is precisely Kohut's ability to value these traumatic states and their repetitive retelling, to believe in a mastery of the wound residing at the far horizon of its reliving—that gives his own dramaturgy of psychoanalysis its distinctive flavor.[12] In this sense, Kohut would only agree with the Proustian exhortation to "love your own demons." The dissonance between more and less archaic drafts of the self occurs at splits or rifts within it—and these are the sites of the improved communication or de-concealing (Heidegger is not irrelevant here)[13] that empathic psychoanalysis can provide. In concluding this brief prospectus to a literary deployment of Kohut, I return to those so intimate gaps, boundaries, and borders, of the "horizontal" and "vertical" varieties, at which repression and its linguistic/psychoanalytical response, are concentrated. As Kohut notes, Freud himself distinguished between horizontal and vertical forms of repression in the ego. The first of these corresponds to what we understand by repression in general: the submersion of the grandiose self through its relegation to a subliminal level, "in a repressed and/or negated state. Since we are here dealing with a horizontal split in the psyche which deprives the reality ego of the narcissistic nutriment from the deep sources of narcissistic energy, the symptomology is that of narcissistic deficiency (diminished self-confidence, vague depressions, absence of zest for work, lack of initiative, etc.)" (*AS*, 177). Vertical splitting, on the other hand, accounts for the coexistence of "more" and "less" grandiose versions of the self literally beside one another—and for the at times abrupt transitions between corresponding overstimulated and relaxed moods.

> The patients' overt attitudes are, however, inconsistent. On the one hand, they are vain, boastful, and intemperately assertive with regard to their grandiose claims. On the other hand, since they harbor (in addition to their conscious but split-off grandiosity) a silently repressed grandiose self which is anaccessibly buried in the depths of the personality (horizontal split), they manifest symptoms and attitudes which resemble those of the first group of patients, but which are strongly at variance with the openly displayed grandiosity of the split-off sector. (*AS*, 178)

Nowhere does Kohut achieve a more suggestive formulation of the existential manifestations of the more prevalent, vertical splits. In the third diagram (Figure 2) incorporated into the body of *The Analysis of the Self*, Kohut graphically illustrates the distinction and psychoanalytical interplay between the two varieties of self-fragmentation and broken-down communication between self-fragments. I reproduce it with Kohut's commentary.

What is most important about this diagram is not its limitation of the subject to a single horizontal and/or vertical split, or its relating to the traumatic circumstances for both kinds of split to attitudes on the part of the mother—but rather to delineate between two different versions of psychological repression or blindness. The horizontal alignment has been well-rehearsed by the classical literature of psychoanalysis. It corresponds to the scenario of individuals being unaware of their own drives, to the extent that other people can discern their drives more clearly than they can, the situation, in other words, of irony, literary as well as clinical. Kohut's vertical splitting of the self is more congenial to the unique psychological temperament of our contemporary age, the subjective experience of emptiness. Through this vertical splitting, Kohut's exemplary subjects, themselves habituated to radical inconsistencies of structure and amorphousness, to "structural whiteout," and to major abdications of idealization in role-modeling and family responsibility, harbor in themselves self-fragments cut off from one another. Kohut's characterization of the transitions of the self between its split-off vertical fragment comprises an original scenario

## Diagram 2

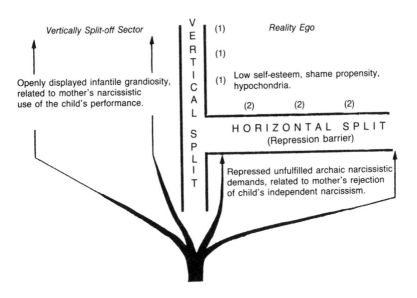

The arrows in the diagram represent the flow of narcissistic energies (exhibitionism and grandiosity). In the first part of the analysis the major therapeutic effort is directed [at the points marked (1)] toward taking down the vertical barrier (maintained by disavowal), so that the reality ego is enabled to control the formerly uncurbed infantile narcissism in the split-off sector of the psyche. The narcissistic energies which are thus prevented from finding expression in the vertically split-off sector (left side of diagram) now reinforce the narcissistic pressure against the repression barrier (right side of diagram). The major effort in the second part of the analysis is directed [at the points marked (2)] toward taking down the horizontal barrier (maintained by repression), so that the (self representation in the) reality ego is now provided with narcissistic energies, thus doing away with the low self-esteem, shame-propensity, and hypochondria which had prevailed in this structure so long as it was deprived of narcissistic energies. (*AS*, 185)

Figure 2

for psychoanalytical intervention and a suggestive way of revising our understanding of subjective and interpersonal experiences. The narrator of Musil's *The Man without Qualities* notes how sexual excitement can, in a matter of seconds, transform the partners into crazed versions of themselves.[14] Such is the snapping in and out of isolated fragments of the self along Kohut's vertical split(s). This helps explain why so much narcissistic malingering can be acted out in the sexual sphere.

Both Kernberg and Kohut furnish compelling accounts of psychological experience—and its psychoanalytical "feedback"—in the age that Walter Benjamin characterized in terms of the "decline of experience" and the "loss of aura."[15] The prognosis for psychoanalysis is as hopeful in Kohut's version as its circumstances are bleak in Kernberg's. I close this introduction to their work and to the conceptual modifications necessitated by an object-relations point of view with a passage from Kohut illustrative of how his upbeat point of view might actually be warranted. Kohut is speaking for him "self" here. Nowhere is the dissonance and interplay between "disparate personality attitudes in depth" more lucidly formulated. Nowhere is the psychoanalytical collaboration "at such 'vertical' barriers" (AS, 183) better outlined, in the formidable task confronting it, and in the possibilities for improved communication between relaxed and grandiose counterdrafts in the evolving edition of the self.

> What is the nature of the analytic work which is performed at such "vertical" barriers? What are the activities of the analyst that enhance the correlated endopsychic transformations? The substance of the psychological task is clearly not the classical one of "making conscious" with the aid of interpretations. It is akin to the abolishing of the defense mechanism of "isolation" as it occurs in the analysis of the obsessional patient. But, while the circumstances here bear a certain resemblance to those in obsessional neurosis, they are by no means identical. In the narcissistic personality disturbances (including, especially, certain perversions) we are not dealing with the isolation of circumscribed contents from one another, or with the isolation of ideation from affect, but with the side-by-side existence of disparate personality attitudes in depth; i.e., the side-by-side existence of cohesive personality attitudes with different goal structures, different pleasure aims, different moral and aesthetic values. It is the aim of the analytic work in such cases to bring the central sector of the personality to an acknowledgment of the psychic reality of the simultaneous existence (1) of unaltered conscious and preconscious narcissistic and/or perverse aims, and (2) of the realistic goal structures and the moral and aesthetic standards which reside in

the central sector. The innumerable ways by which the increasing integration of the split-off sector is brought about defy description. But as a concrete and frequently occurring example I mention the overcoming of the often severe resistances—mainly motivated by shame—which oppose the patient's "mere" description of his overt narcissistic behavior, of his conscious perverse fantasies or activities, and the like. To say "mere" description is, of course, based on a profound misunderstanding of the dynamic relationships which prevail in such individuals. The informed analyst will understand how difficult it is for the patient to accept the split-off sector as truly contiguous with the central one. (*AS*, 183–84)

CHAPTER 7

# Object-Relations Theory:
# Alice Miller

No introduction to the current theory of narcissism and both its individuality and cultural manifestations could fulfill its responsibility without a serious reference to Alice Miller, author of works including *The Drama of the Gifted Child* (1981)[1] and *Thou Shalt Not be Aware: Society's Betrayal of the Child* (1986).[2] The story Miller narrates is very much in line with Kohut's tale of deficits in empathy and mirroring. Her account confirms the subjective emptiness (she calls it depression) and ongoing grandiosity and contempt that are the legacy of Kernberg's pathologically narcissistic and borderline patients. Her claim on a unique corner of this collective enquiry consists in the rigor with which she recounts the evolution of the psychological ills of our times from the perspective of the subject who is both its product and victim: from the point of view of the child.

Alice Miller's story is endowed with the simplicity characteristic of those syntheses most conducive to a profound regrouping of the empirical data. Those who have had the fortune to pursue the fashions in literary theory over the past twenty-five years have come closest to the principles of her genealogy in their encounter with Nietzsche. Within the parameters and conventions of psychoanalytical thought, it is Miller who continues the tradition of anger and disbelief with which Nietzsche regarded the perpetuation of European repression and moralism.[3] According to Miller, these psychosocial restraints show no signs of abating. The breeding ground of the abuses of narcissism is an altruism and sense of responsibility that early in life distanciates individuals from their emotional reactions and impels them in the direction of Winnicottian "false self."

> They have all developed the art of not experiencing feelings, for a child can only experience his feelings when there is somebody

there who accepts him fully, understands and supports him. If that is missing, if the child must risk losing the mother's love, or that of her substitute, then he cannot experience these feelings secretly, "just for himself" but fails to experience them at all. But nevertheless . . . something remains. (*DGC,* 10)

When our children can consciously experience their early help-lessness and narcissistic rage they will no longer need to ward off their helplessness, in turn, with exercise of powers over others. In most cases, however, one's own childhood suffering remains affectively inaccessible and thus forms the hidden source of new and very subtle humiliation for the next generation. (*DGC,* 70)

Kernberg and Kohut, while they bring the psychoanalytical understanding of the interpersonal field to a new level, continue the Freudian tradition in which fieldwork, case studies—told from the psychoanalyst's point of view—corroborate and amplify the current theoretical model of choice. Among the many distinctions of Miller's work is the tenacity with which she holds to the enter-prise of narrating—always from the child's perspective—the ma-nipulations and oversights by which adults, as paradigmatic special agents, revisit and perpetuate the narcissistic wounds of their own early years. It is in this sense that the economy of narcissism keeps us "Prisoners of Childhood," the title of *Drama of the Gifted Child* in its first edition. In Miller's account of a by now familiar story, always very much from the perspective of the child, the gifted are, ironically, most susceptible to the wounding in both the passive and active modalities of the verb because their very gifts constitute a refuge in which they can overcompensate for the excesses of abuse and neglect. "The person who is 'grandiose' is admired everywhere and needs this admiration; indeed, he cannot live without it. He must excel brilliantly in everything he undertakes, which he is surely capable of doing (otherwise he does not attempt to do it). He, too, admires himself—for his qualities: his beauty, cleverness, talents—and for his success and achievements. Woe betide him if one of these fails him, for then the catastrophe of a severe depression is immanent" (*DGC,* 38). Here Miller betrays a detachment from her narcissistic clients that we have observed in Freud, Kernberg, and Kohut as well.

But Miller never strays far from childhood as the scene of the narcissistic crime; in this resides much of her distinction and the unique focus she brings to bear on the psychoanalytical enterprise. For Miller, child abuse, in its aggressive and sexual facets, is a very real thing. If psychoanalysis—and the wider culture of psychoanalytical thought that includes scholarly studies such as the present one—would only focus upon and recapitulate the disastrous events from early life, it might achieve a concentration often otherwise lacking and avoid its own predilections to overintellectualization. The intellectual world was shaken some years back by Jeffrey Masson's contention that Freud had revised his own theory of childhood sexuality: he ended up ascribing adult hysteria to childhood "fantasies" of sexuality instead of actual (abusive) experience.[4] Miller's concern with this flap is not in the interest of scholarly precision, but out of her awareness of how much continues to be at stake, even in the contemporary world, in the denial of the multifaceted abuse that defenseless children continue to receive.

> The general public tends to doubt the prevalence of sexual abuse of children by older siblings and adults and to deny its lasting effects, because the necessary repression of what one knew as a young child blocks any later insight into this subject. Furthermore, it is not in the best interest of adults, once they are in a position to take over the active role themselves, to uncover the motives behind their actions. But most important, the principles of "poisonous pedagogy" insist that parents' actions toward their children be regarded as loving and beneficial and that children be denied the right to protest. (*TSN*, 158).

The actuality of child abuse, what Miller calls, in a chapter title, "The Vicious Circle of Contempt" (*DGC*, 64), the Nietzschean recurrence by means of which the victims of childhood perpetuate its abuses—these are the data that motivated Miller's writing career, and also her withdrawal from those (institutional) aspects of psychoanalysis that perpetuate the Big Lie, that would deny to child abuse its own reality. Surely, from a certain theoretical point of view, this would tinge Miller's work with advocacy; it would implicate her in the reification of certain selected aspects of experience. Yet Miller has anticipated these objections in her particular account of intellectualization: "It is easy to see why some professors, who are quite capable of expressing themselves clearly, will use such complicated and convoluted language when they present their ideas that the students can only acquire them in a fog of anger and diligence—without being able to make much use of them. These students may well have the same sorts of feelings that their teacher once had and was forced to suppress in relation to his parents. If the students become teachers one day, they will have the opportunity to pass on this unusable knowledge" (*DGC*, 109–10).

Miller would hold the abuses of narcissism very much to their childhood scenes and origins. This focus endows her thinking on the psychoanalytic enterprise with a very distinctive flavor. "Slings and arrows" of recent vintage may have psychoanalytical significance, but their primary value consists in their serving as screens behind which lurk moods and memories of truly venerable lineage. In a passage to which I will refer again during the reading of the film, "The Silence of the Lambs," that follows in chapter 16 below, Miller articulates the tenets of a Freudian orientation to childhood experience to which she still holds:

1. Everyone is shaped (this does not mean determined) by his or her childhood.
2. Neuroses are rooted in childhood.
3. The methods of free association and of the analytic setting (couch, rule of abstinence) make it possible for the drama of childhood to be reenacted in the transference and for a maturation process that has been blocked by neurosis to begin.
4. Changes in personality occurring during analysis do not stem from "corrective emotional experience" but from insights that the patient arrives at by repetition, remembering, and working through the relevant material. (*TSN*, 51–52).

Given the bizarre manifestations that can arise during "the revival of the introjects, and learning to come to terms with them, with the help of the transference" (*DGC*, 19) the above rules of thumb endow psychoanalysis with a possibly unexpected determination. Moods, behaviors, and manifestations seemingly of the most recent provenance are rooted in the (structurally) tragic conditions of childhood. To the degree that psychoanalysis can, eschewing moralism and "reeducation," conjure up these past events and moods, it can free the client from the prison house of childhood and from the compulsion to repeat the self-perpetuating cycle of abuse.

Millerian psychoanalysis is a setting in which the client is released to undertake a very empathic and open-ended "repetition, remembering, and working through." The analyst must come to terms with his/her own unconscious identifications with authority and its Big Lies; s/he must resist his/her impulse to perpetuate the wounds resulting in his/her own choice of a profession. In the debate over educationalism to which I will return in chapter 16, in which Kohut and Kernberg were engaged, Miller comes down squarely on the side of Kohut's extreme reticence to threaten the environment of empathy with any external, proven wisdom.

In crucial senses, Miller's work affirms certain of the attitudes at the heart of an object-relations approach to psychoanalysis: the agonizing symptoms as the way out as well as the way into the "disease"; an orientation to accessing, reassessing, and in this way "mastering" the particular narcissistic wounds of childhood; and understanding that since the repressed material is by its nature traumatic, the "road" or "pathway" of psychoanalysis will be rocky long before it "smooths out" or takes a turn for the better; a sense of the therapeutic alliance as a collaboration between two individuals who have acknowledged the tragic dimensions of human experience and endeavors; a dimensional sense of the difficulty in effecting changes, of the time and shared patience and tolerance that repetition, remembering, and working through require.

The breeding ground of narcissistic disturbances or "pathologies of the self" is a family situation oriented toward the parents' needs, vestiges of their own early wounds, rather than toward the optimal conditions for the child's personal growth: empathic, tolerant mirroring and self-unfolding:

> The parents have found in their child's "false self" the confirmation they were looking for, a substitute for their own missing structures: the child, who has been unable to build up his own structures, is first consciously and then unconsciously (through the introject) dependent on his parents. He cannot rely on his own emotions, has not come to experience them through trial and error, has no sense of his own needs, and is alienated from himself to the highest degree. Under these circumstances, he cannot separate from his parents, and even as an adult he is still dependent on affirmation from his partner, from groups, or especially from his own children. The heirs of the parents are the introjects, from whom the "true self" must remain concealed, and

so loneliness in the parental home is later followed by isolation in the self. Narcissistic cathexis of her child by the mother does not exclude emotional devotion. On the contrary, she loves the child, as her self-object, excessively, though not in the manner that he needs. (*DGC*, 14)

Psychoanalytical working through and the therapeutic alliance arise in the context of this familial and cultural breakdown in the parenting function, of the counterfeit bearing and emotions to which the child has been lead through this role-reversal. Much of what Miller has to say about the therapeutic process itself is illuminating. Psychoanalysis is articulated in several stages, each with its own pitfalls, distortions, and triumphs.

In the majority of cases, it is not difficult to point out to the patient early in his analysis the way he has dealt with his feelings and needs, and that this was a question of survival for him. It is a great relief for him that things he was accustomed to choke off can be recognized and taken seriously. The psychoanalyst can use the material the patient presents to show him how he treats his feelings with ridicule and irony, tries to persuade himself they do not exist, belittles them, and either does not become aware of them at all or only after several days when they have already passed. Gradually, the patient himself realizes how he is forced to look for distraction when he is moved, upset, or sad. (*DGC,*17)

Miller, like Kernberg and Kohut, is struck by how few sufferers of narcissistic disturbances will seek out any sort of therapeutic intervention. This is because the personality disorder, or what Kernberg would call the borderline organization, is itself a homeostatic or self-perpetuating system of defense: its internal tactics are quite successful in informing those who have taken it on as a coping mechanism exactly how far they can go in maintaining a grandiose lifestyle while also seeming to adhere to social norms of humility, altruism, and conformity to the rules. Miller writes: "A grandiose person will only look for an analyst if depressive episodes come to his aid and force him to do so" (*DGC*, 50). In the situation of personal grandiosity, those exquisitely painful and bizarre symptoms, that Poe would have ascribed to his "imp of the perverse," constitute, in one of their facets, blessings: they are the manifestations inducing an individual to take his/her grandiosity before the High Court of measure (meaning, the Social Contract), personified by the figure of the psychotherapist in the role of social mediator.

Once initiated, however, psychotherapy brings with it quick relief, yet this initial improvement, as Miller understands, is possessed of its own limitations. Psychotherapy's initial curative effect, as described in the immediately preceding passage, is a matter of a reconciliation with previously concealed facets of psychological life; results from the satisfactions of taking the false self in hand, in bringing the trial to Court. As comforting as this initial reconciliation may be, it is succeeded by therapeutic dramas of far more ambiguous value, whose underlying tactics and transvaluations of value are masterpieces of subterfuge:

> The analyst must take on a second [function] as soon as the transference neurosis has developed: that of being a transference figure. Feelings out of various periods of childhood come to the surface then. This is the most difficult stage in analysis, when there is most acting out. The patient begins to be articulate and breaks with his former compliant attitudes, but because of his early experience he cannot believe this is possible without mortal danger. The compulsion to repeat leads him to provoke situations where his fear of object loss, rejection, and isolation has a basis in present reality, situations into which he drags the analyst with him . . . so that afterward he can enjoy the relief of having taken the risk and been true to himself. This can begin quite harmlessly. The patient is surprised by feelings that he would rather not have recognized, but now it is too late. . . . Now the analysand must (and also is allowed to!) experience himself in a way he had never before thought possible. (*DGC*, 17–18)

The phase that psychotherapy enters when the first glow of its empathy and understanding fades is one of misplaced and untimely, but devastating recognitions. The recognitions that ultimately prove capable of displacing a grandiose lifestyle may result only from the most misguided acting out, yet they are recognitions. They belong to a theoretical-psychoanalytical model for the emergence of knowledge whose ultimate source is the Hegel of *The Phenomenology of Spirit*. The recognitions to which the patient leads him/herself out of an ultimate dissatisfaction with the cycle of contempt and shame, facilitated by the therapist's empathy are revolutionary, at the same time that they are poorly timed and outrageously staged (acted out). Miller's description here of the therapeutic misadventures endemic to a process in which vital human measures and assurances emerge only when it is too late bespeak her own excitement at and involvement in the therapeutic process. The dénouement of the process, as she describes it, is a triumphant one, at least in dramatic terms. Yet at no time does she give in to yet another grandiose fantasy: that psychotherapy has somehow arrived at an intimate truth, whether the truth-content of a lifetime, or a "true self."

> The true self has been in a "state of noncommunication" as Winnicott said, because it had to be protected. The patient never needs to hide anything else so thoroughly, so deeply, and for so a long time as he has hidden his true self. Thus it is like a miracle each time to see how much individuality has survived behind such dissimulation, denial, and self-alienation, and can reappear as soon as the work of mourning brings freedom from the introjects. Nevertheless, it would be wrong to understand Winnicott's words to mean that there is a fully developed true self hidden behind the false self. If that were so, there would be no narcissistic disturbance but a conscious self-protection. . . . It is only after it is liberated in analysis that the self begins to be articulate, to grow, and to develop its creativity. Where there had only been fearful emptiness or equally frightening grandiose fantasies, there is now unfolding an unexpected wealth of vitality. This is not a homecoming since this home had never before existed. It is the discovery of home. (DGC, 20–21)

The ultimate achievement that Miller claims here, although miraculous and wonderful, stops far short of an apotheosis, of Hegelian "Absolute Knowing." Her ultimate claim, and here she echoes Winnicott, is of a homecoming, a recognition of the adequacy of non-grandiose conditions. Dying, Emma Bovary may come close to this recognition when she understands that life with Charles Bovary would have been "good enough."

Yet the thrust of Alice Miller's psychoanalytic theory is less of a "making do" than a setting aside of a defensive lifestyle and set of strategies. Her enterprise shares with the work of Kernberg and Kohut two vital movements: a discernment of grandiose manifestations and their underlying causes, and an articulation of the conditions under which these tactics can be productively abandoned and replaced. She devotes major sections of her writings to such literary figures as Hesse and Kafka, suggesting the applicability of the disturbances of narcissism to esthetic production and the intellectual life. Far outweighing any moral trial to which she subjects the grandiose is a vivid recollection of childhood—its brutalities and its letdowns—that she sustains despite society's wariness with regard to child abuse and the general ruses of memory. She is an important advocate of the beaten child who survives in many of us, and she corrects the current discourse of psychoanalysis of any tendencies to cold and moralistic detachment to which it may, in moments of misrecognition, revert.

# CHAPTER 8

# Robert Musil, The Man without Qualities: Setting

In the wake of the preceding introduction to the recognition of a new subject on the part of the psychoanalytical field, a readjustment toward individuals who do not necessarily manifest personalities in the conventional sense of the term, it will hopefully not be too jarring if we shift our attention to Robert Musil's *The Man without Qualities* (*Der Mann ohne Eigenschaften*). This is a major work of early twentieth-century encyclopedic fiction, ranking alongside Proust's *Recherche*, Joyce's *Ulysses* and *Finnegans Wake*, the body of Kafka's novels, and Mann's *Dr. Faustus* and *The Magic Mountain*. In two particular ways it stands out from more or less contemporary efforts to assemble vast historical and epistemological backdrops to the drama at hand: while *Ulysses* and *The Magic Mountain* also incorporate certain scientific discourses or models either operative in or illuminating the "action," Musil' work is the most comprehensive in insisting upon the inseparability of scientific or philosophical rigor from linguistic suggestibility and esthetic power. Musil may well be the encyclopedic novelist who best understood the interdependency between prolixity and minimalism, dynamism and entropy, free-associative indirection and prepositional finitude necessarily interjected in any representational setting for the technological, demographic, sociopolitical complexities of advanced Western twentieth-century experience.[1] Secondly, Musil's characterization in *The Man without Qualities* is so vivid, and his central unifying event, a campaign to celebrate the ideology and contributions of Austrian culture, so ingenious, that the novel is able to shift into a social commentary strongly reminiscent of the Frankfurt School without in any way losing its formal concentration or thrust. In the enterprise of social commentary, Musil is not alone; Walter Benjamin, for one, highlights and celebrates Proust's gifts as a social critic. To this writer's mind, however, no other novelist succeeded quite so well in opening up the genre to the pointed interplay of linguistic, conceptual, demographic, technological, ideological, and mass psychological factors for whose discursive elaboration we revere Adorno, Horkheimer, Benjamin, and Marcuse.

Musil's formal training was in Engineering. He maintained lifelong interests in experimental and theoretical Psychology. While the engineer in him questioned certain pivotal Freudian beliefs, such as in an unconscious, important aspects of his big novel are structured by Freudian concepts. In this regard, he is in the position of psychologists who, while they shifted Freudian values, emphasizing social or object-relations at the expense of the classical waystations on the path of psychosexual development, nevertheless remained somehow within the psychoanalytic field. For the purpose of the present essay on character in literature and psychology, I shall emphasize Musil's importance as a harbinger of the departure—in both planes—away from fixed notions of subjectivity, its drives, and its dysfunctions and toward the notions of personality disorders and borderline states. The clarification of these newer concepts is a process still taking place; and as of this writing much lies ahead in terms of their empirical verification and delimitation. Yet "borderline" is a term that stands out in *The Man without Qualities*, and its significance is strikingly close to that with which a contemporary Viennese, Otto Kernberg, has embued it.

The psychological developments that we may extrapolate from *The Man without Qualities* are thus important ones. Musil stands at their head. Admittedly, this is a focused rather than a comprehensive approach to a very broad novelistic canvas.[2] But it is an approach that has a certain specificity, if you will, personality, of its own. It gains in definition what it loses at the level of idealization.

The great comprehensive joke spanning Musil's novel—and it parallels one at the heart of Proust's *Recherche*—is that the title is completely misleading. If any character in the novel may be considered a personage or surrogate of qualities, it is Ulrich, the "man without qualities." Conversely, the characters with whom he interacts, presumably the foils to Ulrich's imputed vacuity or amorphousness, turn out, one after the other, to be possessed of the emptiness stated in the novel's title and prophetic of contemporary understandings of personality disorders and borderline conditions. Even Ulrich, at one point in his meditations, acknowledges his own awareness of this irony: "Which had to confess to himself, smiling, that for all this he was after all, a 'character' even without having one" (1:175). Given the novel's pronounced gravitation, at the levels of theme and characterization, to a certain borderline, one, admittedly slanted, access that the novel offers into its complex workings is to be read in its own terms as the story of a working intellectual's largely conflictual interactions with characters of lesser quality, or perhaps more accurately, with characters not possessing at the fictional moment of the novel, the same degree of "cohesion of the self" (Kohut) or "true self" (Winnicott). Put differently, *The Man without Qualities* may be read as an allegory of the problematic relations in which both thought-through intellectual work and well-formed selves (and these two entities are apposite to each other) find themselves enmeshed. The story, paying all due respect to the idiosyncratic and antagonistic features of the intellectual self, is told from the intellectual's point of view. Self and sense of self as evidenced in the capacity for productive intellectual "working through" are indeed the bones of contention in the novel, no longer the penis of the Freudian universe or its enlargement in Lacan and others to the notion of the phallus within the symbolic domain.

In this scenario, I do not want at all to posit Ulrich as some kind of transcendent or totally cohesive "self." Ulrich, as opposed to Kernberg's pathological narcissists and borderline patients, is defined by his *inabilities* to bring about certain forms of resolution. The most prevalent imagery in the novel is one of forces, vectors, waves, attractions, and repulsions within a physical field. Ulrich, whose family name is playfully withheld from the reader, is as subject to the novel's play of forces as any other character.[3] He is unable to resolve his own gravitation to abstraction and scientific thought with his absorption in discrete experiences. The novel represents him as subject to a wide array of sexual charges and counterforces, some of a disastrous nature, but with which he, as yet another element within the field, nonetheless interacts.

Something within Ulrich is fundamentally antipathetic to naive idealization. This something is his rigor as an intellectual, the precision also at the root of Wittgenstein's rage for distinction making. Nor is Ulrich very successful at the polarizations of value so prevalent in borderline personalities and rigid state ideologies. The name "Ulrich," then, designates a thinking and critical scene one of whose prominent features is its *inefficiency*, its refusal to compromise a certain specificity and autonomy. Ulrich is by no means perfect. Certain of the values upon which he meditates, such as incest as a release from dissimulation and seduction within the sexual sphere, are positively horrifying. But precisely in this active imperfection, which he describes in the second part of the Second Book as an active passivity, and which is akin to the "less-than-perfect mother" that the child confronts in D. W. Winnicott's scenario for development,[4] precisely in this capacity for imperfection and uncommensurability is Ulrich's tension with the other major characters, who become particularly intelligible to us through psychoanalytical considerations of narcissism, personality disorders, and the self.

Whatever in the novel's narrative cohesion is not supplied by the personage of Ulrich enters by means of two overarching events, or rather events in a state of becoming that span the novel, which is set in 1913–14, on the verge of World War I. One of these is the Collateral Campaign, a celebration of Austrian achievements and national values planned for 1918, when Emperor Franz Joseph will reach the seventieth year of his reign. The Collateral Campaign has been placed under the direction of Imperial Liege-Count Leinsdorf, and Ulrich, at his father's insistence, has had himself appointed executive secretary to Leinsdorf. The large committee to plan the jubilee combines, in Leinsdorf's words, "cultural and capital" (1:115), an elite of moneyed and cultured interests. For an aristocrat such as Leinsdorf, or for German industrialist Paul Arnheim, with whom Ulrich will engage in a spirited antagonism, "culture" and "capital" are joined in a metonymic relationship. For an intellectual such as Ulrich, the cooperation of interests, the substitution of intellectual for economic captial, comprises a highly problematical softening of esthetic, scientific, and philosophical rigor.

The second event lending the novel whatever narrative cohesion it has to offer is the trial of one Christian Moosbrugger, whose brutal murder of a prostitute, an act of dismemberment, has both horrified and captivated Austrian society. Moosbrugger is a daunting physical presence. In the public eye, he is as charming and affable as he is in his private life psychopathic. Moosbrugger is an embodiment of the subjective emptiness that for Kernberg epitomizes contemporary psychopathology. At his center is a void. He passes without transition from heartless murder to the crowd pleasing manipulation of his own image through the media. Possessing no self and no ideals, he is capable of stunning feats of polarization and reversal. He manifests precisely none of the introspection that Ulrich feels compelled to bring to some scientifically responsible conclusion and in which the other characters, at least for specific purposes, sometimes engage. Moosbrugger is the novel's starkest, but by no means solitary, embodiment of the borderline state. His trial is a disquieting counterweight to the Collateral Campaign, its phantasmatic subliminal repetition. While the Collateral Campaign may be described as a futile retrospective exercise in the idealization of very real national processes, tendencies, events, and accomplishments, the trial confronts Austrian society with the vacuum or voiding out of these very ideals.

The counter-events of the Collateral Campaign and Moosbrugger's trial furnish the novel with a very resonant and flexible narrative unity enabling Ulrich's awareness and relations with other characters to unfold and serving as a platform for its at times stunning critical commentary, which attains social, psychological, philosophical, and literary-theoretical dimensions.

If one could argue that Ulrich is Robert Musil's most immediate and telling—though by no means exclusive—fictive surrogate in the novel, this central character is fated, until the Third Book at least, to a certain painful solitude, one chastened by intellectual honesty. (If a "man without qualities" is supposedly Musil's answer to the predispositions to narcissistic and borderline lifestyles that he sees emerging in the sociopolitical, economic, technological, and demographic conditions of twentieth-century life, then even this anti-narcissist succumbs to the martyrdom of a certain delicious solitude.) It is nevertheless quite striking that when Ulrich emerges from his alienation, it is to interact with a set of characters all demonstrating, to some degree, the traits that have become associated, in the literature of clinical psychology and psychoanalysis, with the economies of pathological narcissism and the borderline personality. In terms of the admittedly slanted reading we are giving this meganovel, we can say that the vast majority of the figures with which Ulrich comes into contact are characterized either by the impulsive, decentered acting out exemplified by Moosbrugger or by problems of excessive idealization that prohibit the realization of their interests or desires. At the advent of contemporary psychology, Musil's novel becomes an allegory of a working intellectual's interactions and struggles with the less clearly defined selves, operating in accordance with a variety of institutions and interests, around him. (This scenario is party to certain narcissistic and martyr-like overtones of its own. If it is accurate, however, it may be "read out" of other contemporary works as well: I think, for example, of Stephen Dedalus's falling out with Buck Mulligan in *Ulysses*,[5] or of the societal disapproval expressed both to Swann and Vinteuil's daughter in Proust's *Recherche*.)[6] This working-through of the conflict between a relatively centered and exploratory self and the diffuser "selves" that it both captivates and injures is nowhere more evident than in Ulrich's rivalries with other characters, a tension in no short supply throughout the novel.

*The Man without Qualities* concerns the period 1913–14, and was written roughly during the last twenty years of Musil's life (1880–1942). Although the lag between the period of historical representation and composition is not a great one, the text is infused with the major irony implicit in the historical novel genre: the characters, regardless of how intelligent or well-informed, blindly grope toward the historical outcome about which the reader knows more than they do.[7] The actuality and interpretation of represented events are under the charge, reordering, and revision of the author. The characters, even Ulrich and Arnheim, in different ways bellweathers of their age, are at a disadvantage. Yet the peculiar temporality of the composition of this novel is unusual. Had Musil written about a period with an ostensibly more "closed" accounting, say the one from Goethe to Napoleon (both important paradigms and counterinstances to Ulrich's thinking), the generic irony would be more manageable. But in 1942, shortly before he died, Musil knew a great deal more about the longer-standing implications of the events telescoped into the time framework of the novel than he did in the early twenties, when he began composition, or in 1930, when he published the First Book of the work-in-progress (2:127). By virtue of this unusually complex temporality of writing, making the novel a cross between "safe" historical retrospection and evolving chronicle, certain of its characters, notably Ulrich and Diotima, "grow" in knowledge and interpretative capability as the narrative proceeds toward its unfinished ending.

Crucial to the novel's historical framework and thematic is the rivalry between the two national and administrative centers of the German-speaking world, Germany and the Austro-Hungarian Empire. When the novel begins, Kakania, the scatalogical nickname for the conflict ridden Eastern European imperial confederation, can posit a legitimate claim as the senior of the two German nations. By the time Musil died in Switzerland, the fates of Austria, the Slavonic societies, and the Jewish characters in the novel, were sealed, at least for a certain interim, adding yet another remarkable irony to the states of affairs crystallized in the novel proper.

However history intervened in the composition of the novel, both the "living" history of the events 1914–45 and the author's ordered historical recapitulation, there is little doubt, in terms of the novel's literary-epistemological-scientific domain, of Musil's encyclopedic aspirations. Through the inherently unrealizable comprehensive goals of the Collateral Campaign, Musil ironizes the possibilities for such panoptical hindsight; yet he still incorporates a treasury of the most prevalent artistic, literary, philosophical, and scientific influences upon Austrian culture during the period within the fictive time frame. At the outer parameters of these influences are the Kantian sublimity in esthetics and a Hegelian historiography revolving around such world-historical men as Goethe and Napoleon, and on which nationality manifests the spirit of a people.[8] In the more immediate range, Ulrich, either by virtue of his own interests or through the fellow surrogates with which he interacts largely acrimoniously, must cope with such factors as the music of Wagner, the estheticism of the Rossettis, the philosophy of Nietzsche, Frege, and Wittgenstein, and quantum physics and relativity. Ironically, the most powerful *literary* influence on the novel may well be *Also Sprach Zarathustra*: Ulrich's extended discourses are set off from the evolving action in full relief. They are invested with a certain seriousness and surrounded with significant details of setting reminiscent of Zarathustrian parables.[9] Musil also engages in an ongoing dialogue with the encyclopaedic authors of his day. In *The Man without Qualities* he addresses the sweeping social setting prevalent in the novels of Thomas Mann, in which major historical events and influences reverberate throughout the narrative levels circumscribed first by the central, then the peripheral characters. When the rivalrous action of the first two volumes gives way to the (even) more meditative sibling reunion of the Third Book, a Proustian mood of (possibly ironic) retrospection coincides with the opening of a temporal dimension to Ulrich's experience.

Ulrich may be exonerated from qualities, then, but he still bears an enormous historical and narrative burden for the novel. He is an exemplary, though no longer so young, child of his times. He is situated at a powerful, but also ominous nexus of sociopolitical, historical, intellectual, and even physical forces (as the extensive references to waves and fields attest). He can afford to react to the death of his father indifferently (indifference is a prevalent, but mostly jarring emotional response in the novel), because he is more importantly the progeny of an era and a set of theoretical models. The decisive birthmark he bears is his refusal to succumb to "splitting," whether of an intellectual (between science and literature) or psychological (between "good sense" and eroticism) nature, even if this flies in the face of long-standing esthetic tradition. The narrative is quite cognizant both of the forces militating for such splitting during its historical moment and of the significance of Ulrich's "shaking them off." In terms of the narrative's "Frankfurt School" style of intellectual-social criticism, "to possess a double mental personality has long ceased to be the sort of trick that only lunatics bring off. On the contrary, the speed at which we live today, the possibility of political understanding, the ability to write a newspaper article, the ˙igour required to believe in new movements in art and literature, and countless other things, are wholly founded on a talent for being at certain hours convinced against one's own conviction, for splitting a part off from the whole content of one's consciousness and for spreading it out to form a new state of entire conviction" (2:107). The age Ulrich both exemplifies and sums up (for better and for worse) is one in which the domains of art and the spirit have no recourse but to acknowledge their foregone scientific (i.e., in terms of this novel, critical) dimension.

Although Ulrich is told by different characters that he should write down his thoughts on various topics (2:231, 430), he repeatedly repudiates the activity and social role of writing. (This is another Proustian irony.) As a purveyer of existing artistic traditions and conceptual models, Ulrich's bearing is one that Foucault would call archaeological. In the contentious skepticism he directs at inherited cultural baggage concerning nationality, idealism, and idealization, spiritualism, and theology, among other topics, his attitude is implicitly deconstructive.

So endowed with writerly talent is Musil that he will not shy away from even the riskiest and most problematic tasks. In chapters 15 and 16, the narrator, initiating a critical function that will be taken over by Ulrich, sketches out a historico-intellectual backdrop for the particular time and place of the novel. This overview, with all the dangers of overgeneralization with which it is fraught, describes an age beset by ambivalences also reminiscent of Benjamin's "Theses on the Philosophy of History," particularly as they are concentrated in the figure of the "Angelus Novus."[10]

> Out of the oil-smooth spirit of the two last decades of the nineteenth century, suddenly, throughout Europe, there rose a kindling fever. Nobody knew exactly what was on the way; nobody was able to say whether it was to be a new art, a New Man, a new morality or perhaps a re-shuffling of society. So everyone made of it what he liked. But people were standing up on all sides to fight against an old way of life. Suddenly the right man was on the spot everywhere; and, what is so important, men of practical enterprise joined forces with the men of intellectual enterprise. Talents developed that had previously been choked or had taken no part at all in public life. They were as different from each other as anything well could be, and the contradictions in their aims were unsurpassable. The Superman was adored, and the Subman was adored; health and the sun were worshipped, and the delicacy of consumptive girls was worshipped; people were enthusiastic hero-worshippers and enthusiastic adherents of the social creed of the Man in the Street; one had faith and was skeptical, one was naturalistic and precious, robust and morbid; one dreamed of ancient castles and shady avenues, autumnal gardens, glassy ponds, jewels, hashish, disease and demonism, but also of prairies, vast horizons, forges and rolling-mills, naked wrestlers, the uprisings of the slaves of toil, man and woman in

the primeval Garden, and the destruction of society. Admittedly these were contradictions and very different battle-cries, but they all breathed the same breath of life. If that epoch had been analyzed, some such nonsense would have come out as a square circle supposed to be made of wooden iron; but in reality all this had blended into shimmering significance. This illusion, which found its embodiment in the magical date of the turn of the century, was so powerful that it made some hurl themselves enthusiastically upon the new, as yet untrodden century, while others were having a last fling in the old one, as in a house that one is moving out of anyway, without either one or the other party feeling that there was much difference between the two attitudes. (1:59)

This passage is in the tradition of panoptical ambivalence established by the first lines of Dickens's *A Tale of Two Cities*. It is riven by contradictions, but held together by "the same breath of life." The unifying factor is an underlying montage superimposing the reading, dreams and ideas of the 1913–14 period, when the century, although young, has lost its first blush of newness, upon its public life and popular culture. Within each arena incorporated by this superimposition, double messages are rife. Appeasement of existing conditions stands side by side with active resistance, decadence alongside the grandiose philosophical transcendence embodied by the Nietzschean *Übermensch*. The setting in which the mood transpires, the architectural foundation or dramatic scaffolding on which its action takes place, is already hopelessly split.

Historically and literarilly, the novel is the extension of a moment conditioned by splitting. One epiphenomenon of this pervasive atmosphere of contradiction is a sudden blurring out of focus, a going out of whack. Musil inscribes into the novel's very historic-phenomenological underpinnings, then, the vacuousness and structural whiteout of borderline conditions.

Something imponderable. A prognostic. An illusion. Like what happens when a magnet lets the iron filings go and they tumble together again . . . or when a ball of string comes undone . . . or when a tension has slackened . . . or when an orchestra begins to play out of tune. No one could have established the existence of any details that might not just as well have existed in earlier times too; but all the relations between things had shifted slightly.

Ideas that had once been of lean account grew fat. Persons who
had previously not been taken altogether seriously now acquired
fame. What had been harsh mellowed down, what had been
separated re-united. . . . Sharp borderlines everywhere became
blurred, and some new, indescribable capacity for entering into
hitherto unheard-of relationships threw up new people and new
ideas. These people and ideas were not wicked. No, far from it.
It was only that the good was adulterated with a little too much
of the bad, the truth with error, and the meaning with a little too
much of the spirit of accommodation. (1:62)

This passage describes a comprehensive moral, intellectual, and
relational meltdown. It is itself spoken from a narrative perspective
of some detachment and even superiority, as if appropriate fame
or the adulterations of values could be adjudicated. To step outside
the Vienna of 1913–14 is to understand that a perceptive and
judgmental *trompe l'oeil* had taken place, that historically, certain
unsettling and unsettled borderline phenomena originated amid its
confusion of structures and lassitudes. Yet Ulrich von _____ is
very much of his time and place. " 'One can't be angry with one's
own time without damage to oneself,' Ulrich felt. And indeed he
was always ready to love all these manifestations of life" (1:64). It
is perhaps Ulrich's preeminent quality to subject his self to his
time's confusions. The very ambivalences described and demonstrated by the above two citations would constitute a serious threat
to the very cohesion of a less substantial self. The mission upon
which the novel dispatches Ulrich is to observe, witness, and even
*become* his age's confusion while retaining enough integrity to
register his own critical commentary upon it. Given the particular
stresses upon the Vienna of 1913–14, this assignment is a formidable one, but in a certain sense it is paradigmatic of the predicament in which all of us who write with a critical eye are enmeshed.

# CHAPTER 9

# The Man without Qualities:
## An Inter"personal" Reading

If Ulrich were a psychoanalytical subject, which of course he is not (he *is* a literary surrogate), we would be applying an object-relations approach to him. That is, by examining the nature of his inter"personal" relationships with other surrogates, we would be "teasing out" the lineaments of the current psychoanalytical understanding of the narcissistic personality disorders at least from within the critical infrastructure of Musil's novel.

By way of introduction to this stratum of the narrative, and in the effort of furnishing the passages I shall cite with some context, a bit more should be said on a general level about Ulrich's "inter-character" interactions. Ulrich's return to Vienna at the beginning of the novel after an absence of three years affords him the status of a "free-floating signifier" and endows the relationships he undertakes with an aura of spontaneity, impermanence, and whimsicality, even in the instances of long-standing associations. (It becomes increasingly difficult for Musil to sustain this sense of surprise throughout the Second and Third Books. The emergence of a previously unmentioned sister, however, and the issues of twinning, parity, and de-sexualized mutuality that she raises, at the beginning of the Third Book, does supply needed energy at the end and shifts thematic considerations in important ways.)

Shortly after the beginning of this novel, Ulrich resumes his friendship with Walter, a lifelong compatriot, and his wife Clarisse. Walter has largely abandoned his youthful preoccupations with music and painting in favor of an administrative position "in some government office dealing with the fine arts" (1:53). Clarisse is a creature of the wild, unruly enthusiasms in the arts and contemporary intellectual movements. Among her obsessions are Nietzsche, for whose imagery and ideas she serves the novel as a lightning rod, Moosbrugger, and a contemporary intellectual guru named

Meingast (his name translates to "my guest"), who does indeed visit the couple for extended periods of time and who sexually abused Clarisse when she was an adolescent. Clarisse approaches ideas, people, and events with a musical (Wagnerian?) attitude that Ulrich finds antithetical to rigorous intellectual deliberation.

Ulrich's involvement in the Collateral Campaign brings him in contact with several of his most significant others. His cousin Diotima, Ermelinda, née Hermine, Tuzzi is the social moving force and organizer behind it. Diotima is the underestimated, sexually starved spouse of Permanent Secretary Hans Tuzzi, characterized as a dry, methodical careerist, the only individual of non-noble lineage to have attained authority in the Ministry of Foreign Affairs. Diotima, by virtue of her bourgeois upbringing and her sexual frustration (the novel is quick, despite certain feminist gestures, to invoke this latter condition in explanation of a wide range of female actions), couches the Campaign in terms of extreme but superficial idealism. Although she develops an intense rapport with her cousin, she personifies an idealization that Kernberg, in the psychological sphere, associates with pathological narcissism and to which Ulrich opposes himself in the specificity of his intellectual questioning. The Collateral Campaign's avowed aspiration to idealize Austrian culture, to merge the interests of the state with those of the culture, enables the novel to interrogate the broadest political parameters of artistic and intellectual activity.

Throughout the novel, Diotima finds herself in the throes of an unconsummated infatuation with Paul Arnheim, a German capitalist of Jewish origins engaged in a near-comprehensive range of large enterprises, among them steel, munitions, oil, and the entertainment industry. Where Diotima aspires, through the Campaign, both to uncover and reinforce "the Good, the True, and the Beautiful" (3:251) in Austrian life, Arnheim is a self-proclaimed prophet and embodiment of "the connection between business and poetry" (1:319). A public paragon, and widely published inspirational author, Arnheim systematically dissolves and effaces the border between unrestrained intellectual inquiry and capitalistic avarice. At the same time that Arnheim captivates Diotima's romantic inclinations and the fascination of the press, he arouses considerable resistance on the part of Ulrich and the Austrian powers that be. Indeed, his practical interest in the Collateral Campaign is not disclosed until well into the Second Book.

In several of the novel's more entertaining passages, Ulrich finds himself explaining his various skepticisms to General Stumm von Bordwehr of the War Ministry's Department of Army Education, an unrepenitent soldier of the old school working and living through the transition toward twentieth-century warfare. In representing the War Ministry's interests in the Collateral Campaign, he cannot surrender imposing military order, even upon intellectual matters: his inventory of great ideas, gleaned from the holdings of the Imperial Library, is a parody on a military requisition (2:82–86). Jovial a character and fictive companion though he may be, the General's presence throughout the novel suggests a pervasive militaristic interest in and rendering of even Ulrich's most abstruse intellectual arguments.

Christian Moosbrugger figures in the novel less as an active force than as a horizon of negativity ironically circumscribing certain of the well-intentioned strivings on the part of "better citizens." As will be argued below, the narrative descriptions of his latest pathological act, the sadistic, if not premeditated murder of a prostitute, are significant, from a psychological point of view. But apart from his activity on the night of the crime, we see precious little of Moosbrugger. We catch a few glimpses of him as he mugs for journalists. His role in the novel—appropriately, given his psychological fragmentation—is less that of a character than a notion (or phantasm) in other characters' minds. In this regard, though, his role is central.

Curiously, female characters infatuated with Ulrich have a tendency to become obsessed with Moosbrugger. On a psychological level, Ulrich must "share" two of his women also with Moosbrugger. Both of them happen to be married. Clarisse, Walter's wife, who adopts both seductive and punitive attitudes toward Ulrich (on several occasions, she incites Walter to kill him), comes to regard Moosbrugger as a Nietzschean martyr, who must be protected from society's hypocritical moralism. Bonadea, Ulrich's longest-lasting mistress, functions as a comical double (and fool) to Diotima. Although she cannot quite claim Diotima's social rank, she flourishes where Diotima can only demurely abstain, in bed. Like Diotima, Bonadea is married to a high official. Her interest in Moosbrugger does not result from active identification as does Clarisse's, with some psychological justification. Bonadea takes up Moosbrugger's cause as a way of intertwining herself into Ulrich's business affairs and personal associations. (She knows that Ulrich has requested sympathetic consideration of the Moosbrugger matter from Count Stallberg, an eminent jurist loosely affiliated with the Campaign).

For two imporatant female characters, then, the supplement to marriage becomes split between Ulrich's erudition, a sustained resistance to simplification of any sort, including the moral variety, and Moosbrugger's nonmanagement of his primary drives and processes. The alternatives to marriage as an overall model for civility and propriety become limited to the extremes of rare cultivation and psychopathic acting out. Public debate regarding the Moosbrugger case focuses on the theme of mental competence and its implications for punishment. As the novel progresses, however, the lack of ego integration, splitting, and impulsiveness with which Austrian society grapples, explicitly in relation to the Moosbrugger trial, become displaced to historical developments so central and pervasive as to become, with great irony, transparent.

Tangential to Ulrich's primary professional and social commitments and the novel's wider historical fiction are his interactions with two microcosmic but significant groupings: Leo Fischel's family and the alliance of Rachel and Soliman, respectively, Diotima's and Arnheim's personal servants. All these characters are limited to a social stratum below that of the major players in the Collateral Campaign. Fischel is called Director of the local Lloyd's Bank, but as a Jew he can aspire no higher than to be its manager. Gerda, the offspring of his mixed marriage, is the only seriously eligible woman with whom Ulrich has an encounter in the novel. As the Third Book ends, she is engaged to marry Hans Sepp, the leader of an idealistic circle of young Germanophile intellectuals. But the novel has allowed us to witness a highly ambivalent sexual encounter with Ulrich, whose underlying tension has accrued over time. Rachel, a nineteen year old Jewish refugee and unmarried mother from Galicia, has attained a good measure of comfort and stability through her service to Diotima. Rachel's sexual explorations in the novel are with Soliman, an African teenager that Arnheim has, on whim, saved from a touring Italian musical company. Arnheim's noble intentions toward his charge waiver somewhat during the novel.

The world of the servants and the Jews (save Arnheim) in the novel is the microcosm to the macrocosm of the weighty affairs pondered and acted upon by the likes of Leinsdorf, Ulrich, Tuzzi, and Diotima. This subliminal domain is minor, in Deleuze's sense of the term.[1] It is where Musil gives us an inkling of the longer-term and historical implications of the events invented, perceived, and misapprehended in the course of the novel.

It is appropriate, in several senses, that I terminate this survey of Ulrich's significant others in the novel, with whom he interacts on a wide variety of levels, with Agathe, the nearly forgotten sister he is fated to encounter upon the death of their father. Agathe not only emerges by surprise, as if an afterthought: her appearance radically changes the novel's drift. Musil is compelled to furnish details of age and separate schooling that would account for such a circumstantial, if not temperamental, distance between them, Agathe's final ministrations to her father, the subsequent funeral ceremonies, and the uncanny mutual affinity she and Ulrich mutually "feel" furnish her with an occasion and justification for abandoning her husband, schoolmaster, and pedagogical theorist Gottlieb Hagauer. The discovery of a sibling to whom he can relate in the manner of a utopia[2] or the "conflict-free sphere"[3] liberates Ulrich from most of the sexual tension and much of the inter"personal" competition motivating him throughout the novel, expressed imagistically by a rhetoric of waves, vectors, and counterforces at whose node Musil often situates him.

Agathe moves into Ulrich's castle-like house, initiating a highly unconventional domestic arrangement, one playing on the borders between incest and familial taboo, between sexual expression and repression. Ulrich initially experiences the arrangement as a relief, a de-cathexis of the prevalent conflicts of everyday life; Agathe is a liberation from the stultification of her second marriage, which she entered hastily after the loss of a young husband, who aroused in her a genuine romantic love.

Despite Ulrich's suspicions toward Goethe and Napoleon as "world-historical men," and toward the broader Hegelian historiography defining the dimensions, conditions, and ideals within such figures operate,[4] there is a pronounced Faustian quality to Ulrich's reconciliation with Agathe. The merger of Ulrich with Agathe shares the phantasmatic dimension and tone of Faust's marriage to Helen of Troy in *Faust II*. In both cases, the central actions are over: Faust has deceived Margarete, and Ulrich has encountered and negotiated a full gamut of contemporary erotic, historical, cultural, political, and even physical forces. The retrospective unions that both male figures enter are exemplary in concept, expansive in dimension, and sublimatory in effect. In certain senses, these belated unions *repeat* what has gone before, but on a displaced plane.

Ulrich and Agathe mentally and physically mirror one another, a point brought home when they meet, after a five year's absence, wearing complimentary traveling suits, "faintly resembling a pierrot's costume" (3:9). In explaining their arrangement to others, they describe themselves as "Siamese twins" (3:275, 281, 286). Kohut, were he to consider their interaction, might well locate it in the mirroring, twinning sector of the narcissistic economy.[5] Ulrich and Agathe see idealized images of themselves in each other. This explains both why their alliance initially comes as such a relief and why it is destined to crumble by virtue of internal stagnation. This is precisely what is happening as the third completed volume of the novel reaches its end.

This third volume, entitled *Into the Millenium* (*The Criminals*), has morality as its predominant conceptual theme, the conflict between sanctioned evil passing for public morality and misapprehended intellectual exploration taken as deviance. Agathe is the last figure included in the present survey of the novel's characterological landscape because she functions as a hinge connecting its discrete experiences to their retrospective recollection, expansion, and emptying. Shortly after the novel begins, we find Ulrich "estimating the speed, the angle, the dynamic force of masses being propelled past, which drew the eye after them swift as lightning, holding it, letting it go, forcing the attention—for an infinitesimal instant of time—to resist them, to snap off, and then to jump to the next and rush after that" (1:7). This is a conspicuously modernistic landscape, whose vectors of force, incidental angles, and discontinuous interactions are reminiscent of jazz, cubism, the Benjaminian city, nuclear physics, vorticism, and Joycean variation.[6] It is within this setting that Ulrich interacts with the characters surveyed above, who function as vehicles in a dodgem-car course or points in a nuclear cloud chamber. Because *The Man without Qualities* is a densely written text, its characterological "points" become locations where its broader themes (culture, history, intellectual work, sexuality, morality) are elaborated. Through Ulrich's at times collaborative and at times tense collisions with the other characters in this field, the issue of self is eventually worked out: its constitution, its critical bearing, the expression in writing, and the attraction and resistance it provokes.[7]

# CHAPTER 10

# The Man without Qualities:
## *Friendship and Persistent Envy*

In the context both of the novel's encompassing framework and of twentieth-century theories of narcissism, extending from Freud to Kernberg and Kohut by way of Lacan, it now becomes possible to work out its inter"personal" reading.

*The Man without Qualities* focuses upon the efforts of a male central character, Ulrich von _____ , to negotiate both his own social and professional worlds and his time. Ulrich may be characterized by a superior integration of his narcissistic self and his work (evidenced in his capability to comprehend and productively comment with critical detachment upon a wide range of historically sociopolitical, esthetic, and economic data). His body is distinguished by trimness and sharp muscular definition, and there are numerous references to his athleticism, suggesting a positive continuity between the physical and intellectual forms of his work (e.g., 1:47–49, 71; 2:397). Among the psychodynamic manifestations of this relatively successful cathexis of instinctual energies in work and the integration of his "self" are Ulrich's social bearing as a man of substance or qualities—this in spite of the novel's carefully seeded joke to the contrary—and a sexual energy occasionally leading him into mischief because it has not yet submitted to the sanctioned fixation of marriage.

In the aftermath of Kohut, it would be naive to suggest that Ulrich is the single non-narcissist in the novel, set upon by a range of psychopaths and pathological narcissists of every degree. It would be more appropriate to argue that Ulrich's skill as a reader of his times and a critic—for that is, ultimately, his work—is a solider and more successful deployment of his own unavoidable narcissism. No more than any other character does Ulrich go scot free of the negative implications of the narcissistic economy. But the novel gives ample evidence of the creativity that, for Kohut, comprises the first of the essential "Forms and Transformations of Narcissism" optimally transpiring over the course of a lifetime.[1] Highly significant in this regard, is Ulrich's choice, in the Third Book, of an all-absorbing mirroring relationship with his sister at the expense of any of the more conventional "torches" he has "lit," whether of the "fulfillable" (e.g., Gerda Fischel, Rachel) or "impossible" (e.g., Clarisse, Diotima) variety.

On a positive note, the novel in general and Ulrich's specific interactions with Leinsdorf, Tuzzi, Diotima, General Stumm von Bordwehr, Arnheim, Fischel, and Agathe afford him (and Musil) a stage or platform for delivering some splendid critical observations on his era: its art, politics, sexuality, science, and industry. Ulrich's observations and criticism constitute the most substantial manifestation of his qualities. They are his pith, the stuffing in his upholstery. The conflicts that Ulrich sometimes freely enters and that are sometimes foisted upon him invariably emanate in some way from this intellectual subject matter. In this regard, such theorists of narcissism as Kernberg and Kohut, despite their apparent differences in tonality, are most helpful in defining the insecurities and injuries that Ulrich both enters and causes.

Let us recall the central position that persistent envy, the result of a feeling of personal emptiness, and idealization occupy in the constellation of factors whose coincidence forms Kernberg's economy of pathological narcissism. If we for the moment leave Moosbrugger aside, as a talismanic extreme of decenteredness and unmitigated pathological and antisocial acting out, the vast majority of the characters with whom Ulrich maintains evolving interactions relate to him either through jealousy, and its impulsive dramatization, or by means of rigid adherence to certain ideals, fidelity to which imposes impenetrable borders. The jealousy and idealization that Ulrich encounters virtually ubiquitously throughout his "social" world roughly correspond to his active and passive roles. Where he is the "hunter," for example, with Diotima and Arnheim, he collides into idealistic structures suspect by virtue of their grandiosity; he becomes the "prey" wherever other characters, for example, Clarisse, Walter, and Bonadea, in their own efforts at self-fulfillment, impose upon him an idealized image of what they themselves lack (e.g., "qualities," the capability of productively enjoying the incommensurate).

If Ulrich's social world increasingly becomes a wasteland, from which he withdraws into a fated idealized relationship of twinning with his sister, this is by virtue of the fact that he encounters envy, and its unpredictable destructiveness, or rigid idealization at virtually every turn. Even Stumm von Bordwehr, a character in the round and good fellow in every sense of these terms, cannot relinquish the rigidity of his military cast of mind. Ulrich may withdraw into the grandiosities of sibling mirroring and moral speculation, but this only after two volumes of conflictual relationships fought out upon the terrain of his integral and fertile, though by no means perfect "self."

As in the complicated analytical vignette related above by Kernberg, the true battleground of *The Man without Qualities* is nothing less than the self and the qualities of integration, focus, inquisitiveness, and empathy making intellectual work possible. The following, congenitally incomplete reading of the novel will focus on the assaults and challenges to the self that Ulrich encounters. It will begin in the domain of the contentious interactions whose context has been outlined above. It will proceed to the idealization serving as an inhibiting factor in interpersonal relationships and resulting in dangerous national self-delusion and blindness at the level of public ideology. My overview of the novel will then take up the exasperating conditions for love on the eve of World War I, an erotic field itself sundered between idealization and debasement. It will conclude with the broadest prospects for self-integration and writing that Musil's novel entertains.

There is no more telling index to the potential for full, meaningful, and forthright adult relationships than the vicissitudes experienced by those venerable friendships among whose precious and irreplaceable qualities numbers the fact that they were formed prior to the onsets of grown-up competitiveness and anxiety. Musil is aware of this without having read Sullivan.[2] He entitles chapter 14, in which he introduces Walter and Clarisse, "Friends of his [Ulrich's, my addition] youth." Ulrich's interactions with these two characters, then, are emblematic for the general possibilities of empathy in the adult field at the same time that they contribute to the broader tapestry. Nothing is more cherished, more saturated with memories of intimacy than the friendship of youth. No promise of a measure of life's comfort held in reserve is more disillusioning when it doesn't pan out.

On the far side of Ulrich's "strange interlude" away from Vienna, his interactions with this couple go from bad to worse. Let us examine them at their optimal state in the novel, shortly after it begins, during chapter 17, "The effect of a Man Without Qualities on a man with qualities." "The music that Ulrich and Clarisse had heard while they were outside, talking, sometimes stopped without their noticing it," this chapter begins. "Walter then went to the window. He could not see the two of them, but he felt that they were only just beyond his field of vision. He was tormented by jealousy. The base intoxication of a sluggishly sensual music lured him back. . . . He was racked by the jealousy of one who is paralyzed and feels how the able-bodied walk; and he could not bring himself to join them, for his anguish left him no way of defending himself against them" (1:65).

Musil's first snapshot of true friendship in the novel is one of anguished separation. Walter hovers between one of his artforms, music, which he has substantially abandoned for the security of an administrative position, and a dual jealous rage directed at his friend, who has remained true to his mathematical predisposition, and at his wife, still faithful to himself. Walter's particular internal tantrum transpires in the context of what Kohut would term a pervasive, ill-defined vulnerability:[3] "He was sensitive, and his feelings were always moved by broodings, full of depressions, billowing dales and hills; he was never indifferent, but saw fortune or misfortune in everything and so always had occasion for vivid thoughts. Such people exert an unusual attraction over others, because the moral motion in which they continuously find themselves is transmitted to these others. In their conversation everything assumes a personal significance" (1:65–66).

Walter personalizes his interpretations of what he hears and sees. His internal moral *Sturm und Drang* exerts an attraction upon others akin to the "certain self-contentment" that Freud isolates in beautiful women and other paradigmatic narcissists. "Strictly speaking, it is only themselves that such women love with an intensity comparable to that of the man's love for them," Freud continues in his 1914 "On Narcissism: An Introduction." "Nor does their need lie in the direction of loving, but of being loved; and the man who fulfills this condition is the one who finds favor with them. The importance of this type of woman for the entire life of mankind is to be rated very high. . . . Another's narcissism has a great attraction for those who have renounced part of their narcissism and are in search of object-love."[4] Though not a beautiful woman, or a child, a comedian, a criminal, or an animal, some of Freud's other narcissist-archetypes, Walter exerts a similar influence. Ten years earlier, his sensitivity and self-absorption had succeeded in routing the competition from Clarisse's largely incestuous erotic field. Clarisse is not without her own voids in self-definition, which the novel goes on to explore. In the context of a mutually anaclitic married relationship, Walter repeats his defensive polarizations of moral value. "With this quality of spreading intellectual preoccupation with oneself, he had also conquered Clarisse and in time driven all rivals from the field. Because with him everything turned into ethical emotion, he would speak convincingly of the immorality of ornament, of the hygiene of simple shapes, and the beery fumes of Wagnerian music, as was in keeping with the new artistic taste; and even his future father-in-law . . . had been intimidated by it" (1:66). Given the amount of narrative material that the novel will devote to the trend-setting and confirming Collateral Campaign, it is extremely significant that Ulrich's paradigmatic friend is described as a slave to fashion rather than a contributor to it, whose personal force derives from a compensatory dramatizing of moral concern. Curiously, this performance is made possible by the embryonic vestiges of a genuine painter and musician residing within him, as his evaluation of Clarisse's playing attests (1:68).

It is in keeping with the mathematics that Ulrich and the novel share that there is an unsymmetrical parity between the judgments by him and those about him; between his *thinking* as performed by himself or projected onto the narrator and his *actions* as witnessed by the other characters and ourselves. If the novel's paradigmatic scene of friendship shows Walter at some disadvantage—as a weakly-defined, compensatory dramatic and upright narcissist—it also exhibits Ulrich's impact upon him. Walter's reactions to Ulrich at this early stage of the novel are important. They become characteristic of Viennese society's ambivalence toward focused, substantial intellectual working-through.

> While looking through the window watching Clarisse come back, he [Walter, my addition] knew half-consciously that once again he would be unable to resist the need to speak badly of Ulrich. Ulrich had returned at the wrong time. He had a harmful effect on Clarisse. (1:68)

> Walter said violently, "Everything is crumbling nowadays! An intellectual pit without a bottom to it! He has an intellect, I grant you that. But he has no notion of the power of an unbroken soul! What Goethe calls personality, what Goethe calls mobile order— that's something he hasn't got an inkling of!" (1:69)

No sooner does the narrative raise the issue of Walter's irritated competitiveness with Ulrich than the bone of contention shifts from a "sexual object," Clarisse, upon whom Ulrich exercises so deleterious an effect, to the issue of the substantiality of the self. In this internal argument, this war of introjections, Walter aligns himself with the Goethean-Hegelian tradition of world-historical men, great personalities, in accusing Ulrich of a certain insubstantiality, secondariness, undependability and supplementarity. Ulrich's dubiousness has already been encountered by those familiar with Derrida's *assemblage* of Western culture's reproaches against writing.[5]

> Walter was frustrated. He searched, he wavered. Suddenly he burst out: "He is a man without qualities!"
> "What's that?" Clarisse asked, with a little laugh.
> "Nothing. That's just the point—it's nothing!" But the expression had aroused Clarisse's curiosity.
> "There are milions of them nowadays," Walter declared. "It's the human type that our time has produced." He was pleased with the expression that had so unexpectedly come to him. As though he were beginning a poem, the words drove him forward before he had got the meaning. "Just look at him! What would you take him for? Does he look like a doctor, or like a business man, or a painter, or a diplomat?"
> "But he isn't any of those things," Clarisse pointed out matter-of-factly.
> "Well, do you think he looks like a mathematician?"
> "I don't know! How should I know what a mathematician is supposed to look like?" (1:70)

"And now just run your mind over the sort of man he is. He always knows what to do. He can gaze into a woman's eyes. He can exercise his intelligence efficiently on any given problem at any given moment. He can box. He is talented, strong-willed, unprejudiced, he has courage and he has endurance, he can go at things with a dash and he can be cool and cautious—I have no intention of examining all this in detail, let him have all these qualities! For in the end he hasn't got them at all! They have made him what he is, they have set his course for him, and yet they don't belong to him. When he is angry, something in him laughs. When he is sad, he is up to something. When he is moved by something, he will reject it. Every bad action will seem good to him in some connection or other. And it will always be only a possible context that will decide what he thinks of a thing. Nothing is stable for him. Everything is fluctuating, a part of a whole, among innumerable wholes that presumably are part of a super-whole, which, however, he doesn't know the slightest thing about. So every one of his answers is a part answer, every one of his feelings only a point of view, and whatever a thing is, it doesn't matter to him what it is, it's only some accompanying 'way in which it is', some addition or other, that matters to him. I don't know whether I make myself quite clear to you?"

"Oh, yes," Clarisse said. "But I think it's very nice of him." (1:71)

These two passages are situated at the dramatic, psychological, and thematic cruxes of the novel. They involve a war of reproaches regarding substantiality. In one corner stands Walter, representing society in a scenario that for Derrida extends back as far as Plato and the Book of Leviticus: accusing Ulrich of appeasing conceptual and moral laxity.[6] From the corner end of the ring, Ulrich exerts the power and attraction, not unappreciated by Clarisse, of open-ended inquiry and a refusal to impose values through a process of polarization. At stake is the issue of quality, whose Greco-Latin roots extend to the question of whatness.[7] The narrative is a player in this epic battle as well. It, informed by and anticipating the wisdom of modern psychology, accords public opinion, the everyday understanding of qualities, to Walter, while it opens the pathway of depth to Ulrich. The narrative referee to this boxing match at the fundamental level of quiddity, whatness, awards quality to both pugilists, only a very different kind of quality. We should not lose sight of the fact that, as many conversations in the novel will bear out, Ulrich's real occupation is not that of a mathematician, although his formal discipline is suggestive, but that of an intellectual and social critic. From a perspective common to Walter, Diotima, and Arnheim, Ulrich is indeed insubstantial, tricky, slippery. But his toleration and even invocation of fluctuation as described in the above passage is part and parcel of his ability to furnish a detached commentary, is a precondition of his writing, whatever form it may assume. This early confrontation between Ulrich and Walter is revelatory, then, of the paradoxical conditions under which writing transpires. Without a doubt, it requires its own self-absorption and a certain grandiosity of its own. Yet the grandiosity of writing is small potatoes when juxtaposed against the ideal miasmas surrounding, among other issues touched upon by the novel, official ideology, commercial hype, sexual mores, marriage, and public morality. The battle of writings, "official" versus critical, becomes a subtle counterpoint of grandiosities.

The early encounter between Ulrich and Walter serves as a paradigm for its tendentious interpersonal relationships. Let us not forget Clarisse's role at this scene, even if it is merely as the gladiators' booty. From Ulrich's (and even Walter's) point of view, Clarisse, whose name implicates clarity, and to the nth degree, operates within a sexual economy of supplementarity. As the novel proceeds, it will record the effacement of the clarity of her gender identification and her absorption into "primary-process thought."[8] Her quintessential role in the novel is as a polarizer, not of values but of men. Having proposed to transform the Collateral Campaign into an Ulrich if not a Nietzsche Year, and being enticed by the "musicality" of Moosbrugger's personality and actions, Clarisse's dramatic apothesis in the novel, the full measure of her decentered impulsiveness, is an attempt to seduce Ulrich, the culminating battle in an extended campaign to bring him and the friend of his youth to the point of homicidal confrontation. She does this in a costume and attitude reminiscent of Louise Brooks in "Pandora's Box,"[9] at a significant moment in Ulrich's life, just after he has learned of his father's death.

> When Ulrich . . . went into his own rooms, he found Clarisse lying on a divan, slightly turned on her side, with her legs drawn up. Her straight slim figure, the boyish cut of her hair, and the

elongated lovely face, supported on her arm, that gazed at him as he opened the door—it made an exceedingly seductive picture. He told her that he had taken her for a burglar. Clarisse's eyes flashed like a rapid firing from a revolver. "Perhaps I am one!" she retorted. (1:441)

The chapter in which this intense seduction-scene takes place (123) is, fittingly, entitled "The Turning-Point." The scene represents a turning point in our understanding of Clarisse and in her flirtation with Ulrich; it comprises the final episode of Ulrich's active sexuality, before he withdraws into a charged but innocent symbiosis with his sister. The scene is framed within a setting of theater machinery evocative of the attic where Young Törless first witnesses and then joins the sadomasochistic fraternal initiations of his youth.[10] "She had some vague idea about the lofts for stage machinery in theatres," the narrative informs us, taking the part of her consciousness. "She pictured to herself how between calls the actresses sat in rafters over the stage, wrapped in shawls, and looked down, watching; now she too was an actress, and the play was going on down there at her feet. In all this her favorite old idea turned up again: life was a drama, and one was there to act it out" (2:243).

Clarisse is of interest to object-relations theorists in this scene because of the impulsiveness of her actions, their dramatic, acted-out cast, and because of the polarized ideation in which she couches her motivations and rationale. She is of interest to feminists because, as a fictive embodiment of the fluctuations of her times, she can only be cast as Pandora, a disseminator of male discord; in flagrantly refusing to bear Walter's child, she is Medea as well; in taking the sexual initiative, she joins other castrating women such as Judith and Salome (both of whom had inspired striking renditions by graphic artists of the period: I think of Aubrey Beardsley, and closer to home, Gustav Klimt).[11]

"You know what an umbrella looks like when the stick's been taken out of it? Walter collapses when I turn away from him. I am his stick, and he's my ____ "what she had been going to say was 'umbrella', but then something much better occurred to her"—he's my shield, my protector," she said. "He thinks he has to shield me. And so that he can protect me properly the first thing he wants is to see me going round with a big belly. Then

he'll take me into believing that a mother with any natural feelings breast-feeds her child. Then he'll want to bring the child up
according to his own ideas. You know all that yourself. He'll
simply usurp rights and have a terrific excuse for turning us both
into philistines. But if I go on the way I have up to now, and keep
on saying no, then it's all up with him! I'm simply everything to
him!"

Ulrich smiled incredulously at this sweeping assertion.

"He wants to kill you!" Clarisse added swiftly.

"What! I thought it was you who suggested it to him?"

"I want to have the child from you!" Clarisse said.

Ulrich whistled through his teeth in surprise. She smiled like
an adolescent who has made an ill-mannered demand.

"I shouldn't like to deceive anyone I know as well as Walter,"
Ulrich said slowly. "It's not the sort of thing I care for."

"Oho? So you're awfully *decent*, are you?" (2:445)

The narrative paints Clarisse here as threatened by the fullness
of pregnancy and the prospect of fulfilling Walter's wish. She retains her power over Walter only by holding his desire in abeyance
and by maintaining her own (physiological as well as metaphoric)
emptiness. She is antinature. The thought of acceding to her
obligations to the matrimonial bond and to nature fills her with
revulsion; but she will accept a child from Ulrich, her phantasmatic
husband, whom she has polarized into God and the Devil.

"Don't you like me? Aren't you fond of me?" she asked. And
when Ulrich did not answer, she continued: "But I know you do
like me. I've noticed often enough the way you look at me when
you come to see us! Do you remember—did I ever tell you you're
the Devil? That's the way it seems to me. Understand me rightly,
I'm not saying you're a poor devil—that's someone who wants
evil because he doesn't know any better. You're a great Devil,
you know what would be good but you do the very opposite of
what you'd like to do! You think the sort of life we all lead is
abominable, and that's why you say, out of sheer contrariness,
one has to go on leading it. And you say in that frightfully decent
way: 'I don't deceive my friends!'; but you only say that because
you've thought to yourselves hundreds of times: 'I should like to
have Clarisse!' But because you're a Devil, you have something
of God in you too, Ulo! Something of a great God! Of one who
tells lies so as not to be recognized! You want me . . ."

> She had gripped both his arms, standing before him with her face lifted to his, her body curving back like a plant that is gently touched at the petals. (2:446)

The narrative moves Clarisse, in this scene, under the aura of the extreme polarization of values and absence of stabilizing structure epitomized by Moosbrugger. Clarisse can only experience Ulrich, in this impetuous and short-lived episode of infatuation, as grandiose extremes of good and evil. This devilishness derives from statements he has made, in keeping with his scientific and esthetic beliefs, to the effect that "the state we live in is full of cracks, through which, so to speak, another state, an impossible one, peers out at us" (2:447). Clarisse magnifies and demonizes a capacity for tolerating ambiguity comprising an important element of Ulrich's intellectual bearing. It affects Ulrich "rather oddly . . . that even in her slim, hard body there was room for all the loosening and soft expansion of a woman's glowing passion" (2:448). Clarisse is aggressive, masculine for a woman. In her impulsiveness, the excitement she sustains and the vibration overcoming her, she becomes a living feminine embodiment of the relativistic force-field in which Ulrich operates.

> Clarisse suddenly came to grips with him. She flung one arm round his neck and pressed her lips to his so quickly that he had no time to resist; he was thoroughly nonplussed. With one quick movement she pulled her legs up under her and slid towards him so that she was practically kneeling on his lap, and he could feel the little ball of one breast against his shoulder. He could not grasp much of what she was saying. . . .
> "I shall kill you if you don't give in!" she said in a high clear voice.
> She was like a boy who in his mingled tenderness and vexation refuses to be put off, so heightening his excitement more and more. The efforts of taming her prevented him from being more than faintly affected by the current of desire in her body. (2:449)

Such are the complexities of relating to the wives of one's friends of youth, one's symbolic sisters-in-law. Ulrich's interactions with Walter and Clarisse set the stage for a certain tendentious interpersonal sphere prevailing throughout the novel. Where Ulrich arouses the antipathy of Dr. Paul Arnheim, whose uneventful flirtation with Diotima does not offer much as an alternative to

the benighted state of matrimony, the issue at stake will again be
the matter of the self. Whereas Ulrich will jokingly call for a "ter-
restrial secretariat for Precision and the Spirit" (2:366), and will
not relinquish the "streak in him of the harsh, cold, and violent"
(2:359), Arnheim is an unremitting expansionist (2:107) whose
drive and success are backed by his rather fuzzy boundaries. "But
now something happened that had never happened before: there
was a man who could talk to each of them in his own language,
and this was Arnheim. . . . It was understandable that he could talk
to big industrialists about industry and to bankers about finance;
but he was capable of chatting just as freely about molecular physics, mysticism, or pigeon shooting. He was an extraordinary
talker; once he had begun he did not stop, any more than a book
can be finished before everything has been said that has to be said
in it" (1:221–22).

Among Musil's most striking tours de force will be reversals of
his own distinctions, and of characters seemingly opposed to one
another, as when the narrator accuses "novelists" of doing exactly
what Musil's own novel has done, dissolving "exceptions," such as
Moosbrugger's horrific murder, "into a matter of subjectivity"
(1:302). To be sure, both Ulrich and Arnheim are split, the former
between his toleration of ambiguity and his exactitude; the latter
between "business and poetry" (1:319; 2:107). But in this inter-
change of identities, it is Arnheim who seeks to appeal to all interests, to reconcile avarice with high ideals and refined taste. He
demonstrates an unusual propensity for "being a paragon" (2:102).
"He possessed the gift of never being superior in any detail, in
anything that could be put to the test, but of always coming to the
top in every situation, by means of a fluid, perpetually self-
restoring equilibrium" (1:228). "Arnheim put his finger on the
place where the redeeming idea, the idea that would create order
in all these complications, was to be sought: it was somehow sym-
pathetically connected with the concept of increased turnover"
(1:128).

On an individual level, Arnheim furnishes an example of an
intellectual hypocrite, who professes high cultural and esthetic
values while harboring deepest suspicions toward the inevitable
ambiguities that these fields set into play. As the representative of
a social class, he dramatizes high-powered capitalism's need to

legitimate itself within the intellectual and cultural spheres. Arnheim "had at every opportunity praised some of these particularly pure poets, because it was the thing to do, and on some occasions had even given them financial support; but actually, as he now became aware, he could not endure them or their inflated verses" (2:125). At one point Arnheim attempts to absorb Ulrich's intellectual power into his array of enterprises by trying to hire him (2:417–28).

Arnheim and Ulrich may both curry for Diotima's favor, while the chief hostess of the Collateral Campaign undergoes her own idealistic delusions, identity crises, and campaigns of sexual liberation, mockingly couched in Freudian and proto-feminist rhetoric.

Arnheim is wounded late in the Second Book, that Count Leinsdorf prefers Ulrich's viewpoint, on the need for rigor in cultural matters, to his own (2:368). But with Arnheim as was the case with Walter, conflict with Ulrich centers on the integrated self's ability to tolerate ambiguity and to remain in communication with its incommensurate facets. "For with the passing of time," Ulrich "had developed a certain readiness to adopt negative attitudes, a flexible dialectic of feeling that was inclined to tempt him into discovering defects in what was generally approved of and defending what was considered beyond the pale. . . . Ulrich was a man whom something compelled to live against its own grain, although he seemed to let himself float along without any constraint" (1:176). Capable of detached, negative, that is, critical scrutiny, Ulrich is nonetheless a man at odds with himself. The dynamic tension with himself is a source of his own insight and energy. This is in sharp counterdistinction to the phenomenon that Ulrich finds in Arnheim "like a rainbow that one can seize hold of at each end and really feel under one's hands. He talks about love and economics, about chemistry and canoeing trips, he is a learned man, a landowner and a stock-jobber. In short what we all are separately he is in one person. But this is what amazes us. You shake your head, sir?" (1:223). The ability to tolerate ambiguity, to have undergone the development beyond the stark polarizations of infancy and early childhood toward a continuum of values and experience, is an essential feature of salutary psychological life for the full gamut of object-relations thinkers: Klein, Fairbairn, Bowlby, Winnicott, Kohut, and Kernberg.[12] This is the test to which Musil regularly subjects Ulrich, one at which he succeeds, even in states of some disequilibrium. His antagonists tend either to have broken this continuum into polar opposites (Clarisse) or to have emptied it of its substance (Arnheim), the latter a prefiguration of Woody Allen's Zelig.

# CHAPTER 11

# The Man without Qualities:
# *Idealization and Repression*

It will be instructive at this point, if bearing in mind the centrality of rigid idealization to narcissistic disturbances from Freud and Lacan through the object-relations theorists, we briefly survey its forms and loci in the novel. A good deal of this activity is concentrated in the figure of Diotima, a.k.a. Ermelinda Tuzzi, who also serves as social doyen to the Collateral Campaign, a "Grecian figure swathed in an almost imperceptible plumpness" (1:125). Diotima's familial relationship to Ulrich as his cousin suggests that deconstructive criticism and naive social accommodation are not so far apart in prewar Vienna as they might be. The Collateral Campaign is an intensification of the ongoing resolving function[1] through which a culture ideologicallly sanctions its existing forms and institutions. That Musil partially personifies this second-degree celebration of existing values in a physically sumptuous high-official spouse of refined social acuity but no great intellectual depth again hints at the author's underlying sexual ambivalences.

Idealization is, without a doubt, the preponderant intellectual theme in the First and Second Books of the novel. More than any particular character, it constitutes the nemesis against which the man of intellectual quality rages. The theme and activity of idealization are balanced, in the Third Book, only by the darker moral issues that confront Musil as twentieth-century history proceeds: what can be the morality of a congenitally flawed world? In the most general terms, the vicissitudes of idealization in the novel are as follows. Diotima, an exaggerated creature of high ideals, becomes the social custodian to Austrian culture's celebration of its own idealized image of itself. In this process, she encounters Arnheim and aligns herself with him. Under Permanent Secretary Tuzzi's concerned and watchful eye, they act out an infatuation for one another that turns out, in the end, to be no more than a Platonic mutual teasing. The dramatic impetus for much of the dialogue between Diotima, Arnheim, Stumm von Bordwehr, and Tuzzi derives from Ulrich's critical, negative, and questioning attitude toward idealization. The novel quite explicitly specifies that, within the economy of narcissism, the pollyanish idealism we confront in Diotima, Arnheim, the Campaign, and several minor characters, is an innocuous variation upon the dramatic obliteration of idealistic structure underlying Moosbrugger's and Clarisse's impulsive behavior.

> In this position Tuzzi now had many people coming to him, wanting something of him, and from this moment on, almost to her own surprise, something happened to Diotima: there opened up in her a store-house of memories of 'spiritual beauty and grandeur,' which she had allegedly acquired in a cultured parental home and in the great cities of the world, but in fact doubtless as a model pupil at a girl's high school; and this she began carefully turning to account. The sober but singularly reliable intelligence of her husband inevitably attracted attention to her too, and now, as soon as she became aware that her intellectual merits were appreciated, she began with great enjoyment weaving in little 'high-minded' ideas at suitable places in her conversation, all with utter naivety, like a moist little sponge oozing out again what it has soaked up to no particular purpose. And gradually, while her husband continued to ascend, more and more people came seeking association with him, and her home became a 'salon,' gaining the reputation of a meeting-place for 'society and intelligentsia.' And now, in intercourse with people who were of some consequence in various fields, Diotima also began seriously discovering herself. Her correctitude, which went on minding its P's and Q's and paying attention just as in school, accurately remembering what it learnt and blending it all into an amicable unity, practically of its own accord turned into a mind, simply by extension. (1:111)

The narrative emphasizes the middle-class origins and accoutrements surrounding Diotima's high-mindedness, but where the Campaign is concerned, such pretensions have achieved the status of cant. Count Leinsdorf, for example, official administrator for the Campaign, was convinced that 'the people' was 'good.' It was not only his many officials, employees and servants that were dependent on him, but so too, economically, were countless other human beings, and he had never come to know 'the people' from another side, except on Sundays and holidays, when as a bright, jolly, bustling crowd it came pouring out from behind the scenery like the chorus in the opera. Anything that did not fit in with this conception he therefore attributed to 'subversive elements'; to him it was the work of irresponsible, callow and sensation-seeking riff-raff. Having been brought up in a religious and feudal atmosphere, never exposed to contradiction in intercourse with middle-class persons, not without reading, but, as a result of having spent a sheltered youth being educated by priests, all his life long unable to see anything in a book but agreement with or erring divergence from his own principles, he knew the outlook of people who were at home in this epoch only from the controversies going on in Parliament and the newspapers. (1:101)

It is from this vantage point of detachment from the stresses and strains, among them ethnic, facing Austrian society, that Leinsdorf will be incredulous when the Germanophile populations rebel against the Campaign (Chapter 120; 2:403–15).

The narrative, once it has identified a congenitally inflated or bankrupt idealism as the denominator common to the Collateral Campaign and to the cult of (world-historical) personality shared by Walter and Arnheim in their repudiation of Ulrich, takes delight in analyzing this idealism, from its soul to its body, in Ulrichian style. (The very term Collateral Campaign hints at the economic dimensions of this empty self-overvaluation.) As the initial committee-deliberations take place, Arnheim insists that "It was not a democracy of committees, but only individual strong personalities, deeply versed both in reality and in the realm of ideas, that would be capable of conducting this Campaign!" (1:126).

From the Campaign's inception, then, it is apparent that it functions as a meeting-ground for the public and private idealisms and ideologies of influential individuals, the State, and its economic systems. The Campaign mobilizes—and exposes to scrutiny—sanctimonious State self-justification, the grandiose personal ambition of the economic "movers and shakers," and capitalism's pronounced tendency to legitimate itself by drawing upon the already existent treasury of ideal-structured canon in religion, art, and folklore. This does not prohibit Ulrich and the narrative from exposing the delusional qualities of this thought purified of imperfections. There are as many blindnesses in the novel as there are private idealistic agendas:

> After this preamble it must be said that what Diotima's great idea amounted to was simply that Arnheim, the Prussian, must take over the spiritual leadership of the great Austrian Campaign, even although this Campaign had a jealous sting aimed at Prussia-Germany. But that is only the dead verbal body of the idea, and anyone who thinks it incomprehensible or ridiculous is maltreating a corpse. As for the soul of the idea, however, it must be said that it was a chaste and proper one; and for all eventualities Diotima attached to her resolve, as it were, a reservation in favour of Ulrich. She did not know that her cousin had also made an impression on her—although at a far lower level than Arnheim and screened by the effect of the latter—and she would probably have despised herself if it had become clear to her. (1:127)

In terms of practical considerations raised by a national celebration of Austrian values and the *Realpolitik* of relations between the two Germanic powers, Diotima's fixation upon Arnheim as an institutional and personal savior is nothing short of a disaster, a major let-down, of defenses and good sense. She is able to maintain this ill-considered fata morgana throughout a long segment of the novel, and in full view of Austrian high society, because Arnheim satisfies on the level of narcissistic fantasy what common sense and her not inestimable husband will not. Diotima's delusion is microcosmic for Austria's. In domain after domain incorporated by the novel, including finance and defense (interests observed, respectively by Fischel and Stumm von Bordwehr) Austria operates according to fantasmatic rather than analytically-perceived versions of its interests. Musil equates the nation's political version of psychogenic fugue with the sexual fantasies and inhibitions entertained by the high-ranking housewife of an official whose sexuality still conforms to the carefully hoarded and scheduled bordello-escapades of his studentdom (1:119–20).

Diotima's fantasmatic union with Arnheim may represent an escape from domestic and sexual tedium but it only intensifies the bonds of the narcissistic economy endowing both characters with their distinctive qualities. The title to chapter 45 formulates their quickening acquaintanceship as a "Silent Encounter between Two Mountain Peaks."

> Neither Diotima nor Arnheim had ever loved. Of Diotima we know this already. But the great financier too possessed a—in a wider sense—chaste soul. He had always been afraid that the feelings he aroused in women might not be for himself, but for his money; and for this reason he lived only with women to whom he, for his part, gave not feelings but money. He had never had a friend, because he was afraid of being used; he only had business friends, even if sometimes the business deal was an intellectual one. So he was wily in the ways of life, yet untouched and in danger of being left on his own, when he encountered Diotima, whom destiny had ordained for him. The mysterious forces in them collided with each other. What happened can only be compared to the blowing of the trade winds, the Gulf Stream, the volcanic tremors in the earth's crust: forces vastly superior to man, related to the stars, were set in motion between the two of them, over and above the limits of the hour and the day— measureless, mighty currents.
>
> At such moments it is quite immaterial what is said. Upward from the vertical crease of his trousers Arnheim's body seemed to stand there in the solitude of God in which the mountain giants stand. United with him by the wave of the valley, on the other side Diotima rose, luminous with solitude—her dress of the period forming little puffs on the upper arms, dissolving the bosom in an artfully draped looseness over the stomach and being caught in to the calf again just under the hollow of the knee. The strings of glass beads in the door-curtains cast reflections like ponds, the javelins and arrows on the walls were tremulous with their feathered and deadly passion, and the yellow Calman-Levy volumes on the tables were silent as lemon-groves. Reverently we pass over their opening words. (1:217)

I quote this passage at length not only because it thematically corroborates the awesome and romantic rhetoric in which two powerful but self-absorbed characters would imagine their mutual infatuation to themselves, but in order to follow the momentum in an exemplary bit of Musil's narrative exploration to its completion. The first paragraph sets out the conditions of isolation shared by Diotima and Arnheim, though it is told mostly from Arnheim's point of view. It ends on a note of destiny: "mysterious forces" greater than them both compels their collision. The second paragraph explores the enlarged dimensions in which they imagine themselves and the mythic setting in which they picture their encounter taking place. It is notable for its rhetoric of sublime awe and the irony with which this grandiose plane can find expression only in small social details: strings of glass beads and yellow Calman-Levy editions. This is a grand love indeed, bigger than the both of them, as the movies once said, but its vulnerability is the one common to the forms of idealization questioned by Ulrich in the novel. This love, holding itself aloof from the field of waves, collisions, attractions, seductions, and disasters in which Ulrich operates, is destined never to be fulfilled. "There was something in Ulrich's nature that worked in a haphazard, paralyzing, disarming manner against logical systematization, against the one-track will, against the definitely directed urges of ambition" (1:300). The options for sexuality that Viennese society, viewed through the cloud-chamber of the novel, has reserved for itself are significant. The possibilities break down into a Platonic "silent encounter between two mountain peaks" or the dismemberment of a streetwalker by a psychotic with borderline features. Within the setting of cultural splitting and polarization that prevails in Kakania, there is either no sexual fulfillment or a sexuality of degradation and primary-process thought.

# CHAPTER 12

# The Man without Qualities:
## Eroticism and Critical Detachment

Before we proceed to the non-idealized model of love in the novel, the one so devoid of ideational content that it takes our breath away, now is perhaps the time to ask: Who is Ulrich? In what do his qualities consist? It has been suggested above that much of the productive dialogue in this heavily dialogic[1] novel is powered by Ulrich's questioning attitude to the idealizations that his respective interlocutors represent. May we typecast him as the novelist's resident deconstructor? Do the activity of questioning and tolerance for ambiguities of valuation condemn him, like God in the Middle Ages, to an existence of negative attributes?

The persistent idealization that Ulrich encounters in his fellow characters—from the grandeur of Arnheim and Diotima's barren love, to Walter and Arnheim's cult of great men, to Strumm von Bordwehr's faith in the universal application of military order, to the banal slogans of the Collateral Campaign—these particular manifestations point to an overall consideration of the status of ideals in the modern world. How can there be ideals, ask Musil and Ulrich, in an age of intense nationalistic competition, of free and easy sexual expression, of military technology placing entire borders under machine-gun control, of unheralded speed and realism in transportation and communications? What will be the revised nature of the ideal in twentieth-century culture, asks Ulrich. For the first two Books, combining an intense esthetic sensibility with a demanding analytical rigor, Ulrich critically confronts every significant manifestation of idealism placed in his path. The Third Book, however inconsequential it may appear to be, can be read as Ulrich's attempt to respond to the problem of idealism in constructive, if not positivistic terms. Ulrich's cloistered twinning relationship to his sister in this Book is destined to failure by its own success. Withdrawing from institutional politics and the win-or-lose eventualities of active sexuality is "too good to be true." For this reason, Ulrich and Agathe's experiment in noncompetitive living is ending as the Third Book concludes. This interlude has furnished a context, however, for an extended exploration of a morality for our times, "even today splitting into these two components . . . mathematics and mysticism—practical ameliorization and adventuring into the unknown" (3:12, 122).

In this sense, the novel implicitly posits a correlation between critical detachment and quality, between deconstructive questioning and breaking the constraints of the narcissistic self-aggrandizement, that is, if the ever-present pitfalls of grandiosity can be avoided. There is something in Ulrich's sensibility intended to be exemplary if not ideal. This something is confounded by its openness to simultaneous thought-models and language games functioning on different planes, pulling in skewed, if not opposed directions. Ulrich is distinguished as much by the anomalies he embraces and joins, as by the coherence he establishes. He is both the critical observer of and contributor to a distinctly non-unified field of energy and interpretation. The difficulty of extrapolating a coherent Ulrich-model is the difficulty of reducing a sequence of differentiated interactions in context to a single format.

Drawing on an ambiguity explored by Wittgenstein in the latter pages of *The Blue Book,* Ulrich is both a critical observer, a roving "eye" on his times; and, as the "senior" surrogate, the prevalent "I" that the novel offers as an internal counterpart to the reader. There are inevitable confusions growing out of this templating. The strongest technical reproach that could be directed against Musil from a writerly point of view would be a fairly prevalent symbiosis confounding the ostensibly objective point of view of the narrator with Ulrich's critical commentary, a confusion between the novel's structural I and the I (and eye) of the central, perspectivally dominant surrogate. "Ulrich's" narcissistic Achille's heel is revealed when he retreats from the political and sexual tensions of his "external" world into the negative safety of an idealized (although articulate) bond to his sister; Musil's becomes discernible in his own (or rather his narrator's) inability to "let go" of Ulrich, Ulrich's status as an extension, whether of the narrator or Musil.

The figure of Ulrich haunts this novel, inhabits it on every plane; yet is, congenitally and necessarily, in keeping with his world and times, difficult to express. The indescribability of the sensibility necessary to cope with the violence, speed, and arbitrariness of twentieth-century living conditions becomes one of its preeminent characteristics. There are passages, however, where Musil succeeds brilliantly at holding out to the reader whatever "handles" on Ulrich are available.

If there is any preeminent reason for Ulrich's elusiveness, it is the combination in his "character" of three not easily resolvable primary traits, indeed, ones often seeming exclusive of one another. Ulrich is at the same time markedly suspicious of systematicity and particular systems, whether conceptual, political, or psychological; curious and open regarding the incommensurate and the asystematic; and analytically rigorous ("scientific") in his thought and problem solving. Among the very first things we learn about him is that as a schoolboy "in his essay on Love of Country Ulrich wrote that anyone who really loved his country should never think his own country the best" (1:15). At a young age, Ulrich already challenges reigning structures of authority. In questioning one form of authority well, Ulrich is freely accorded the intellectual authority that gets him appointed Honorary Secretary to the Collateral Campaign. A turning point in the novel occurs in chapter 40 of the Second Book, when, at a time when he is being sought for this appointment, he is arrested for interfering in the arrest of a drunkard.

> It is not difficult to give a description of this thirty-two-year-old man, Ulrich, in general outline, even though all he knew about himself was that he was as far from all the qualities as he was near to them, and that all of them, whether they had become his own or not, in some strange way were equally a matter of indifference to him. Associated with his intellectual suppleness, which was based simply on a great variety of gifts, there was, in him, a certain bellicosity too. He was of a masculine turn of mind. He was not sensitive where other people were concerned and rarely tried to get inside their minds, except when he wanted to understand them for his own ends. He had no respect for rights when he did not respect those whose rights they were, and that happened rarely. (1:175–76)

Such is the rebellious Ulrich, whose "masculinity" is acted out in a pronounced athleticism opposing itself to the "flabbiness" (1:71) of the Walters of the world. The performative mode of Ulrich's masculinity of mind is his scientificity of thought.

> The comparison of the world with a laboratory reminded him of an old idea of his. Formerly he had thought of the kind of life that would appeal to him as a large experimental station, where the best ways of living as a human being would be tried out and new ones discovered. The fact that this whole complex of laboratories worked more or less haphazardly, without any directors or theoreticians, was another matter. It might even be said that he himself had wanted to become something like a dominant spirit and master-mind. And who, after all, would not? (1:177)

Ulrich's sensibility is constituted by a dynamic tension between its rigor and its empathy, its openness to the incommensurate. One way the narrator chooses to describe this tension is to speak of a doubled Ulrich, a split central surrogate to go along with a doubled Moosbrugger and Bonadea (Ulrich's married and longest-standing mistress). Musil's splitting his characters along the vertical fissure of simultaneous self-fragments, or along the rift between the signified and signifier in the Saussurian sign, suggests that for him, as for Proust, no sooner is there character in literature than character is, always already, doubled, sundered. A list of characters in Proust's *Recherche*, extending from Swann and Odette, through Legrandin, Françoise, Vinteuil, the latter's daughter, Madame Verdurin, Jupien, and Charlus, are structured by this doubling: superficially, these characters may appear banal, or magnanimous, or cruel; but coexisting with these surface phenomena are deep structures at once contradicting and illuminating them: I think of Françoise's pleasure in killing the chickens she transforms into culinary artwork; the posthumus filial devotion, at the level of art, shown by Vinteuil *fille* to Vinteuil *père*.[2]

As the narrative of chapter 40 dramatizes, the trajectory extending from mistaken arrest to honorary appointment can be dramatically brief and uncertain. On its way, we encounter "two Ulrichs . . . side by side" (1:180):

> The one looked around, smiling, and thought: 'So that's where I once wanted to play a part, against such a stage-decor. One day I woke up, not snug as in mother's little basket, but with the firm conviction that I must accomplish something. I was given my cues, and felt they did not concern me. Everything was filled with

my own intentions and expectations, as though with flickering stage-fright. But in the meantime the stage revolved without my noticing it, I got a bit further on my way, and now perhaps I am already standing at the exit. In next to no time it will have turned me right out, and all I shall have spoken of my great part will be: "The horses are saddled." The devil take the lot of you!'

But while the one walked through the floating evening, smiling at these thoughts, the other had his fists clenched in pain and anger. He was the less visible of the two. And what he was thinking of was how to find a magic formula, a lever that one might be able to get a hold of, the real mind of the mind, the missing, perhaps very small, bit that would close the broken circle. This second Ulrich had no words at his disposal. Words leap like monkeys from tree to tree; but in the dark realm where a man is rooted he lacks their friendly mediation. The ground streamed away under his feet. He could hardly open his eyes. Can a feeling blow like a storm and yet not be a stormy feeling at all? If one speaks of a storm of emotion, one means the kind in which man's bark groans and man's branches fly as though they were about to break. But this was a storm with a quite calm surface. It was almost, but not quite, a state of conversion, of reversion. (1:180–81)

This doubled Ulrich is at once playful and scientific, in search of Wittgensteinian formulae but open to the storm, indifferent in a distinctively twentieth-century way, but capable of genuine spontaneity and emotion. The two Ulrichs described in the above passage constitute the complementary playful and rigorous flanks of his critical confrontation with idealism. Even more striking than the *difference* between the antagonistic qualities and attitudes that Ulrich combines is the communication between them. Ulrich is internally fragmented, sundered, but the different positions asserting themselves within his sensibility are intensely, explicitly related to each other. The very substantial mental work that Ulrich is performing during his meandering walk is framed by the insubstantiality that Sir Arthur Eddington discovered in the core of the seemingly solid physical universe.[3] "A higher sense of his own ego came into conflict with an uncanny feeling of not being quite firmly fixed in his own skin. And the world too was not quite solid; it was an unsteady mist, continually becoming distorted and changing its shape" (1:183). Anger, wonder, play, and very deliberate and structured thought are actively involved in Ulrich's sensibility, in predicating its reactions to ideas, politics, and sexual stimulation. It is the openness and expressiveness of the positions struggling both for dominance and consensus within Ulrich that must count as the quality of qualities, the qualification earning him the position of Musil's roving reporter and roving eye on his age.

The detachment of Ulrich's mathematics severs him from the naive idealists; and his Nietzschean openness to incommensurability separates him from nationalists, priests, and moralists. The narrator, always struggling with the dissonance of Ulrich's qualities, finally seizes on literature and reality as the arenas where their *Auseinandersetzung* takes place; they will never abandon their "strained relationship" (2:361).

> This urge to make an onslaught on life, and so to dominate it, had always been very marked in him, however it expressed itself: whether as a rejection of the existing order or as a varied striving after a new one, or as logical or moral demands, or even merely as an insistence on keeping the body in good fighting-trim. And everything that, as time went on, he had called Essayism and the Sense of Possibility and of Fantastical, as opposed to Pedantic, Precision, the demands that history should be invented and that one should live the history of ideas instead of the history of the world, that one should clutch hard at everything that could never be quite realized in practice, so that one might ultimately reach a stage of living as if one were not a human being at all, but merely a figure in a book, a figure with all the inessential elements left out, the essential residue of it undergoing a magical integration—all these terms in which his thoughts had expressed themselves, and which were anti-realistic in their abnormal epigrammatic intensity, had one thing in common: they brought an unmistakably ruthless passion to bear upon reality. . . .
>
> This inactive half of his personality showed itself most clearly, perhaps, in his involuntary conviction that the active and busy half was no more than provisionally useful—a conviction that was like a shadow cast upon the active half. In everything he set about—which meant physical passions just as much as intellectual ones—he had finally come to see himself as one held captive by preparations that would never be finished; and in the course of the years his life had run out of the sense of necessity as a lamp runs out of oil. His development had evidently split into two roads, one lying on the surface, in the light of day, and one

dark and closed to traffic; and the condition of moral standstill that had settled down upon him, which had been oppressing him for a long time (and perhaps more than was necessary), could be explained only by the fact that he never succeeded in joining up these two roads. (2:360–61)

In such passages as the ones cited above does the narrator attempt to establish the "operating system" or "deep structures" that will account for Ulrich's particular positions and actions. Like Derridean deconstructions, Ulrich's debunkings of the Here and Now (1:343) and love as animate (2:317), will be both esthetic and mathematical in thrust, will draw on a wide range of poetic and logical figures and operations. The greatest risk to which Ulrich exposes himself, his greatest claim on literary heroism, is the manifoldness of approaches, positions, and postures that he manages to sustain without lapsing into the closure and splitting that dominate whom and what he addresses.

# CHAPTER 13

# The Man without Qualities:
## An Early "Borderline Character"

What are the erotic conditions prevailing in such a world of naive idealism and skepticism, of such randomness and design? The above discussion of Clarisse suggests that sexuality, in the ages of Ulrich and borderline phenomena, is a strikingly polarized affair, abrupt and impulsive in its dynamics, colored by Victorian sanctimony and unprecedented license at its extremes. Marriage is at once a contemptible wasteland and an unavoidable socioeconomic arrangement. The long tradition in which women are polarized between Madonna-like purity and identity-dissolving seductiveness and evil has reached one of its major pinnacles. The split sexual messages during this first age of practical erotic freedom structure the characters of those who hear and heed them.

I reserve the analysis of Moosbrugger for this section of the discussion because the crime bringing him to the attention of Austrian society is of a sexual nature. This brutal murder is a sexual crime, but it is integrally related to the epistemological conditions responsible at once for Ulrich's thinking and his institutional and personal encounters. Characterized by the narrator with a rhetoric of borderline phenomena, Moosbrugger consists of all the shocks, collisions, impulses, and paradoxes working at odds in Ulrich's sensibility, but minus two crucial ingredients: integration and introspection. Ulrich constitutes an intellectual field in which the chaotic forces of his era will play themselves out, for better or worse. In the figure of Moosbrugger, we encounter all the chaos, the vast and as yet unbounded energy available to the historical moment, but minus the remorse, the self-consciousness, and even the self that would furnish some medium of coherence and consistency. A creature of effaced internal structure, Moosbrugger inhabits a borderline of recognizable human cognition and behavior. Love, *chez Moosbrugger*, is a horrifying specter of intimacy devoid of any idealistic structure whatsoever; intimacy exposed and vulnerable to primary-process violence.

It is in keeping with Moosbrugger's role as a talisman and anti-model for Austrian culture that we see little of him: we witness the crime that comprises the occasion for his current trial, and we observe his antics in jail and before the court. The narrative of the prostitute's murder explicitly raises the issue of the boundaries between Moosbrugger's and his victim's selves:

> But when he paid, there again the thought was: What was he to do if she was still waiting outside? There are such thoughts that are like string winding itself in endless nooses round one's arms and legs. And he had taken only a few steps out into the dark street when he felt the girl at his side. Now she was no longer humble, but brazen and self-confident; nor did she plead any more; she was merely silent. There and then he realized that he would never get rid of her, because it was he himself who was drawing her along after him. His throat filled up with tearful disgust. He walked on, and, again, the thing half behind him was himself. It was just the same way that he always met processions. He had once cut a big splinter of wood out of his leg himself, because he was too impatient to wait for the doctor; it was very much the same, the way he felt his knife now, lying long and hard in his pocket.
>
> But with an almost more than earthly exertion of his conscience Moosbrugger hit upon yet another way out. Behind the hoarding along which the street now led there was a sports-ground; there one could not be seen, and so he entered. In the small ticket-booth he rolled up, with his head pushed into the corner where it was darkest. And the soft, accursed second self lay down beside him. So he pretended to go to sleep at once, in order to be able to slip away later. (1:82)

Moosbrugger does not experience his companion as a partner or an other, but as something detestable in himself, an extension, something that must be extruded. Logically as well as physically, Moosbrugger subjects the woman to impossible, paradoxical conditions, ones surrounding a double bind:[1] she is external to him, an extension, but she has invaded his body, and must be surgically removed from him. Her crime does not consist of any sexual mischief, but "insult[ing] a man . . . clutching at him" (1:82–83).

The woman so evil that she must be annihilated is there, but not by virtue of her own volition. Moosbrugger "was drawing her along." The woman is not properly a she but an it: "the thing half beside him was himself." The woman is not an integral individual to Moosbrugger because he is not one to himself. Destroying the woman is tantamount to a self-performed operation, excising a self-fragment which, through splitting and devaluation, has become equated with evil and sickness. The operation is asocial, unsanctioned, performed before the doctor arrives. The woman's dismemberment is described as a cutting away of Moosbrugger's own self: "she fell with her head inside the booth; he hauled her some way out, on to the soft earth, and stabbed and stabbed at her until he had cut her completely away from himself" (1:82). Moosbrugger's conviction that his victim has entered his body is reminiscent of Adolf Hitler's paranoid fantasy, as related by Kohut, that "the Jews had invaded the body of Germany and had to be eliminated" (*AS,* 256). The dissolution of Moosbrugger's "self"-boundaries, the extreme polarization of his values, the abrupt splitting "he" achieves within himself, and the violence of his "object" relations are all phenomena discussed productively by Kernberg as well, in his diagnosis and treatment of severe borderline patients.[2]

No less striking than the violence of Moosbrugger's crimes is that of his social performance, which can be so disarming at its affable extreme that it has convinced courts to pardon prior, equally psychopathic assaults. Musil is as interested in Austrian society's fascination with Moosbrugger, its not fully explicit desire to condone and even reward his behavior, as he is in this particular character.

> During the proceedings Moosbrugger made quite unpredictable difficulties for his counsel. He sat there at huge ease on his bench, like an onlooker, calling out "Hear! Hear!" to the public prosecutor whenever he made a point of Moosbrugger's being a public menace and did it in a way that Moosbrugger considered worthy of himself. He gave good marks to witnesses who declared that they had never noticed anything about him that pointed to his being not responsible for his actions. "You're a queer customer," the presiding judge said from time to time, in a flattering way, and conscientiously pulled tighter the noose that the accused had laid round his own neck. (1:83)

In society, Moosbrugger displays a flair for the dramatic incon-
sistent with the profile of a psychotic killer. He can be affable, and
even entertaining, as the occasion permits. In the extract immediately above, Moosbrugger has leveraged the judge into a familiar,
quasi-protective bearing toward him. Through his character Musil
explores the semiological disparity between signified (character)
and signifier (behavior) prevailing under borderline conditions.
Musil has not neglected, though, to inscribe the pervasive core of
annihilating emptiness around which Moosbrugger's violence dis-
sipates itself. The ultimate fate of Moosbrugger's madness is not
entertainment but blankness, the silence of cultural illiteracy, a
concern surfacing elsewhere in the novel. "He envied all the people
who had learnt when young how to talk easily," the narrative says
of Moosbrugger. "With him the words stuck like rubber to his
gums" (1:282). For Moosbrugger, "the subjective experience of
emptiness" is linguistic a well as structural and moral. The pervasive Kernbergian envy also registers itself in these lines. The final
substantial vision that the novel offers of him is of perceptual and
cognitive blankness; the play completely removed from a once
tense elastic.

> Now almost all the time he had the feeling of being spread out
> like a big twinkling pool that nothing could disturb, though he
> had no words for this.
> The words he had were: h'm-h'm, uh-uh.
> The table was Moosbrugger.
> The chair was Moosbrugger.
> The barred window and the bolted door were himself.
> He did not mean that in a way that was at all crazy or
> unusual. It was simply that the elastic had gone. Behind every
> thing or creature that tries to come quite close up to one there
> is an elastic band, stretching. Otherwise, of course, in the end
> the things might go right through each other. And in every move-
> ment there is an elastic band that never quite lets one do what
> one would like to. These pieces of elastic now all at once were
> gone. Or was it merely the hampering feelings as of elastic?
> (2:111)

If elastic is emblematic of internal tension and self-definition in
Moosbrugger, it is gone. This character represents an extreme of
vacuousness and inconsistency whose juridical process forces
Austrian society into a confrontation with its own borderline

features. With regard to this psychoanalytical rhetoric, Musil is nothing less than prophetic. "Moosbrugger was one of these borderline cases known to jurisprudence and forensic medicine, and even to laymen, as cases of diminished responsibility" (1:287). Moosbrugger represents a certain extreme and horizon for Austrian society in the novel. No character but Clarisse even approaches him in agitation, erraticism, and impulsiveness, and yet, strangely, in sexual mores, Moosbrugger comprises the extreme of deviance nevertheless qualifying the "normative behavior in the novel." With the exceptions of Count Leinsdorf and General Stumm von Bordwehr, whom we know exclusively in their official capacities, every major character is split, sexually, in a pronounced way, whether the division is between sublimated and casual eroticism or between marriage and its supplements. The overarching economy of sexual ambivalence, whether in the complementary forms of Diotima's marriage-weariness or Bonadea's need for serial deception, or as Ulrich's unmystified adventurism, comprises the household brand of a polarization acted out by Moosbrugger with no remorse or restraint. The petty economy of household sexuality is the setting where Moosbrugger's grandiose impulses and contradictions become domesticated, and where they reach the proportions and levels of distraction we recognize so well from our everyday lives.

Bonadea spirits Ulrich away from the scene of a chance crime at which he happens to be mugged. Since at the time of this modernistically haphazard occurrence, Ulrich is engaged in a bestial affair with one Leona, an occasional prostitute (a not insignificant detail in connection to Moosbrugger), Bonadea is a "good idea" in more senses than one. When Ulrich bonds to Bonadea, two weeks after meeting her, he detaches himself from Leona. His on-and-off-again affair with Bonadea comprises the primary outlet for his sexuality and desire until the surprise emergence of his sister.

A married woman of significant social stature, Bonadea is in a particularly delicate situation. It is in her figure that the narrative bridges the erotic tension felt by an individual and the sexual tension characterizing a time and a place.

Bonadea lives out the desire experienced by Diotima in the manner of grand tragedy in a comic mode. The narrative specifies that she is as capable of domestic attachment and trite idealizations as any other legitimate member of her society:

She was the wife of a well-respected man and the fond mother of two fine little boys. Her favourite idea was that of the 'paragon'; she applied this expression to people, servants, shops and feelings, whenever she wanted to speak well of them. She was capable of uttering the words 'the true, the good and the beautiful' as often and as naturally as someone else might say 'Thursday.' What was most deeply satisfying to her craving for ideas was the concept of a tranquil, ideal mode of life in a circle formed by husband and children. . . . She had only one fault, and this was that she was liable to be stimulated to a quite uncommon degree by the mere sight of men. She was by no means lustful; she was sensual in the way that other people have other troubles, such as sweating of the hands or blushing easily; it was apparently congenital, and she could never do anything about it. When she got to know Ulrich in circumstances so romantic, so extraordinarily stimulating to the imagination, she had from the first instant been the destined prey of a passion that began as sympathy, after a brief but severe tussle went over into forbidden intimacies, and then continued as an alternation between the pangs of sin and the pangs of remorse.

But Ulrich was only one of heaven alone knows how many cases in her life. Men—as soon as they have grasped the situation—are generally in the habit of treating such nymphomaniac women little better than imbeciles, who can by the most trivial means be tricked into stumbling over the same thing time and time again; for the tender aspects of masculine self-abandonment somewhat resemble the growling of a jaguar over a hunk of meat, and any interruption is taken gravely amiss. The consequence was that Bonadea often lead a double life, like that of any citizen who, entirely respectable in the everyday world, in the dark interspaces of his consciousness leads the life of a railway thief. (1:43)

Bonadea, a sexually active female, whose attitude toward men and the fulfillment of her desire is similarly an active one, is alienated from her time by being ahead of it. (Musil's empathic treatment of her may also be regarded as an advance, historical and beyond some of the other characterizations in the novel.) The health of her appetite in matters sexual, however, relegates her to the stealth of a railroad thief, to a shadow life in the form of a succession of intense, but fated dangerous liaisons; to the world of Proustian inverts.

In the implicit map charted by the novel, it is as inevitable that Bonadea should bind herself to Diotima as that she should be the ideal mistress for Ulrich. Bonadea becomes a second natural link, besides kinship, making Diotima's compulsive idealizations contiguous with Ulrich's relentless deconstructive debunking. It is precisely the impossibility of the affair, its fatedness, that makes Bonadea's liaison with Ulrich the "ideal" expression of his own shiftlessness. And yet the guilt and remorse of which she is also capable links her to Diotima's divided values and her growing awareness of and anger at the limited sexual options open to women. The examplarity of Bonadea's situation is explored in chapter 109, "Bonadea, Kakania, systems of happiness and equipoise," in which as a gesture of solidarity, Bonadea literally clothes herself after Diotima (a costume she will abandon before the next—and final—call she makes at Ulrich's castle).

> Bonadea's system had hitherto consisted in leading a double life. Her ambition was satisfied by the fact that she belonged to a family circle that could be referred to as of high standing, and in her social intercourse too she had the satisfaction of passing for a highly cultivated and well-bred woman. But there were certain lures to which her spirit was exposed that she gave way to on the pretext that she was the victim of an over-stimulated constitution or, alternatively, that she had a heart that led her into committing follies. . . .
>
> But there had been one fault in the working of this system: it divided Bonadea's life into two conditions, and the transition from one to the other was not made without heavy losses. For however eloquent the heart might be before one of her lapses, it was equally discouraged afterwards, and she whose heart it was constantly being flung to and fro between a psychic state that was maniacally effervescent and one that drained away in inky blackness, two states between which there was rarely a middle state. Nevertheless, it was a system. That is to say, it was not a mere play of uncontrolled instincts, to be compared, for instance, with the way that people once used to see life as an automatic squaring of accounts between pleasure and pain, with a certain balance on the side of pleasure, but included a considerable number of intellectual arrangements for taking these accounts. (2:270–71)

Duplicity is not merely the mode through which a sexually active woman shares sensuous pleasure with a man. More than "a mere play of uncontrolled instincts," duplicity constitutes a system, the system that will allow itself to be read if the reader will only join Ulrich's (and the narrator's) double work of analyzing and imagining beyond. There is a duplicity in this scene as well: thematically, it describes the ruses civil men and women undertake in order to achieve a certain satisfaction. Critically, it elaborates the (accounting) system, "an automatic squaring of accounts between pleasure and pain" according to which the novel could operate both as representation, as (world) picture, *and* as the conceptual system whose chapter headings possess the form and finality of logical propositions.

The coincidence between the novel's representational explorations and its critical commentary constitutes its allegorical dimension. As an allegorical novelist, Musil engages simultaneously in conjuring up a world, systematizing its traits and tensions, and in delivering a deconstructive commentary on its constitution as well as its blindnesses. The very act of writing, then, is implicated in the duplicity at whose successful cunning, in Ulrich and Bonadea, we smile and at whose extreme dissociation, in Moosbrugger, we recoil. The writing of *The Man without Qualities* demands the allegorical double vision of systematization with observation, of criticism with action, of articulating and denuding ideals.

Chapter 109 brings the Kakanian society in which Bonadea satisfies her desire through duplicity to a systematic accounting. The domestic economy of pleasure and pain expands itself first to the overall purview of cultural criticism and then to the metacritical awareness of the interplay of semiological systems. It is not accidental that in such a chapter Bonadea should don a new costume, one closer to the ideal trappings of her culture, or that the same chapter should offer a cultural commentary, in the best tradition of the Frankfurt School, on the mystifying power of clothes.

> This Bonadea, gazing at herself in the looking-glass, wearing a new dress, was quite incapable of imagining that a time might come when instead of leg-of-mutton sleeves, long, bell-shaped dresses, and a curl in the middle of the forehead, one would wear knee-length skirts and have one's hair cropped like a boy's. Nor would she have denied the possibility of it; her brain was simply incapable of absorbing such a notion. She had always dressed the way a lady must dress, and every six months, when she contem-

plated the new fashions, felt a reverence as though face to face with eternity. Even if an appeal to her power of reasoning had forced her to admit the transience of these things, it would not in the least have diminished her reverence for them. . . . And this was why it was so comical to see Bonadea without clothes on; she was then denuded of all ideal coverings too and was the naked victim of an inexorable compulsion that overwhelmed her with the non-human violence of an earthquake. (2:273–74)

Briefly, through this outfit, Bonadea will reconcile herself to the societal ideals exemplified and enforced by Diotima. But the novel, as the above passage is aware, is as capable of stripping away ideals as it is of dressing them in the emperor's new clothes. The novel is a contextual world in which clothes and window-dressings can look other than as "strange tribes and excrescences." In context, these accoutrements, so monstrous "lifted out of the fluidity of the present" become enchanting "when seen in combination with the qualities they bestow on their wearer" (2:275). In terms of Musil's allegory, the novel is a costume in which the author dresses a time and place, and its representative characters. As a coordinated environment, the novel idealizes events and details which would otherwise be random, but in its capabilities for social criticism and metacommentary, the novel strips naked the very constraints on which it has based its coherence. The novel splits and polarizes itself. It indulges in its own pathological narcissism.

Such objects are like debtors who pay back the sums we lend them with fantastic interest; and in fact there are only debtor-objects. This quality that clothes have is also possessed by convictions, prejudices, theories, hopes, belief in anything, thoughts; indeed, even thoughtlessness possesses it, in so far as it is only by virtue of itself that it is penetrated with a sense of its own rightness. All of them, by endowing us with the properties that we lend them, serve the purpose of placing the world in a light that emanates from us, and fundamentally this, precisely this, is the task for which everyone has his own special system. By exercising great and manifold skill we manage to produce a dazzling deception by the aid of which we are capable of living alongside the most uncanny things and remaining perfectly calm about it, because we recognize these frozen grimaces of the universe as a table or a chair, a shout or an outstretched arm, a speed or a roast chicken. (2:275)

Dressing up in its own metaphorics of dressing, the novel delivers a simultaneous thematic, social, and metacritical accounting. Disinterestedly, in its own terms indifferently, it seeks out and exposes the multiple deceptions, in style, rhetoric, and morality enabling social and individual existence to go on. Its own performance, however, is sustained by the very deception it decries on thematic and tendentious levels. The novel indulges in, its existence is predicated by the deception it debunks as a stripping away of the ideal facade. The very existence of the novel is a deceitful and symbiotic double life. Its essence, were we to allow ourselves to speak of such, would be the coincidence of lived experience and "dazzling deception," of "the most uncanny things" and "perfect calm."

As a novelist of his era, Robert Musil bases his uncanny simulacrum of the world upon the rampant nationalism, time-devouring technology, and ideological kitsch that he observes. He dispatches Ulrich to a world of growing political instability, pollyanish delusions, and unstable personal relationships. Musil is uncannily accurate as an avatar of the unique psychological landscape prevailing from his age to ours. Ulrich and the other characters negotiate a human landscape in which the conditions of pathological narcissism and other personality disorders are already well-entrenched.

By Musil's own account, the novel is of the deceptions it exposes and debunks. *The Man without Qualities* assumes responsibility for the psychopathology it chronicles and in which it takes part. In this sense, it establishes, at least within the parameters of twentieth-century literature and art, a privileged relationship prevailing between the literary enterprise and any self-aware linguistic discourse and the conditions of narcissism and the borderline.

# CHAPTER 14

# The Man Without Qualities:
## *Sibling Mirroring*

*The Man without Qualities*, then, successfully accounts for itself, both as an artifact of novelistic representation and social commentary and as a portrayal of the psychological and existential conditions under which writing arises. It is unique in even enjoying the latter conditions. It is not unusual for writing to self-aggrandize itself in internalizing a dull or obtuse audience for itself within the confines of its projects; or to present its apprehensions as themselves transcending and superseding the status quo of human thought as systematized by sociopolitical institutions or bodies of knowledge. An encyclopaedic novel, that will dare, however, to explore the condition of personal and intellectual emptiness that preconditions so much writing, also admitting the social wear and tear of having ideas in settings in which they are at once prized, envied, and reviled—such a work is a *rara avis* indeed.

In an essay that has presumed to read a modernistic novel framed within a setting of high modernism in terms of theories and relations of the self, an essay deploying a concept of the self no less than twenty-five years after simplistic understandings of self-representation in language (or subjectivity) first underwent its current severe methodological scrutiny, I would like to pause over the distinction between the theoretical and existential statuses of writing, writing as thought through and writing as lived through or acted out. As a literary construct or category, the self (or its more technical, in a structural sense, predecessor, the ego) currently finds itself in a condition of extreme disrepute, something like the notion of presence.

It will hopefully not be too farfetched to assert that there is at least a classically psychoanalytical element or tinge to Jacques Derrida's deconstructions of such notions as presence, identity, and the truth. In reactivating the long-standing conceptual treasury and apparatus surrounding widespread assumptions about the status and dynamics of language, Derrida inspires and instructs readers to "see around" the entrenched biases. Indeed, after a reading of his basic deconstructive texts, common sense notions of intention, presence, essence, and identity in language will never be the same again. Derridean "conceptual psychoanalysis"consists in making explicit the biases underlying ideational repression, exposing attitudinal underpinnings that have become so integral to long-standing metaphysical inventions as to have become invisible or transparent. But to say that henceforth readers and writers need never concern themselves with their selves, something Derrida certainly never says, would be tantamount to asserting that henceforth the children of readers and writers should be raised by "absence." (Note that a rhetoric of biological reproduction and familial responsibility has crept into my discourse.)

The self joins presence as a construct, which, although needing every refinement and statute of limitation upon its use that can be mustered, does not entirely disintegrate in the wake of the theoretical and methodological scrutiny dedicated to it. Purely scriptually defined, the self is the reference of our signature, a subject to which Derrida has returned.[1] With all the qualifications regarding unity, identity, certainty, and essence that can be applied to it the notion of the self hovers about us, if, as nothing else, a perspectual framework, in a state of constant revision, through which we apprehend and articulate the world. We can say that the self is the person whose book or article we hope gets published when we submit it to a publisher. The self is the person we bring along to a session with a psychologist or psychiatrist, who "joins the conversation" on our behalf.

Although whimsical, my examples here are not entirely haphazard. To say that an individual has severely questioned or curtailed the notion of self as applied to herself or himself on a theoretical or intellectual level does not imply that s/he has done so elsewhere, or everywhere. It is even theoretically possible, though I cannot personally document this, for an individual who has entirely dispatched or renounced the concept of the self on an intellectual level, to movingly articulate and dramatize in a clinical setting certain symptoms whose location would be something very like a self, if the self did not exist. We say of the existential conditions of writing that they invade novels and other modes of fiction more than we would ever dare expect. We honor them in artforms from which, through conventions of verisimilitude that still persist, we can detach ourselves. But where the existential conditions of writing enter the discursive or critical work, a faux pas has been committed, an embarrassing noise has been made.

Personality disorders, as they are currently understood both clinically and theoretically, may refer back to the status of a self and its objects, but the self they address has lost the unity and consistency of its structure. Individuals with personality disorders do not possess a self or a personality in any conventional or simple sense of the word. The theories of object relations and personality disorders implicitly if not explicitly inquire as to whether human thought and behavior necessitate the possession of a single and integral self. Disorders of the self, and the theory, diagnostics, and therapeutics addressing them, thus already incorporate certain of contemporary critical theory's questions into the natures of intentionality, representation, and immanence. Terms such as "difference," "dissemination," "duplicity," and "supplementarity" can be readily interjected into descriptions by object-relations theorists of the clinical conditions facing them.

Musil's novel operates both at the level of "dazzling deception," that is, fictive representation and modelling, and at that of social and theoretical commentary. By virtue of its scope, it is free, representationally and critically, to incorporate the existential analysis of writing we so judiciously exclude from our own scholarly-theoretical discourse. It is therefore free to remind us, of what we might, in the narcissistic absorption of writing, forget: that the suspension of limits edifying in the theoretical sphere, "essential" to it, may not store so well in the existential. Moosbrugger and Clarisse, the novel's most "borderline" characters, are indeed fascinating as fictive constructs. There is something in the facility of their "thought" and "action" that may even be important to Ulrich's bearings as a critic, Musil's writing of the novel, and to writing in general. Yet within the novel's existential allegory, these characters and others exhaust Ulrich through their decenteredness and jealousy, ultimately sap his ability to think clearly and creatively.

Musil's novel, if not contemporary scholarship, is free to suggest that what is energizing, edifying, and inspiring at the levels of theory and esthetics may be nothing less than disastrous at the levels of the "self" and its existence. Does this mean that writing may be hazardous to your health? No, on the contrary, it is writing's internal ethics to supersede itself, to expose its internal points of fixity, to subject its constructs to the never-ending ebb and flow of its dynamics. Is carrying over or acting out the dynamics of writing within the existential sphere a disaster? Perhaps not always, but literature, from Sophokles and Shakespeare through Poe, Melville, Dostoyevsky, Kafka, and Camus, is filled with instances where this proves to be the case.

In addressing the role object relations play in psychoanalytical theory, should contemporary critical theory devote enormous energy in challenging the existence of a self or something quite close to it? I suspect not (1) because its overall inquiry into subjectivity has been so powerful and convincing that any rigorous conceptualization of self is already conditioned by it; and (2) because, as suggested above, self belongs to those concepts, such as "other" and "presence," that do not entirely disintegrate just because they are amplified. Where does, from a critical theory point of view, the Kohutian concept of the self need to be revised? Probably in the implicit belief that a single, immanent sector of the self is more "real" (more primary, authentic, essential) than those archaic self-fragments with which it, under a variety of stressors, temporarily exchanges identities. While psychological therapeutics surely wishes to establish the dominance of the working-through self-sector so that psychological integration and equilibrium may be finalized, the literary "imp of the perverse" whose domain extends well beyond Poe, delights in the uncertainty and imbalance made possible through a heterogeneity of selves or equally weighted self-fragments.

This is one context in which it is possible to interpret the Third Book of Musil's work. While the unexpected reunion of Ulrich and Agathe has interesting utopian and incestuous overtones, their association is above all a mutually therapeutic interlude from the self-effacing tenor of their lives. Although from the perspectives of sensationalism and sensuality, to which the novel has conditioned us through its explicit scenes, the siblings' moralizing discussions represent quite a comedown, their subject matter is as meta-existential as the novel's lurid material is metapsychological and metacritical.

A hypothetical alliance of siblings, in which both partners take "time-out" from the involvements and self-effacing conditions of their lived experience in order to interact with each other therapeutically, is the scenario for psychotherapeutic work that Musil chooses over a more realistic representation. Given the limited geographical, characterological, and dramatic potentials in the formal psychoanalytical setting, it is not difficult to understand, for novelistic reasons, why he disguised therapy in the trappings of quasi-incest (a questioning attitude to psychotherapy may herein lie as well). Although the therapeutic alliance does not exhaust the siblings' encounter, however, and constitutes far from its "only" meaning, the "repair work" that Ulrich and Agathe undertake for each other surely embraces a therapeutic dimension.

Above all, Ulrich and Agathe relate to each other empathically. They feel free to express the most controversial and "inadmissible" ideas to each other, concerning suicide (3:83, 353), homicide (3:79–81, 88–89), and incest (3:92–93, 324–28). They are more tolerant and accepting of each other than any two other characters in the novel. In this sense, they furnish each other with a psychological haven. They mirror and twin each other (explicitly) in a Kohutian sense.[2]

In chapter 25 of the Third Book, a particularly intense one, Ulrich and Agathe explore the narcissistic dimension of their mutually empathic relationship. Agathe exclaims to Ulrich "Considering, that I'm supposed to be your self-love, you treat me rather roughly!" (2:280), while Ulrich admits to "this desire for a *Doppelgänger* of the same sex, this craving for the love of a being that will be entirely the same as oneself and yet another, distinct from oneself, a magical figure that is oneself and that does nevertheless remain a magical figure as well and is more than any figment of the imagination" (3:282). In terms of the self-effacing and unbalancing conditions that they face, each sibling serves the other as a supplement. Ulrich supports Agathe in her efforts to liberate herself from an oppressive marriage of convenience to Gottlieb Hagauer; while Agathe diverts Ulrich (if not saving him) from the contentious wear and tear of the Collateral Campaign and his already competitive friendships. The Third Book devotes considerable resources simply to recording their discussions; it would not do so if some dramatic development were not contained simply in the speech-act itself. I would argue that therapeutic reintegration and restoration is precisely the "work" accomplished through the recording and reading of these sessions.

As the narrative suggests, the sibling alliance may be short-lived, as psychotherapy invariably is. Existentially and fictively, Ulrich and Agathe's shared withdrawal is artificial, dramatic—as psychotherapy is. In so modernist a work, the emergence of the protagonist's long-lost sister has the feel of a deus ex machina to it, but this contrivance offers a neutralization of sexual tension necessary for the elaboration of psychotherapeutic conditions.

The Third Book explores a utopic supplement to the generally idealized, exploitative or hostile object relations dramatized in the first two Books. Any possibilities of restoration that it holds out, transpire, again, at the level and in the site of the self, the constantly self-revising observational perspective of lived experience.

CHAPTER 15

# Borderlinity and Contemporary Culture: The Silence of the Lambs

Within a span of representational styles extending from hyper-realism to the most imaginative special effects and a synesthesia incorporating multiple, above all, visual and aural elements, film has, since its inception, functioned as a splendid medium for the depiction and cultural evaluation of grandiosity. The intervention of film into everyday life is in itself, for the above-mentioned reasons, momentous. We have become so habituated to the representational devices and dramatic conventions of the cinema, its extension in television, and the various forms of popular music that these have acquired the status of a nature to us, as Roland Barthes noted early on in the set of sociopolitical and cultural conditions defining the present age.[1] Even the most casual review of these media and artforms suggests how conducive they are to the treatment and working through of grandiosity in its social-psychological manifestations. A comprehensive exploration of this theme would furnish an occasion for yet another *livre à venir,* one well-worth writing and reading. Before terminating this introductory inquiry into the complicated influence of grandiosity upon literary production and culture then, I would like to devote a few pages to its cinematographic role.

A film such as Orson Welles's "Citizen Kane" (1941) serves, in terms of a discussion differentiating between the values of various psychoanalytical models, as an ideal artifact. A Freudian interpretation of this film might well focus on Charles Foster Kane's earliest family configuration and on the realization of his instincts and desires, as reflected in his choices in profession and artworks for his collections, and in his relationships with wives and lovers. Surely crucial in this regard is the weakness in his father's character and power depicted in the crucial scene in which Walter Parks Thatcher becomes his *foster* parent; a lack of power and authority aggravated by the displacement of Kane's vast windfall *around* his father; this event strengthens an oedipal alliance between the young Kane and his mother evident in the scene in which the traumatic early displacements in Kane's life take place.

Young Kane's immense and unanticipated wealth is the stuff both dreams and nightmares are made of. News of this event literally brings the curtain down on the scene of Kane's childhood, his early memories, and his first attachment. He shoves his famous sled, "Rosebud," into the midriff of the man who is literally snatching him away from his home, in the most profound sense of this word. While there are surely a multiplicity of Lacanian readings to this artifact, a very basic one would pursue the trajectory of "Rosebud" as a signifier, an element of language tinged with Kane's early experiences of unanticipated gain, loss, and undesired separation through a number of scenes and "events" in his "life." The first phase of Lacanian readings might have satisfied itself with equating Kane's consciousness to a certain number of linguistic processes; with elaborating the role and nuances of "Rosebud" within the Lacanian equivalents of Freudian intrapsychic agencies such as the Imaginary, the Symbolic, and the Real. Lacanian approaches of, say, the past five years, would extend this fundamentally linguistic allegory, based upon a parallelism between consciousness and language, to a New Historical account of the saga of an evolving post-Cartesian subject. Within this ongoing tale, such constructs as the *petit objet a*, the Real, the *point de capiton*, and the *sinthome* are as important as they were during the initial phase of Lacanian studies, but they are also referred to a progress report on the evolving Subject, who in Hegelian terms is *us,* our (wo)man in the text. This elaborated Lacanian reading would surely be sensitive to the coincidence between Kane's life and history and the mass media (newspapers, political sensationalism, twentieth-century opera) in which he participates. Such a current Lacanian reading might well pursue "Rosebud" as a symbolic manifestation of a desire never realized by Kane through all his quests for power, cultural centrality, and appropriate objects for his desire. It might treat the Colorado snow that is so pervasive during the childhood scene and that recurs in the "snow"-filled paperweight that Kane drops during his first appearance and at the literal end of a misguided but important life as an element of the Real framing the multifaceted history.

Fascinating though it might be, such a reading would subordinate the object relations abounding throughout the story to the schematic trajectories of the signifier as they illuminate the History of the post-Cartesian Subject. (Such readings, as they are being produced today, are indeed fascinating, effecting masterful coordinations between linguistic analysis, historical awareness, and the techniques making the contemporary media possible.)[2]

A gloss on "Citizen Kane" from an object-relations point of view would surely take off from the loss of a beloved and crucial transitional object, the sled identified by "Rosebud," and it would pursue Charles Foster Kane's life in the context of the narcissistic wounds suffered at this point. It would take into account the lack of empathy toward young Kane's inclinations and desires at this crucial moment, and then would note the adult Kane's blindness toward his second wife's hesitations about becoming an opera star. The older Kane will suffer a deficit in his ability to constructively mirror the needs and wishes of his significant others perhaps owing to the removal of his loving, if unsophisticated father, his best source of positive mirroring.

An object-relations reading of "Citizen Kane" would surely chronicle the evolution away from a healthy grandiosity early in his career, evident in his idealism, his muckraking style of journalism, and his devil-may-care attitude, and toward increasing isolation, shame (prompted by his scandal-ridden political campaign), and social hostility. By the end of his career, in terms of the film narration, Kane is "aloof, seldom visited, never photographed." The young Kane, on the other hand, is an American original. We are as attracted by his brashness, his conviction that no challenge is too big to be surmounted, his belief in a major social contribution that is his to bestow in the beginning of his career as we are put off by his increasing remoteness, depression, and emotional volatility at the end.

It would be possible to argue that Welles devotes the outset of his cinematographic career to an exploration of a particularly American, culturally-mediated grandiosity, a dream fueled by an unprecedented technological and social expansion at the beginning of the twentieth century that coincided with the improvisations of modernism. The cinematographic techniques and devices for which Welles is best known, including his panoramic low-angle shots and his persistence under conditions of dim lighting, consti-

tute his technical response to the unlimited expectations and underlying depression of American "manifest destiny." As a documentary voice-over notes Xanadu, the Florida castle to which Kane
ships the *objets d'art* that he collects with unconscious desperation
is named Xanadu, after Coleridge's "pleasure dome" of "Kubla
Khan," acknowledging the source of this particular grandiose
vision to the sublime of Romanticism. Documentary reportage of
Kane's death depicts the construction of this palace at the beginning of the film. Kane retreats to this palace directly after the termination of Susan Alexander Kane's operatic career by an attempted
suicide. (Her chief operatic role has been in Ernest Reyer's
"Salammbô.") Pictures of Xanadu are accompanied by a film music
of ponderous, deep tones.

Mood at the very beginning of the film is colored precisely by
this music. The first images are: barriers to Xanadu, first simple
fences, then ornate gates, indicating the exclusive nature of Kane's
domain. The first objects we see illustrate Kane's voracious acqui-
sitiveness; his need to fill in his own personal void and vacuousness
with things that never rise above being poor substitutes for his first
thing, his transitional object, his connection to the love and "continuity of Being" (Winnicott) that he lost when sudden wealth
deprived him of a home. We see, in succession, monkeys enclosed
in the "biggest private zoo since Noah"; gondolas imported from
Venice (the shape of "Rosebud" is oddly gondola-like, and as a
child Kane is utterly uninterested in a substitute that his guardian,
Walter Thatcher gives him); we see an entire golf-hole imported to
Xanadu on whim; a Renaissance wall, a Gothic interior with win-
dows. These examples of unbridled quest and compulsion lead into
a snow scene, which turns out to be the artificial, internal snow
scene in the paperweight that Kane drops as he utters, "Rosebud!"
and expires. In light of the rest of the film, it is clear that Kane lost
everything of importance (in object-relations terms) in the Colorado snow when his mother turned him over to Thatcher in the
name of wealth and a certain, uniquely American, destiny.

Kane's rough-hewn but loving father bitterly inquires into the
law's right to interfere with his natural paternal roles and functions
during this scene, when it is revealed that seemingly worthless rights
to a goldmine were bequeathed exclusively to Mrs. Kane by a
lodger at the family rooming house. The audience wonders, along

with Kane senior, about the circumstances surrounding Mrs. Kane's claim to the lodger's thoughtfulness. The hard decision as to the nature of young Charles's patrimony—whether it will be the natural environment of his family or the dreamworld, the phantasmatic domain of his wealth—falls to Mrs. Kane, a hard character in her own right, as played by Agnes Moorehead. Kane's mythical transformation as a child is, then, accompanied by devastating loss, in object-relations terms: the loss of empathy, of adequate fathering, the disclosure of hard practicality in the personality and worldview of the nurturing mother.

There is a parallelism between two musical scenes in the film, one during which Kane celebrates the hard-won success of *The York Daily Inquirer*, a paper he has raised from obscurity to the best selling daily in New York. He has just succeeded in luring the winningest team in New York journalism over to his own staff. Surrounded by a marching band and squadron of showgirl cadets, Kane prances and mouths the honorific popular song that is the tribute accorded to major celebrities, "What is his name? Charlie Kane?" In this scene, his character displays what Kernberg and Kohut would both consider a healthy exhibitionism and a grandiosity in the service of the ego, one in which an alliance has been achieved between an ambitious individual and the energies and positive self-concepts of which he is capable. The musical scene with which this contrasts is the opera that Kane has arranged (he's even built the opera house) to display a musical virtuosity on the part of his second wife that only he can see. This event caps a series of events in which Kane has lost his wife, Emily, to Susan Alexander through the politically-motivated disclosure of his sexual escapades; has disregarded his second wife's lack of talent and the good advice of the operatic experts whose services he has purchased; and displays a pronounced inclination to regard his wife exclusively as an extension and tool of his own fantasies and projections. The scene ends with a close-up of Kane's face with an intensely resolute expression as he single-handedly prolongs the half-hearted applause his wife has received for her starring performance. Kane's applause resounds hollowly. The enclosure of his visage in a close up, not entirely dissimilar to his famous political poster, signals that he is utterly alone. The production itself, as well as Kane's relation to his wife and advisors, furnish instances of grandiosity gone wrong: contempt toward significant others, splendid isolation, residing within a domain of self-confirming projective fantasies. "That's when you have to fight'em," Kane responds to Susan's lament, "You don't know what it is to know that people are—that a whole audience just doesn't want you." Susan describes the devastating impact of humiliation *after* she has tried to end her life with an overdose of sleeping medication. Kane's obtuseness in the face of public opinion comprises one vital element in his narcissistic life-philosophy.

The persistant acid test to which the film puts Kane's capacities for meaningful human interaction is his lifelong association with Jedidiah Leland, a college roomate who becomes a drama critic in the Kane newspaper chain. As Kane's aspirations grow grander, as he departs farther from his youthful "Declaration of Principles," it falls to Leland to articulate the terms of societal restraining norms, to issue the standard moral (Kohut would say "educational") reproaches against grandiosity. In general, Leland is quite right: Kane's love is ultimately for himself; he dictates the terms of the altruism that he professes. Yet the film leaves open the possibility that some of Kane's original dedication, idealism, and unselfishness persist. Kane finishes the inebriated Leland's scathing review of his wife's operatic performance as Leland would have written it; the film makes clear that Kane enters his first marriage, even though its passion is short-lived, out of genuine love.

The relationship between Kane and his oldest friend serves the film as an occasion for dramatizing the excesses of the narcissist and the reproaches that society has in store for him/her. "You talk about the people as though you own them. As though they belong to you, goodness," accuses Leland after Kane loses the Illinois gubernatorial race because his political foes have publicized his infidelities with Susan Alexander. He continues:

> As long as I could remember, you've talked about giving the people their rights, as if you could make them a present of liberty, as a reward for services rendered. . . . You don't care about anything except you. You just want to persuade people that you love'em so much they ought to love you back. Only you want love on your own terms. It's something to be played your way, according to your rules.

Such is the criticism that the lifelong friend, whose fate has risen and fallen more than once with the tide of Kane's enthusiasms and infatuations, delivers. Leland's pronouncements are indicative of the field that object-relations theory covers, although their directness deprives them of any value they would possess in a therapeutic situation.

The synesthetic representational capabilities of the cinema (and video) are almost capable of "bringing grandiosity to life." There is a privileged relationship between the hyperrealism and sensationality of these media and the psychological representations of magnificence. At least since the science-fiction fantasy of Meliès (1902), the cinema has represented the sublime and the grandiose. Yet I would like to add a historical and clinical component to this observation. In the years since the Freudian model of human psychology asserted itself with the most compelling authority, popular media have manifested increasing fascination with the so-called personality disorders. The cinema has, in other words, chronicled either an increase in the prevalence of certain psychopathologies or a heightening in popular awareness of psychological conditions for which prior understandings of neuroses and psychoses have become beside the point.

In the spring of 1992, "The Silence of the Lambs" (1991), based on a novel of the same title by Thomas Harris, won a number of Academy Awards, including best film, best director, best actor and best actress. I would argue that the controversy surrounding this film and its popularity arise in part from increased public awareness of and fascination with the borderline personality and its conditions. I would like to devote a few pages to the substantiation of this argument in a reading of the film and the novel, but I could have addressed a number of parallel recent artifacts as well: David Lynch's 1986 film, "Blue Velvet" and a television series, "Twin Peaks," extending his exploration of psychological and cultural bipolarity; both the original and remake of "Cape Fear" (1961, 1992), in which an ex-convict torments a lawyer whom he believes to have wronged him many years after the fact. For purposes of economy, I will focus my discussion on "The Silence of the Lambs," but popular culture in the United States and beyond is replete with artifacts devoting considerable resources to a working through of the non-Freudian psychopathology whose structure and driving force is that of the borderline.

*The Silence of the Lambs*, the novel as well as the film, may be taken as an artifact of the Vietnam War, an event in the history of the United States whose moment consists in the fact that it has not yet been assimilated into our culture, even now. As those of us who lived through the era and its politics knew, profound cultural continuities underlay and undermined the apparent conflict between pacifist politics on the domestic front and the conduct of the War itself. It makes perfect sense to remember this War as the War of psychedelic art and culture. At the same time that department stores in Boston, Chicago, and Los Angeles were dispensing psychedelic shopping bags to their customers, American belligerents were consuming vast quantities of marijuana, hashish, and hallucinogenic drugs. Among the many virtues of Francis Ford Coppola's "Apocalypse Now" is its depiction of the *continuity* between the military theater of operations and the domestic culture that had seemingly arisen in arms against it. To the degree that this latter film loosely modeled itself after Conrad's novella, "Heart of Darkness," it is a vital touch that the character corresponding to the harlequin, who has penetrated close to the heart of anomie, which is also the borderline of subjective emptiness, is a manic photographer in full hippy regalia.

Jame Gumb, the sociopathic serial killer of women in *The Silence of The Lambs*, and I do not yet differentiate between the novel and the film,[3] is a holdover, creation, and in some sense victim of the Vietnam War. He stalks his prey with infrared nighttime viewing instruments originally deployed against the Vietcong. He stuffs the larvae of Death's-head Moths into the mouths of the female cadavers he has "harvested" in his efforts to assemble a prosthesis of the upper female torso, made of genuine human flesh, to drape over his own male body. (He is evidently not yet entirely satisfied with his own physiological constitution. This pervasive dissatisfaction with the self and its limits is what links his Vietnam War references to the current cultural moment in the 1992 United States.) Jame Gumb, in other words is a composite, of aspects of the War that our culture has thus far failed to resolve or assimilate:

its psychedelic derangement, its penetration to the barely known frontiers of the known world, the defeat of U.S. strategy and technology, the gnawing emptiness that accompanies the debunked assertion of mastery and knowledge. (The last stillshots in the film of the subterranean environment, utterly devoid of commonality with middle-class American manners, in which Gumb torments, skins, and murders his victims, are of a Vietnam battle helmet crossed with an American flag and of a rotating oriental fan depicting butterflies. It should be also noted that the film, not the novel, adds Nazi imagery—graffiti, a blanket—to the repository of Gumb's military paraphernalia.)

In both the book and the film of *The Silence of the Lambs*, it falls to Clarice Starling, female trainee in the FBI, to unravel the displacement of violence from the War to the serial killings and dismemberments and also to collar the perpetrator. Given the preponderant bias of Western fiction and the U.S. cinema, this is a significant responsibility to assign to a woman (or female subjectivity). Her involvement in the bizarre case begins when an FBI section chief enlists her as a go-between between the Agency and the single consciousness deranged and brilliant enough to possibly shed some light on the nature (if not identity) of the perpetrator. This individual is a psychiatrist, Hannibal Lecter, inhabitant of a psychiatric prison especially fitted out for psychopathic freaks. Book and film thus both establish the locus of psychiatric or psychological insight as a potential house of madness. The psychiatrist in these artifacts is not an agent of social welfare, justice, and moral responsibility. He is, rather, a psychopath (in the heart of sanctioned society) every bit as destructive and dangerous as the marginal (historically, geographically) pervert and killer. The FBI hopes that the psychiatrist will function as the errant arrow whose wild trajectory will lead in the direction of another deranged missile. Hannibal Lecter thus plays the role that Lacanian psychoanalysis assumed in relation to the International Psycho-Analytical Association; of the Department of Psychiatry to the rest of the Medical School Faculty. He represents the potential evil of derangement when it has penetrated to the heart of the social institutions of moral control. The grandiosity of his threat makes him a descendant, by way of the sublime, of the Kantian "original genius" in the *Critique of Judgment*.

*The Silence of the Lambs* offers us the scenario of a woman solving deranged crimes against women that are themselves, in some not entirely clear way, outgrowths of the Vietnam War. In order to fulfill this function, she must enter collusion with a psychopath, Lecter, so brilliant and sick that he can guide her along her murky path. It is left to her, in effect, to "clean up" the excesses of both the Vietnam War and the aggressive male sexuality that have done so much to benight our politics and culture. The skills at her disposal are very much critical ones. (She has majored in Psychology and Criminology at one of our venerable institutions, the University of Virginia.) But what kind of psychopathology is she confronting in her travails? I would like to argue that Thomas Harris's novel, in revolving around a doubled male psychopathic figure (encompassing Lecter and Gumb) spans the distance and development from the Freudian psychopathology to that articulated by the borderline of the personality disorders. The novel, from its outset, describes Hannibal Lecter in terms familiar to this latter psychopathology, while Jame Gumb remains understandable in terms of the "drive/structure" model at the heart of the Freudian model of subjectivity. (Both characters' names, Lecter deriving from the German verb, "to lick," and Gumb bespeak the primitive oral range that for Otto Kernberg is fundamental to the personality disorders. "Lecter" is also homonymic with "lector.")[4] Lecter is a voracious reader as well as a consumer of taboo food. He therefore encompasses both sides of the frontier between instinctual and linguistic models of subjectivity.

In what does the spectacle of "The Silence of the Lambs" consist? I would argue that the ultimate focal point of the book and the film (the Barthesian *punctum*) is the spectator's confrontation (mediated by the FBI) with languages of purely private significance.[5] What separates Lecter and Gumb from other villains is not merely the violence of their crimes but their lack of concern with expressing themselves in publically acceptable or even comprehensible terms. Their acts confront the audience with primary-process thought explained or domesticated to no degree whatsoever. The directness and unlimited scope of their violence parallels the initial incomprehensibility of their symbolic actions. Lecter is a character who, under constraint, demonstrates rationality, control, and even insight; but the release of his constraints is tantamount to the unleashing of primitive, nonspecific violence. The same character who, an instant before, was handcuffed or in a stretcher, attacks anything in sight, preferably orally, almost *on principle*. Gumb's violence is a bit more elaborate. Expressed on a literary plane, the idea of inserting an exotic insect pupa in the throat of a corpse one has disfigured is a powerful, one is tempted to say, pregnant image. The female victims are in a sense impregnated by the yet larval seed of Vietnam. Vietnam exposed the political and economic contradictions in the American ideology. The Vietnam era opened up the cognitive and psychological abyss of drugs. The historical menace of the book and the film is expressed in the insect image that powers and holds them together: we might like to think that the War is over, but it remains within us, unrealized, in a state of potentiality. The film takes care to depict Gumb in his infrared gear as an insect after Officer Starling capitalizes on her training in shooting him first. There is something Hithcockian, in the terms of Slavoj Žižek's discussions of this filmmaker,[6] in the resolutions to the literary and cinematographic works and their dual psychopathic characters. The violence unleashed by the Lacanian Real upon the symbolic order of normality is only beginning as the artworks end. Vietnam has penetrated, impregnated our consciousness, without our awareness of this change, this implantation. Lecter remains in freedom at the end. In the film, he has lured hospital director Chilton and Barney (in the book an orderly with whom he gets along) to some Caribbean setting, where he plans to kill and devour them.

The ultimate spectacle of *The Silence of the Lambs* is the *nonmediation* of utterly private imagery, or in other terms the *acting out* of what certain psychoanalysts might call "primary-process thought." The critical efforts of the FBI are the closest thing we have in the book and the film to a force of rationalization or cultivation of such images and impulses; and by the time things enter the bailiwick of the FBI the possibility for the the type of compromise over which the traditional ego has jurisdiction is fairly much of a lost cause. In Saussurian terms, both Lecter and Gumb offer the extreme in the particularity possible in the *parole* without the wider, more enduring purview of the *langue*. In theoretical terms, this is the ultimate allure of these artifacts: not cannibalism, transsexuality, and necrophilia, which, although situating certain taboos whose violation is sensational, exhaust themselves at the thematic level. In whatever form, the artifact, *The Silence of the Lambs,* confronts its audience with the spectacle of unqualified private language. This is the borderline in its linguistic and most theoretical form.

In at least one crucial sense, "borderline" is the subjective registration and dynamic of the Derridean "trace," "mark," "re-mark," and other infrastructures indicative of the manner in which writing articulates consciousness before consciousness can undo this anomalous fact. Derrida spends so much effort in his early works in a meticulous delimitation of idealization because the ideal, whether mythologized in artifacts or institutionalized in schools of learning, is an environment not conducive to writing. The borderline is a condition as well as a place; it is a place where deconstructive "awareness" can meet with psychoanalytical theory in establishing a cultural critique of the conditions in which we think and interact.

I have elsewhere written that the twentieth century begins and closes with the apprehension that consciousness, reality, truth, and other ideological notions are structured by the dynamics of language rather than the inverse. This is a viewpoint that Derrida articulates with greater focus and authority than anyone else. Within this context, artifacts by Saussure, Kafka, Joyce, Stein, Freud, Proust, Musil, Benjamin, and others serve as harbingers of this realization of the primordiality of language in culture before there are theories capable of tracing out the implications of this priority. From within the perspective of this understanding of twentieth-century intellectual history, reductive though it may be, such movements as structuralism and even existentialism literally intervene between the literary and much later theoretical acknowledgments of the formative role of language in cultural, intellectual, and even psychological life.

As opposed to other prevailing theoretical models currently acknowledged by literary academic discourse, object-relations theory allows us to trace out the interpersonal grounds and implications of literary and other intellectual work. It furnishes terms for the choice of literary and other linguistic artifacts as significant spheres of personal endeavor. It provides some public articulation and forum for the narcissistic wounding not only motivating literary-critical production but also configuring the institutions in which intellectuals work. The political dimensions of object-relations theory consist in the leverage that this model affords in the reconsideration and reformulation of the goals and modes of operation qualifying intellectual institutions and enterprises.

The borderline articulated by object-relations theory and surveyed by *The Silence of the Lambs* is both the scene of writing par excellence and the predominant mode of subjectivity and interpersonal relations as the century ends. Entering a cultural studies mode myself, I am arguing that the conditions of writing, as deconstructionists elaborate them, have finally caught up with the postmodern condition itself; and that a whole host of artifacts, "Twin Peaks" and both versions of "Cape Fear" as well as *The Silence of the Lambs*, chronicle this development.

*The Silence of the Lambs* tells the story of a female investigator as she interprets and attempts to trace to their cause a series of murders committed by one psychopath, and understood in a special way by another. It is significant that the investigator lost her mother during infancy and her father as an adolescent, in the line of duty as a criminal justice worker. The role of villainy is divided between a marginal survivor of the Vietnam era and the holder of an esteemed medical position and privileged training. The artifact also contains the story of the training of a female professional. The educational function in film and text is divided between an exemplary male role model, Section Chief Jack Crawford, and the psychopathic psychiatrist, whose instructions to Starling issue with oracular authority. (Lecter's written and oral communications with Starling issue with the subliminal authority of introjections; more on this below.) While Lecter is an embodiment of primary-process thought, Crawford's sexuality is neutralized (only in the novel) by the terminal illness and eventual death of his wife, Phyllis-Bella. Starling thus learns both from an idealized male mentor and one whose acting out, intruding upon her own symbolism and thought processes, is consistent. By virtue of this characterological splitting, the artifact becomes a dual *Bildungsroman*, with a female subjectivity at its center, of our own era.

The story is also a thriller, or tale of detection. In this dimension, it compares the ineffectual efforts of male investigators, under the direction of Crawford, to the ultimately successful results that Starling, the star of our story, achieves. In what consists Starling's qualifications to be the heroine of this adventure? Starling is above all a redeemer: of her ill-equipped father's death during her childhood (he was a nighttime deputy in a small town); of the underclass constituting the American "silent majority" (*SL,* 290); of the slaughtered lambs and horses with which she identified as a foster child under care of her grandparents (is it appropriate that her film role was played by an actress named Foster?); of women, both as exiles from the nexus of power and wealth and as the targets for sexual crimes.

In what does the spectacle of borderlinity consist? The "drill" here is not to demonstrate that two fictive surrogates in the novel, Lecter and Gumb, possess attributes corresponding to the narcissistic and borderline personality disorders; to assert that these syndromes amount to the characters' essence or content. I am arguing that the spectacle of literary and filmic artifacts is the phenomenon of the borderline itself. The parallelism that can be demonstrated between a psychoanalytical model probably implicit in Freud himself, and developed over the clinical experience of thinkers including Klein, Lacan, Bowlby, Winnicott, Mahler, Kernberg, Kohut, and Alice Miller—between this model and the inventions of a contemporary writer of thrillers, is a phenomenon in its own right. Allowing for intermedia and cross-disciplinary slippage, the correlation between a psychoanalytical theory and popular artifacts suggests a wide cultural context for the borderline at the present moment.

In what does the borderline spectacle consist?

My remaining comments will address themselves to this question, approaching it from the perspectives of psychoanalytical theory, the notion of introjection, and the current cultural climate in the United States and similar economies.

1. Hannibal Lecter speaks to Clarisse Starling from the borderline of psychological, social, and cultural experience. This means, in terms of the current theoretical model, that his consciousness is divided between sharply divergent states that have not been integrated. His interpersonal relations are characterized by what Kernberg terms "omnipotence and devaluation," in other words, his treatment of people is limited to the extremes of adulation and contempt. His contempt is emotionally draining to its targets. Lecter's remarks to Starling are introjective in nature, that is,

characterized by aphoristic truncation and an exaggerated sense of immanence that we celebrate today in the Romantic poets. Starling is susceptible to Lecter's interjects, for, as the narrative records, an introjective commentary is taking place in her own consciousness. Aware of the introjective nature of consciousness in the novel, the narrative has Crawford warn Starling, "You don't want any of your personal facts in his head" (*SL*, 6). Lecter is aware of the affinities between himself and Starling. He ends his last communication to her, "Some of our stars are the same" (*SL*, 367). Lecter thus represents the unresolved borderline in Starling, and through her, as the previously disenfranchised, persecuted, and innocent, in the audience.

> "When he [Lecter] spoke again, his tone was soft and pleasant. 'You'd like to quantify me, Officer Starling. You're so ambitious, aren't you? Do you know what you look like to me, with your good bag and your cheap shoes? You look like a rube. You're a well-scrubbed, hustling rube with a little taste. Your eyes are like cheap birthstones—all surface shine when you stalk some little answer. And you're bright behind them, aren't you? Desperate not to be like your mother. Good nutrition has given you some length of bone, but you're not more than one generation out of the mines, *Officer* Starling.'" (*SL,*22)

The above dialogue, in both novel and film, occurs toward the end of the first interview between Starling and the prisoner. Despite the trainee's legitimate trepidations (she has heard vivid warnings about the prisoner from Crawford and hospital director Dr. Frederick Chilton), the interaction has gone as well as could have been hoped. The two characters negotiate his filling out a questionnaire; discuss his pictographic recreation of Florence from memory; his and other prisoner's exaggerated olifactory senses (Miggs has told her he could smell her genitals; Lecter has analyzed the scents she uses); and Lecter has noted her wearing her "best bag."

Given Starling's reasonable expectations of encountering a deranged lunatic, the first interview nevertheless goes as well as could be expected, that is until the diatribe whose beginning I cite above. Lecter's devastating devaluation of Starling thus begins with some suddenness. It emerges from otherwise polite conversation (the novel takes some care to establish that Lecter, while cannibalistic and savage in his violence, maintains a demeanor of utter

courtesy). At the beginning of the novel, Lecter's physical movement is limited by the constraints of an utterly rigorous isolated
physical confinement. The novel and the film focus attention on
Lecter's verbal savaging of Starling, his attacks on her poverty and
her cultural history and background as the arena in which his
violence transpires. Like Kant's Original Genius, Lecter possesses
vast and intimate knowledge of his "subject" from the briefest of
acquaintances and the briefest of encounters.

Starling's authority over Lecter is minimal; and he has in short
shrift demolished any socioeconomic privilege she might claim.
There are limits, then, on the degree to which Kernberg's scenario
of the borderline patient who alternately idealizes and deflates the
fetishized figure of the analyst applies here. But even with this
qualification, Lecter furnishes in this scene a marked instance of
what Kernberg refers to as "omnipotence and devaluation": he
recognizes Starling's status and achievements and an instant later
brutalizes her psychologically through an utterly confining characterization; as a pathetic "rube" clawing herself up from a detestable
background through the FBI. Kernberg and others have described
the emotionally draining impact of working with patients with
marked personality disorders. It would not be exaggerated to argue
that this utter devaluation is the most extreme abuse she suffers
early in the novel and film, more devastating than Miggs's hurling
his smegma at her.

In the context of this uncanny personal attack (uncanny in its
fusion of grandiose detachment and immediate intimate knowledge), Starling's reply, "Are you strong enough to point that high-
powered perception at yourself?" is nothing less than heroic. Starling qualifies as an American heroine because she does not allow
any ingrained sense of disadvantage or shame to derail her desire
to put her intelligence and other gifts at the service of U.S. society.
So does her African-American roomate, Ardelia Mapp, who hails
from a housing project in Baltimore. But what we have here is a
battle of the intelligences: Starling's homegrown, humble talent,
seeking no more than to find an appropriate deployment in a needy
society versus the genial, innate, borderline apprehension of the
corrupt practitioner, the psychiatrist who turns his privileged training and knowledge against society. As spectators to this conflict,
we root for characters such as Starling and Mapp, but as readers

we cannot gloss over the danger that non-humble, privileged (economically as well as technically) knowledge poses.

Starling is a psychological as well as a dramatic heroine. She counters Lecter's classical borderline devaluation, a splitting her into "all-good, all-bad" facets corresponding to the failed integration of his own contradictory conceptions and impulses, with a splendid and accurate return salvo. In effect: "Your insight may be uncanny, but you can't apply it to yourself." Though not a psychiatrist, she is not without her own psychological weapons.

Lecter does not merely split Starling, subject her to alternate idealization and devaluation, and display the uncanny insight linked by a number of theorists to personality disorders and borderline organization. His cannibalism corresponds to what Kernberg terms a primitive "oral rage" (*BCPN*, 41); building on the work of Klein and Winnicott, theorists such as Kernberg and Kohut, in their developmental accounts of the predisposition to personality disorders, emphasize double messages embedded in the mothering (whether by males or females) that infants and young children receive (*BCPN*, 41). (Jame Gumb obsessively reviews a film clip of his mother in a 1948 beauty contest.) The film version of "The Silence of the Lambs" capitalizes both narratively and dramatically on Lecter's oral rage. When she first arrives at the Baltimore State Hospital for the Criminally Insane, Starling is shown a photograph of the results of one of Lecter's dental assaults; when the psychiatrist breaks out of his confinement in Memphis, we, the audience, witness both the image of a bitten up face and the "moustache" of blood around Lecter's mouth (not unlike the traces of milk left on a young child). Kernberg emphasizes as well a "shift toward primary-process thinking" (*BCPN*, 24) in his borderline patients. Surely this is yet another way to describe the horror and allure of Lecter's actions and personality. One moment he is all culture and courtesy; the next he is a creature and agent of thoughts and desires that Freud would consign to the primitiveness of the id.

Surely the Lecter of both artifacts gives evidence of "bizarre forms of perversion" (*BCPN*, 11); we may describe his more bizarre actions in terms of a Kernbergian "lack of impulse control" (*BCPN*, 23) and a dearth of "developed sublimatory channels" (*BCPN*, 23). Lecter gives ample evidence of "early forms of projection, and especially projective identification" (*BCPN,* 29–33). He, and later Gumb, are not merely cannibalistic in a physical sense. Their psychic cannibalism consists in their ability, through "projective identification," to project themselves within the mentality, the hopes, desires, and values, of those targets from whom they extract (symbolic) food and whom they split into idealized and degraded facets. Speaking of psychiatric patients, Kernberg describes the dynamic in the following way: "This leads such patients to feel that they can still identify themselves with the objects onto whom aggression has been projected, and their ongoing 'empathy' with the now threatening object maintains and increases the fear of their own projected aggression. Therefore, they have to control the object in order to prevent it from attacking them under the influence of the (projected) aggressive impulses; they have to attack and control the object before (as they fear) they themselves are attacked and destroyed" (*BCPN,* 31).

In his narratively transcribed thoughts, Jame Gumb thinks of Catherine Baker Martin, a senator's only child, as "The material . . . lying on her side, curled on her side" (*SL,* 205), an "it" (*SL,* 283). "Experience has taught him to wait from four days to a week before harvesting the hide" (*SL,* 206). Hannibal the Cannibal Lecter imaginatively projects himself into the minutest psychic recesses of individuals he can then treat with utter brutality and cold calculation. For Jame Gumb, Catherine Baker Martin changes instantaneously from an individual with a very specific identity and social significance into a dehumanized source of skin. The sensationalism of the film functions above all on a psychological plane. We are confronted less with the spectacle of murder and cannibalism than with the spectacle of a mode of thought and functioning radically different from that characterstic of most "average" spectators. The spectacle of *The Silence of the Lambs* is the spectacle of the late twentieth-century borderline.

**Introjection.**    From Melanie Klein on through Fairbairn, Bowlby, Winnicott, and Kernberg, introjection describes the process whereby the language and attitudes of significant others help form the psyche and are represented in it. Introjections constitute both a *phenomenon* (there are times at which we experience more introjections than others) and a *process* (inherently projective in nature), by which we psychically "play back" perspectives about ourselves and others that we have collected from the outside world, above all from significant others. I have above suggested the close affinities between introjections as a psychological phenomenon and some of the most striking literary forms and artifacts. Among the literary phenomena with the most telling introjective qualities we would have to number prayers, condensed lyrical poetry, the commentary provided by the chorus in classical tragedies, and, in twentieth-century literature, the spilling over of characters' thoughts and attitudes into the narrative, a practice that has been described as the "interior monologue," "erlebte Rede," or "discours indirect libre."[7] In "Structural Derivatives of Object Relations," Kernberg includes introjections among "identification systems" (*EPOOR,* 360–67).

The notion of introjection resides at the locus where contemporary object-relations theory comes closest to matters of language and representation. Introjective thought involves the internalization and memorization of very fundamental object relations and their psychological repercussions. Roy Schafer has furnished a canny deconstructive critique of the agencies and activities involved in this internalization. Even with this important reconsideration in mind, Kernberg's notion of introjection as an internal or immanent language of the self derived from representations that significant others have enunciated and memories of formative relationships is important indeed.

The borderline phenomena and pathological narcissism with which Kernberg, Kohut, and Alice Miller are concerned are characterized by an extreme splitting between the subject's "good" and "bad" introjections and by an entrenched inability to integrate the sharply divided positive and negative images of the self and significant others. So far as Kernberg is concerned, "One essential task in the development and integration of the ego is the synthesis of early and later introjections and identifications into a stable ego identity" (*BCPN,* 25). From Kernberg's point of view, the disturbed object-relations characteristic of pathological narcissism and the borderline personality result from a persistence of a polarized thinking characteristic of very early development into later stages. From an object-relations point of view, Jame Gumb's fascination with images of his mother as a beauty contestant from early child-hood, as well as the adoration he maintains for his dog, Precious, at the same time that he starves, flays, and murders his victims, is significant. The simultaneity of Gumb's contradictory attitudes toward his dog and his victims is parallel to the coincidence of Lecter's courteous treatment of Starling (in the film, he offers her a towel, for example, when she is wet), and the sudden eruption of his homicidal rage at his Memphis guards.

What is crucial in addressing *The Silence of the Lambs* is to note (1) that the narrative records Clarice Starling's own introjec-tions (these occur particularly at moments of crisis) and (2) that Lecter's bizarre power over people in part consists of his entering the domain of their own introjections. (Indeed, this would not be a bad way of defining the intervention of a successful empathic psychotherapist: first extrapolating, and then subtly entering and "correcting"—with amplifying interpretations—the shame and horror evoked by one's bad introjections. I have suggested above how Lecter's villainy in part consists of his repudiation of psychi-atry's implicit moral imperative to work in the interest of social welfare.)

It can be said, then, on a general level, that Clarice Starling and Hannibal Lecter share a certain introjective activity. She *experi-ences* introjections. He *penetrates* others' introjections, at the same time that he *acts out,* in deeds of cannibalistic homicide, the con-tents of his own. Introjections constitute not only the subject's most seemingly immanent language; their contents come closest to his or her *private language*, the locus at which personal symbolism is farthest from the the mediating and socializing functions of the Saussurian *langue*. Serial Killer Jame Gumb enters the artifact's play of introjections because his actions and environment consti-tute an utterly private language, one excluded from the exchange of introjections that Starling and Lecter share. If the *spectacle* of *The Silence of the Lambs* is the phenomenon of the borderline itself, the *horror* of this grisly, heroic tale consists in the capability of a marginal subject to crystallize and enact an utterly private language, among whose elements are the female body, skin, the introduction of Death's-head Moths into the corpses of selected female corpses, and the indeterminacy of sexual identification.

Yet curiously, there is a sense in which Clarice Starling and

Jame Gumb serve as doubles of each other as well. Not only do these two characters become the ultimate antagonists in the story. In a sense, the trajectory of Gumb's serial murders of females follows the *map* leading into Starling's past and geographical origins. (Can it be entirely fortuitous that Starling's roommate and sidekick is named Ardelia *Mapp?*) Gumb's murders, situated in such places as Belvedere, Ohio (his home base), Potter, West Virginia, Evansville, Indiana, Damascus, Georgia, and East Memphis, Tennessee, where he abducts Catherine Baker Martin (*SL, 75*), lead Starling in a loop back to her Appalachian roots.

When Lecter, in his last communication to Starling, a note sent to her when he is a free man and she an FBI agent, speculates that "Some of our stars are the same" (*SL, 367*), he may well be referring to the role that introjection plays in their mental lives, she as its subject, he as its penetrator. The novel takes care to record some of Clarice's early "internal" thinking, particularly during early scenes when she is becoming familiarized with her surprise assignment on the "Buffalo Bill" case. *"Clarice is on a roll, Clarice has got control. Quit being silly and call the man up in, lemme see, Number Nine Ditch, Arkansas. Jack Crawford will never let me go down there, but at least I can confirm who's got the ride"* (*SL,* 35–36). Harris italicizes Starling's immanent thoughts to set them apart; in the lines immediately above, through rhyme, he preserves the "primary-process thought" quality of these "private" thoughts. Starling is full of internal reflections when she penetrates a storage space in which the remains of one Benjamin Raspail, an early Lecter patient and Gumb victim, have been preserved in a vintage 1938 Packard. *"Well, a brown recluse spider is the only kind to worry about, and it wouldn't build out in the open,* Starling said to herself" (*SL,* 48). *"Now is when it's important to think. Now is more important than all the crap you tell your pillow for the rest of your life. Suck it up and do this right. I don't want to destroy evidence. I do want some help. But most of all I don't want to cry wolf"* (*SL,* 50). Starling's introjections here are at once in her own interest and in the clipped, authoritative style of commands from an FBI instructor or manual.

The most significant exchanges in the novel as well as the film from an introjective point of view occur in two scenes in which Starling secures information and advice from Lecter regarding the

"Buffalo Bill" case at the expense of granting him entry to her life history and private symbolism. Both within the confines of the Baltimore State Hospital for the Criminally Insane and the Shelby County Historical Society, Starling and Lecter exchange clues and personal revelations with the breathless tension surrounding a game of strip poker. When one partner in the match reaches the limit of a revelatory unit, s/he reminds the other that his/her turn has arrived with the phrase "quid pro quo," "something for which."

It is precisely from this exchange of language, Lecter's borderline discourse "informing" Starling's code of civil order and vice versa, that the artifact derives its title. Throughout the novel and film, we are taken aback by the degree of Lecter's personal involvement in Starling, the degree to which he remains a psychiatrist while the ostensible issue at stake is the serial disfigurements and murders of which he possesses privileged knowledge. Both in Baltimore and Memphis, the grisly conversation concerning desire, rage, transvestism, and the logistics of crime and mental disease is interspersed with the intimacy of a patient revealing herself and of a therapist unblocking associative barriers, undoing Kernbergian splits, in the interest of fuller integration and self-knowledge.

Lecter remains the attentive, rigorous interlocutor even as the story reaches its dramatic climax, that is, when he has fed Starling sufficient information to direct her to the killer and while the time until Gumb "harvests" his victim's skin rapidly dwindles. Even at the story's psychological as well as narrative crisis, Lecter probes his "client" for the circumstantial type of detail—of time, place, sequence—that might trigger a new configuration of meanings, the kind of alternate account by which an entire counter-story of our lives becomes accessible to consciousness. A turncoat when it comes to some of society's deepest engrained taboos, among them regarding cannibalism and homicide, Lecter remains loyal to the etiquettes and procedures of his psychotherapeutic calling. As is noted above, precisely in this conjunction between transgression and steadfastness is situated a good measure of the story's uncanny horror.

Clarice Starling is a victim who by some miracle of character and calling becomes a champion of her fellow victims, not an avenger or a nameless integer, lost in the flock of starlings. Her heroic concern for a doomed horse turns out to mask another instance of messianic identification, this one with a distinct theological coding, an identification with the lambs also slaughtered at her foster parents' farm. The bleak circumstances of her early life form a crucible in which her character is formed—between the surpassing norms compelling her to rise above her circumstances and the restraining norms that enforce the modesty of her calling and aspirations, allowing her to become a true U.S. working-class heroine. Through her identification with doomed lambs and her loyalty to the FBI, Clarice Starling places herself in a position to neutralize the murderer, and in so doing, metaphorically to erase a blot on American history. For in attempting to spare Thomas Harris's fictive lambs, Clarice Starling answers any lingering disquietude we may have that during the Vietnam War lambs of another sort got murdered. It falls to Clarice Starling, using her own insight and possibly with the benefit of Lecter's advice, to duel a cruel murderer. The Vietnam War has served as the cultural framework within whose parameters their psychopathology was formed.

2. The dual literary-cinematographic artifact has much in common with Alice Miller's formulations, in *Thou Shalt Not Be Aware: Society's Betrayal of the Child*, firmly situating the narcissistic wounds at the basis of the psychopathology of the self in childhood. I cited these postulates above in chapter 7, but because they are brief, recite them:

1. Everyone is shaped (and this does not mean determined) by his or her childhood.
2. Neuroses are rooted in childhood.
3. The methods of free association and of the analytical setting (couch, rule of abstinence) make it possible for the drama of childhood to be reenacted in the transference and for a maturation process that has been blocked by neurosis to begin.
4. Changes in personality occurring during analysis do not stem from "corrective emotional experiences" but from insights the patient arrives at by repetition, remembering, and working through the relevant material. (*TSN*, 51–52)

Jame Gumb, as the result of extreme early childhood disturbances, dismembers the bodies of women in a particularly savage attempt to supplement his identity. The artifact allows his malady and behavior to be interpreted both from within the constraints of the classical drive/structure model and in terms of personality disorders, themselves conditioned by what Kernberg terms "the subjective experience of emptiness." (*BCPN*, 213–23). The range of capabilities manifested by the pathological duo consisting of Lecter and Gumb thus polarizes Starling. By virtue of her own childhood desolation, she shares, ever so slightly, in Lecter's ironic detachment; while in killing Gumb she cathartically eradicates her own slight tendencies in this direction (and implicitly the audience's).

In its implicit narrative imperatives, the novel edges the characterization of Gumb toward a drive/structure explanation of his actions. Ironically, in explaining less, the film remains more consistent to a borderline characterization of this character. In a sense, film, with its capabilities for abruptness and unexpected montage, is an ideal medium for the depiction of the "subjective emptiness" which is, so far as I am concerned, the most compelling post-Freudian account of the subjective conditions prevailing (in Western, postindustrial societies) during the present era. In its relative freedom from narrative continuity, film is an ongoing record of "actings out."

It is the novel's historical (or rather, case-historical) dimension that moves it in the direction of the constructs conditioning classical psychoanalysis, even where the details of the history point to a borderline interpretation. Clarice Starling is the public's representative in the artifact. In both artifacts, it is essential that her history be filled in. While she endured the triple narcissistic wound consisting of her mother's death in early childhood, the loss of her father, and the slaughter of the innocent beasts with which she identified, it is essential that she be identifiable from within the purview of classical neurosis as well. Otherwise, she cannot be the audience's surrogate in the artifact. Her history needs to be presented in full, even if manipulatively extracted by Lecter. Her story describes the conquering of her narcissistic proclivities by matching wits with Lecter and by conquering Gumb, a phantasmatic embodiment of borderline organization.

Yet history, where supplied with respect to Lecter and Gumb, will domesticate them, will push them over from the sublime wilderness of borderlinity to the more familiar realm of classical neurosis. And, for reasons intimated immediately above, it is unequivocally in the textual version of the artifact that such historicizing (neuroticizing, if you will) takes place. It is in this context that the book fills in much more information than the film regarding Jame Gumb's relationship with his first victim, Benjamin Raspail and the love triangle in which Gumb, Raspail, and a Swedish sailor named Klaus were at one time involved (*SL,* 172–74). The novel also explains the circumstances under which Gumb became known to Lecter, and even on one occasion met him: Raspail was one of Lecter's psychotherapeutic patients before his arrest and incarceration. By the same token, toward the end of the novel, the text interpolates a series of events rationalizing (though by no means justifying) Gumb's deeds and tendencies: as the double of Starling firmly entrenched on the side of the borderline. Gumb was neglected by his beauty queen, alcoholic mother during the first two years of life; placed in "unsatisfactory" foster homes, he murdered his grandparents at the age of ten (*SL,* 357–59). This segment of the narrative explains as well the role of sewing in his life and its place in the character's internal system of supplements.

In no passage more than the following does the novel indicate its receptiveness to classical psychoanalysis as a base position out of which the borderlinity of bad object relations emerges. In his constantly indirect way, Lecter is intimating to Starling the economy of supplementarity in Jame Gumb's sexual identification:

> "Do you know what an imago is, Clarice?"
> "An adult winged insect."
> "But what else?"
> She shook her head.
> "It's a term from the dead religion of psychoanalysis. An imago is an image of the parent buried in the unconscious from infancy and bound with infantile affect. The word comes from the wax portrait busts of their ancestors the ancient Romans carried in funeral processions. . . . Even the phlegmatic Crawford must see some significance in the insect chrysalis. . . ."
> "The significance of the chrysalis is change. Worm into butterfly, or moth. Billy thinks he wants to change. He's making himself a girl suit out of real girls. Hence the large victims—he has to have things that fit. The number of victims suggests he may see it as a series of molts. He's doing this in a two-story house." (*SL,* 163–64)

In the film, Clarice does not gain this insight, that the perpetrator pursues his victims in order to tailor a female prosthesis of skin, until she sees a sewing dummy in Fredrica Bimmel's house. In the film, the mystery that defies solution until the end is the criminal's motivation; in the novel, it is his identity.

In the novel, Lecter offers Starling a decisive clue into the serial killer's mentality early on, with characteristic courtesy. This crucial intimation is couched in a characteristically Freudian rhetoric of excavation and dialectical revolution. In this passage the language of insects merges into the language of psychological metamorphosis and revelation. The insect imago that Gumb implants into his victims' throats shares the characteristics of the parental image impressed into the unconscious, as it were, before the fact. In terms of this classical psychoanalytical scenario, for both of the unlikely doubles, Starling and Gumb, who experienced infantile trauma, there are ghosts (imagos) of parents lost in early life to contend with. The critical difference between characters, establishing the dramatic tension in the artifact, is that one character, Starling, finds resources in Freudian psychology and in societal values of morality and justice, enabling her to remain on the near side of the sociopsychological borderline; while Gumb's experience is so disturbed that it impels him to act out the supplementation of his own identity with graphic and homicidal rage. The novel thus invokes its Freudian heritage in the background of the drama between its characters' actions and values. Yet the Freudian model is precisely that: a background in which a current phenomenon is introduced to the audience. This current event is the emergence of borderline organization as the prevalent model for subjectivity in advanced Western postindustrial society.

3. As a cultural artifact, then, the thriller has served as a projective device, externalizing object and interpersonal relations into a fictive surrogate world. Civil culture thus "allows itself" to observe the shift from relations characterized by the Freudian system, previously our sole comprehensive model for subjectivity, to ones situated amid the subjective experience of emptiness, the theory of object relations, and the psychopathology of the personality disorders. A now familiar list of factors offers itself in explanation of this shift: increased mobility and familial disintegration; exclusion from economic life and dependency on large bureaucratic organi-

zations in accordance with the trends of late-Capitalism; the decline of opportunities for productive work; an increase in population and longevity; the popularity of media not conducive to reflection or interpretation; the availability of alcohol and drugs as panaceas to the stress created by any and all of the above. Through *The Silence of the Lambs* and similar artifacts, we record our collective journey away from a psychological space whose drives, stresses, and joys may have been only too predictable to a borderline state whose implications are only beginning to be known.

# CHAPTER 16

# *Conclusion*

There has always been a kind of fatal parallelism between my literary surrogates and my life. The first time I saw Orson Welles's film adaptation of *The Trial* was on Mother's Day, 1962. My mother and sister, whom I'd taken to see the film, walked out half an hour after it started. I, on the other hand, was hooked, on Welles and Kafka. I developed asthma shortly after reading Proust as a graduate student. The only world-historical event that came into the neighborhood in Philadelphia where I grew up was a visit to inaugurate a new playground by Fess Parker, at the peak of his reknown as the star of the then current "Davy Crockett" television series by Disney. I never actually did set eyes on the star that summer of 1956 because he was several hours late, and since my parents had recently gotten divorced, the time had arrived for me to be returned home. As an adult, I wrote a study on Hegel.

When I first wrote about *The Trial*, I was a newly formed student of deconstruction. It was quite easy for me to read the entire novel as an appendage to the famous Parable of the Doorkeeper, which could in turn be read as a Derridean scene of writing, a de Manian allegory of reading, or a Lacanian parable of psychoanalysis, with an inbuilt dimension of ethics to boot. After all, in the course of the novel, Joseph K. is increasingly captivated and dominated by the phantasmatic setting of a trial he must undergo for no apparent reason. He becomes ineffectual at work; he withdraws from his family and all other friendly relations. All he gains as a compensation for his social isolation and considerable *angoisse* is the audience of a parable, which comes down, in the end, to a Kantian antinomy setting off an unlimited regress of potential readings. The Kantian antinomy involved is that while the Man from the Country, the subject of the Parable, expended a lifetime waiting at the threshold of a multiple, self-negating, and ultimately exclusive Law, only he could have walked through the Door denied him by the forbidding, father-like Doorkeeper. The next leaves open whether walking through the Door would have comprised either a further imprisonment, enmeshment, or some kind of release. If this escape that exists only on the level of a hypothesis constitutes a release, it would be from the kind of thought-thing that we find in certain of Kafka's parables: an object in which all the pains of life have been amalgamated, and again, enmeshed. I think of such parables as "The Cares of a Family Man" and "A Crossbreed [A Sport]." The logic of *The Trial's* parable runs: only you, by virtue of a process remarkably akin to psychoanalysis, can exit the precincts of the thought-thing comprised by all the pains of your life, which you have invested into certain objects.

When I first read *The Trial* from a professional point of view, the Parable was sufficient to account for the novel as a whole. I entered a surprisingly competitive literary profession, one in which the contentions articulated themselves on fairly fine gradations of difference; in which the investments were introjected into fairly worthless things, at least in economic terms. No stranger has ever burgled my car when it was filled with books, even when I've left it invitingly open.

When I returned, years later, to *The Trial,* I found that I had captured that part of the narrative dealing with Joseph K.'s paradoxical *gain* in the novel, the initiation into the esthetic, that is to say, textual sensibility, to which the events lead him; but that I had neglected the entire context of withdrawal from the social world and the compensatory sense of intellectual superiority that makes it possible for this character, who is at once a Son, a Martyr, and an Artist, to appreciate the Parable. The Parable is a splendid achievement in its own right. Appreciating it is something like appreciating the Church of the Arena at Padua or a great Picasso breakthrough. But what is the context in which the author-surrogate in Kafka finds in artistic and intellectual ability an answer to the misapprehension and indifference he has received from the family; what was the context in which my own critical parables answered to a parallel inventory of outrages and reproaches? The last line of Kafka's *Diaries* is "You too have weapons." I was in search of a theory to supplement the ones that had accounted for the textual message in the Parable. Only through such a theory would Joseph K.'s increasing social isolation in the world, his wild fluctuations between an accusatorial contempt toward virtually anything in the field of vision and an equally pernicious shame, become discernible and comprehensible to me. There was clearly some overlap between the interpersonal conditions of my trajectory through the world and that of the particular literature I was drawn to. In the present study, by referring to classical and Shakespearean tragedies, Musil's *The Man without Qualities*, and several twentieth-century artifacts of popular culture, I have presented the larger traits of the psychoanalytical theory accounting for the interpersonal context in which art, and its critical reception, arises.

Kafka's textual parable overflows with its own paradoxes. One of very few moments of camaraderie in *The Trial* takes place during its quite wonderful ending, when for one brief moment Joseph K. is literally in step with the men who are about to execute him. We feel a strong political, ethical, and psychoanalytical repugnance toward these predatory literary characters.

I would hope to have provided some meditations and suggestions about contemporary object-relations theory, above all as elaborated by Otto Kernberg and Heinz Kohut, and how their psychoanalytical model may be of use to us in understanding certain aspects of literature and in evolving conceptions of ourselves as literary critics. I am situating both of these important psychoanalytical thinkers in a common model despite their ongoing debate over the matter of educationalism. Kernberg, in characterizing treatment of cases in which there is a severe effacement of psychological structure, whatever that might be, provides for a subtle and delicate, but very important element of education in the psychoanalytical process itself. According to him, in certain cases of personality disorders and extreme narcissism, psychoanalysis rebuilds or establishes for the first time structures or awarenesses that were, by virtue of a polarized, neglectful, or in other ways inhuman environment, lacking. Kohut finds this intervention too harsh, this mission too explicit and evocative of resistance. He would substitute empathic support for such a directive intervention. I have suggested in chapter 7 that Alice Miller, yet another compelling contributor to the literature of object relations, ultimately sides with the Kohutian position in this debate.

This major parting of the ways reviewed, I would nevertheless review Kernberg and Kohut's participation in a common model of psychoanalytical thought, one addressing a subjectivity defined by its inconsistency rather than by its blocked drives and unconscious knowledge; by its deficits in coherence and integration rather than by some barrier interposing itself between surface and depth phenomena; by the poverty that such subjects experience in their interpersonal relations rather than by the limits in their introspective ability. Does this subject sound a bit familiar? We have found it virtually wherever we've looked, lording and ranging and creeping and crawling and spewing out its seemingly interminable monologues throughout twentieth-century literature.[1] And even though this model of subjectivity, defined by its tendencies if not laws, toward polarized thinking, and relating to the world alternately by omniscience and devaluation, and consequently relating to other people through self-aggrandizing and self-referential manipulation rather than through Sullivanian collaboration or Albert Camus's notion of solidarity[2]—even though this model of subjectivity becomes the stock-in-trade if not paradigm for twentieth-century literature, its precedents in the history of literature are multiple, large, and particularly vivid. Iago, the real central character in Shakespeare's *Othello*, is a creature of the object-relations model of subjectivity. Always different from him"self," always manipulating the other characters in the play to act out his own ongoing bubbling, Kernberg would say primitive rage, Iago is also the most esthetically interesting surrogate in the play, and his schemes amount to Shakespeare's internalized dramas in the text. Literature has devoted an inordinant amount of attention to such characters, just as in Kernberg's and Kohut's psychopathology, such individuals attract a prodigous amount of attention and concern to themselves.

The subject of polarization, alternate self-effacement and devaluing, and abrupt shifts between the shameful and grandiose facets of its self-presentation has, then, a venerable history in articulate culture; but it is in the twentieth century, the century of psychoanalysis, that its subjectivity enters the very operating system of literary form and production. Kohut, in particular, elaborates the scenario in which subjects flip in and out of the grandiose versions, or drafts, of themselves. This is one of the most compelling accounts both of intrapsychic process and interpersonal behavior that I have encountered. Kohut places on the agenda of psychoanalytical discourse the concept of the grandiose, an absolutely capital construct both within the development of human personality and within the history of culture, a place where individual subjectivity and culture join in a truly meaningful way. The alternation between contempt and shame, between grandiosity and the narcissistic wounds they redress, elaborate, and hide, is a fundamental feature of personal and cultural achievements and failures, even intruding itself within the preserve of literary studies and criticism.

I have attempted to elaborate an object-relations model of literary characterization, subjectivity and interpretation. Not everything in the model is useful to literary work. To my mind, though, three or four of its conceptions are crucial: (1) the constitution of the subject through inconsistency, specifically through erratic fluctuations between overvaluation and devaluation, affectively, contempt and shame; (2) the concept of the subject as a palimpsest, a colloquy of grandiose and mature versions of the self that may be thought of as *drafts*; (3) the notion of introjections, the highly charged language through which, according to Klein, Winnicott, Kohut, and Kernberg very young children learn to store such polarized images of themselves, as a language before language; the language into which children are belatedly born in a Lacanian sense; from a Derridean point of view, a language before the origin preempting any possibility of an original language. Introjection may be regarded as a mode of private thought resulting in persistent and powerful conceptions. Its influence in a wide range of cultural manifestations is formidable. The examples I have cited have derived from artifacts as diverse as *Antigone* and *The Silence of the Lambs*; and, (4) a redefinition in psychopathology from derangement, whether at the level of neurotic quirks or systematic psychotic distortion to withdrawal, the nurturing of what Sullivan terms autism. But I believe that object-relations theory merits and sustains Roy Schafer's critique that you can't blame someone merely for liking to be by him/herself.[3] The withdrawal that Kernberg and Kohut encounter in their patients makes them, to borrow a phrase from Shelley, "remote, serene, and inaccessible." In Kohut's parlance, such a retreat is a return to the childhood scene of a narcissistic wound, one that has never been dressed or redressed. Not only have the symptoms of psychopathology been redefined from behavioral and cognitive derangements, whether on the grand or minor scale; trauma has been revised as well, from the residue of events that, categorically and by their very nature, are traumatic, leaving memory traces that will not be effaced, to injuries to the self, viewed as a spatial surrogate of the Psyche, of an enduring and unresolved nature. When Kafka's Country Doctor finally realizes that he is on the same plane as his youthful patient, so that he lies down on the same pallet, and hears the patient whose complaint he initially dismissed utter: "A fine wound is all I brought into the world; that was my sole endowment" (*CS, 225*), he witnesses the endurance and pervasiveness of narcissistic wounds, as they are formulated by object-relations theory.

At this advanced moment of what is always a provisional exploration, I would like to venture a few speculations as to how this psychoanalytical model applies to the options available for contemporary criticism. Criticism, needless to say, assumes many forms, corresponds to multiple formats, and fills a variety of functions. For Benjamin, argued Mark Crispin Miller in a presentation he made at my university some years ago, criticism consisted in an effort to preserve what was hopelessly lost from culture, either by virtue of human violence, the passing of time, or simply through oblivion itself. For some in the Frankfurt School and early French Structuralism (I think above all of Adorno and the early Barthes), criticism consisted in an erudite, linguistically and philosophically informed polemic directed against prevailing cultures totalitarian in their modes of business and thought. The direction begun by modern Phenomenology and elaborated by deconstruction has been for criticism to make its intervention at the level of the operating system accounting for the history of thought, at least in its Western theater. Deconstruction names, describes, and discloses the points of fixity and give within a certain conceptual repertory. It observes and comments upon the manifestations of these ideas, structures, and infrastructures in a highly context-specific way. The critic, in this mode, orchestrates a transference between highly pervasive concepts with long histories, whose persistence derives at least in part from their ability to disguise and vary themselves—and texts and other cultural manifestations in which these concepts are referred to, repeated, disfigured, effaced, and occasionally obliterated.

Criticism, in other words, has as its purview a continuum or spectrum reaching from the integrative to the polemical, with many positions for mixed models in between. As an example of a polemical stance in criticism, we can take Adorno's fixes on Western logic and ontology or the entertainment industry. Ironically, though, the take on show biz was inspired by Benjamin's musings on the same subject, for example in "The Work of Art in the Age of Mechanical Reproduction," which took as its only stance an integrality to the very end, even while the very end was happening. Even though this magnificent set of thoughts and gestures contains a number of polemical propositions against Nazism, the preponderance of its thrust is precisely an act of integration and synthesis in the face of an inconceivable systematic and institutionalized splitting, one whose certain outcome was the death of all the discriminations that Benjamin continued to make. The advantage of critical integrality, in Benjamin's own words is to "awaken the dead, and make whole what has been smashed" (*I, 257*). Its shortcoming will consist in what the next generation of Marxists will term "repressive tolerance." Polemical momentum clarifies the lines of tension, but will, unqualified, reinforce the splitting that criticism has attempted to undo. Deconstruction is so difficult to discuss in part because its movement consists of a polemic against certain prevailing features of metaphysics in the form of local, exceptionally integral articulations. It lionized itself early on through a small set of propositions whose purpose was to rouse the sleeping, but that was also capable of releasing an enormous amount of resistance and rage. But when we analyze its discourse as a medium of language, as I have elsewhere argued, the integrative effects of its qualifications far outweigh the polemical castings of its argument. This even with certain of Derrida's political choices.

Object-relations theory not only frames certain of the options available to critical discourse; it adds a supplement to preexisting twentieth-century psychoanalytical models for subjectivity. Object-relations theory has added the third term of the economy of narcissism to the preexistent orders of psychosis and neurosis. Pathological narcissism is endowed with an inconsistency and fickleness that we might otherwise associate with psychosis. Yet it blends into everyday criteria of normality with an adaptiveness that neurosis rarely achieves. It is the achievement of Kernberg and Kohut to identify and characterize this third world of psychological organization and structuration. We ordinarily associate the term "psychotic" with a disorder and impulsiveness sharing the qualities that Freud attributed to the id. Yet a perusal of the theoretical and clinical literatures suggests that the world of psychosis and its literary analogy are if anything overwhelmed and overdetermined by structures, laws, and sanctions. Two examples of the psychotic world order coming immediately to mind are the system of rays and commands by means of which God communicates to Daniel Paul Schreber[4] and the hierarchy of Yr (perhaps related to the German *irre*) that dominates Deborah, the heroine of Hannah Green's *I Never Promised You a Rose Garden*.[5] The psychotic, as evidenced in such examples, operates not out of a world of anomie but one of excessive, arbitrary order, whose language, strictures, and compulsions issue from afar. A comical example of psychosis, defined in this fashion, is Lewis Carroll's Queen of Hearts. Political examples of this systematization that has exempted itself from the constraints of reality testing would include certain of the protocols of the Nazi extermination machinery and more recently, "the machine" that for the Khmer Rouge designated its own mechanism for terrorizing and ordering the population.[6] So stigmatized are we by the appelation psychotic that we have not paused and wondered long enough about the dimensions of psychosis that pervade, and in some cases, humorously uplift our everyday lives; we have not yet written, in other words, "The Psychosis of Everyday Life." One of its examples would surely be the systems that we devise in our schemes to win the New York State Lottery and its peer institutions, the only way that most of us will get rich. In effect, we presume to influence in our favor a statistical field of grandiose proportion by devising a number of some private significance to ourselves. Our financial investment in this bit of systematic thought is not great, but enough to disappoint us when our number doesn't come up. Our bureaucratic lives as well consist in negotiations with highly structured systems there before we are, issuing precise constraints on our behaviors and options. Everyone of us who has confronted bureaucratic regulations in a university setting has noted, at one point or another, their arbitrary and highly systematized nature. Fulfilling our administrative responsibilities amounts to negotiating a set of compulsions not arising out of the contingencies of our professional lives; negotiating a system whose rules bring with them a severity also out of proportion to the situations into which the rules intervene. The order of psychosis is with us on a day-to-day basis even though the vast preponderance of us never develop symptoms of a psychotic severity. Vast literatures, both of the clinical and fine arts varieties, have dedicated themselves to dramatizing and explaining this order.[7]

The same is true of the neuroses, a realm of enormous consequence and concentration to Freud. The best way to conceptualize the neuroses, I think, is as localized instances of a system gone awry, a system fragmented into its *Bruchstücke*. Addressing the neurosis does not involve the horror of confronting the grandiosity of a vast machine in full operation, but rather repair work at the level of a particular function out of whack. It is the particularized, localized dimensions of the neuroses that explains the concentration of mechanical, hydraulic, and biodynamic energy that Freud poured into their description. Hysteria and obsessive neurosis constitute complementary his and her versions of the problems arising from libidinal repression. Paranoia, not the only potential psychosis endowed with a neurotic dimension by Freud, results from a series of transformations—in direction, object, and logic—applied to the sexual drive.

The domain of the personality disorders, object-relation theory's contribution to twentieth-century paradigms of literary and psychological subjectivity, also articulates itself at the levels of systematicity and structure. Where psychoses and neuroses situate themselves at the extremes of systematic holism and fragmentation, personality disorders, as characterized by Kernberg, Kohut, and others challenge systematicity by incorporating a strategic, but not uniform inconsistency. Where psychoses and neuroses define themselves by structure, through the structures they incorporate and disfigure, the personality disorders arise from something that is not quite but has some affinity to structure;

bespeak the operation of a certain "soft structure,"[8] a structural indeterminacy also evident in the constitution of certain twentieth-century literary surrogates, such as Camus's Meursault and Beckett's Molloy.

I have argued that the sublime and its literary examples constitutes one of Romantic thought's major efforts at defining, addressing, and delimiting the grandiose. The grandiose resides, both in Kant and in literary and plastic examples from the period, outside, on the slopes of Mont Blanc, or in the body of a creature resulting when the immense forces of nature are harnessed by a biological machine. While the ultimate source of Victor Frankenstein's disproportionate creation may be ideas too large for his own comprehension and well-being, the threat in the novel issues from the outside: from the barren waste of the North Pole and from the force infused into the creature's misshapen body. During this period it is comfortable, or uncomfortable as the case may be, for Caspar David Friedrich to ensconce the grandiosity of nature in unambiguously external landscapes; although by the time of the late Turner, the spatial setting of the paintings has become so unclear that their landscapes are as internal as the reverse. The plot of Coleridge's "Rime of the Ancient Mariner" may be summarized as the weaning of the narrator away from his superiority over nature; but even here, there is a dissociation between the desolation in the external seascape and the psychological isolation within which this esthetic sensibility has confined itself.

It is Kernberg, Kohut, and Miller's achievement and possible notoriety to separate the sublime from esthetic marginality and to install it in psychic process in the form of a state of consciousness known as the grandiose. In Kernberg's writings the grandiose functions more as a distinctive cognitive or emotive state whereas Kohut views it more as a developmental stage, corresponding to when an unassimilated narcissistic wound took place, a psychological scene of the crime to which the subject, under a variety of stressful, repetitive, or ongoing conditions, returns. For Kernberg, psychoanalysis involves a painful and painstaking recognition that a grandiose ideation and lifestyle exist. So successful is the repression of the grandiose ideas at the basis of the behavior it predicates, that their articulation often emerges to the patient in an educative form. Kohut explicitly acknowledges that grandiose ideation must be "marshaled" before it can be worked through and assimilated. The patient makes an alliance not only with the therapist but with the disease. The formulations that Kohut posits of the value of psychological dysfunction to the patient and of the necessity for symptoms in psychotherapy to get worse before they get better are the most compelling regarding these phenomena that I have encountered in the literature.

Ulrich's great psychological achievements, in *The Man without Qualities*, are to maintain an active and aware communication between the constituents of himself and to avoid, even under the fire of jealousy and other aversive stimuli, lapsing into his own grandiosity. Clarice Starling, by the same token, in *The Silence of the Lambs*, journeys to a bizarre hinterland of private fantasy without losing her sense of mission and personal integrity. As we have seen, Thomas Harris's novel "fills in" the contents of her introjections, but she stops short of the borderline in reliving her own serious childhood narcissistic wounds. As the narrative of *The Man without Qualities* specifies, Ulrich is an imposing intellectual presence and an avid debater. It would be most understandable if Ulrich's lucid and creative "working through" were thrown off track by certain of the other characters: by Walter's jealousy and Clarisse's seductiveness and furious posing; by Arnheim's desire to sap his energy and blur his insight while incorporating him into the capitalism-idealism nexus; by the Collateral Campaign's congenital groping in the dark, because there is no way to idealize an existing state of affairs. Yet Ulrich and Starling continue in their interpretative and critical vocations in spite of the distractions and devaluations of their personal contributions they encounter. This critical work goes on because the characters, in spite of the aversive conditions by which they are beset, resist lapsing into their contemptuous and/or depressive defenses.

As has been suggested above, the redefinition of psychological life according to slipping in and out of states of greater and lesser grandiosity, though nothing entirely unforeseen by Freud's own understanding of psychological objects, significantly recasts the

diagnostics, goals, tenor, and stages of psychoanalysis. This scenario also has enormous light to shed on adjacent fields, notably
politics and intellectual history. I would like to terminate this
study of characterization and contemporary psychopathology with
a few brief and admittedly sketchy suggestions on the play of
grandiosity within the spheres of politics and intellectual discourse.

In the light of work by Sullivan, Hartmann, Kohut, Kernberg,
and Miller, the emergence of monster dictators such as Adolf
Hitler on the (Hegelian) "stage" of World History becomes a bit
less mysterious.[9] Such pathologically "strong" personalities have a
propensity for emerging at uncertain and transitional moments in
history. Hitler, as he appears in propaganda films and in news
footage, could not care a jot for the people around him and in his
more and less immediate audiences. But his manifest grandiosity
assures his local audience that he, if no one else, knows exactly
what to do in the face of serious economic pressure and political
fragmentation. Hitler images and personifies social regression in
response to external adversity and internal changes in technology and mores. So did his contemporaneous strongmen, Stalin,
Mussolini, and Franco. The role of tyrants and dictators in history
suggests that religious and political orthodoxies often select personalities of a stern, unyielding bearing to represent them. The
tyrant may well constitute the political correlative to Kant's
Original Genius, that is, may present himself on the Hegelian
historical stage as a lightening rod of absolute truths into the
empirical realm in its political, administrative facet. The most
recent orthodoxy to make a major clamor on the "World Stage" is
that of Islamic Fundamentalism, whose recent popularity stems
from a variety of sources, including its superior delivery of social
services and its extreme disquietude at the expansion of global
communications and market networks and at a general relaxation
of sexual mores. At least as he was represented here in the West,
the Ayatolla Ruholla Khomeni, an important motivating force in
the rise of Islamic Fundamentalism, displayed the same awesome
seriousness and utter self-certainty characteristic of other orthodox
and authoritarian leaders.

The choice of the leaders that societies either select or passively
allow to rule them is, then, directly related to a sense of mastery
or of being overwhelmed by the socioeconomic, technological, and

moral "tide of the times." While societies will opt for dramatized grandiosity in times of instability, no phenomenon is more disarming or hopeful than a society's ability to veer away from the images and figures of absolute power of which it has, during certain historical moments, judged itself in need. This relinquishment of a projected grandiosity was at least in part accomplished in the former Soviet Union through the transition from the classical Communism of Stalin-Krushchev-Brezhnev-Andropov to the more modest vision of Mikhail Gorbachev. While Gorbachev's day is already over, from the perspective of historical scrutiny, he will remain the pivotal figure in the politics of his region, for under his leadership his society opted for a smaller-scale representation of itself and its aspirations. The relatively brief history that has transpired since the ascension of Boris Yeltsin suggests that where large-scale Grandiosity takes a rest, small-scale grandiosity, in the form of local bigotries and histories of animosity, are ready in the wings to take (Hegelian) center stage. What I have in mind is of course the resumption of traditional rivalries in Yugoslavia, Czechoslovakia, and regions such as Georgia and Armenia after a sixty year hiatus, an interregnum to some extent occasioned by Communist visions of uniformity in the Soviet Union. I am curious as to what the duration of these tribal rivalries will be in the age of the "Global Village," but the situations in Northern Ireland and the mideast suggest that the esthetic of "local grandiosity" may have a shelf life as long as that of its imperial correlative.

American democracy has, for a long stretch in its history, earned worldwide approbation for the relatively modest assertion of political ideals themselves prized for their restraint. What was perhaps most astonishing about the Gorbachev-Yeltsin transition was that, at least for a certain time, the majority of the Soviet citizenry seemed to support it, to advocate a reduction in the self-aggrandizing profile and behavior of the nation. The "center stage" of World History shifted from the Western Europe-United States dialectic to the Soviet Union and the sectors of Europe and Asia affected by the voluntary reduction of its hegemony, including the "Pacific rim," where for some time a transformation of classical economic relations had been in effect.

I hesitate to venture further into speculations regarding the interpretations of recent and not so recent political events lest my own observations take on a certain Hegelian grandeur and generality. Yet I am certain that research into nationalistic symbols, images, and self-representations from the perspective of collective grandiosity and shame will yield rich results, especially when undertaken by those better qualified than myself. As this book goes to press, the U.S. presidential campaign is poised between the primary elections and the national nominating conventions of the major political parties. There is at the moment considerable popular consensus as to the obsolescence and superficiality of the world view propounded by George Bush, who has, throughout his administration, presented himself as a "toned down" version of his predecessor, "imperial President" Ronald Reagan. The Democratic frontrunner is a bit short when it comes to dramatic assertions of authority: Bill Clinton is relatively young; he espouses certain affiliations with his 1960s generation, one that has never been assimilated into the mainstream of U.S. culture; and, he is, in terms of the moral perfection that increasingly emerges as a major political prerequisite at a moment of intense media scrutiny, tarnished. In the context of two very human candidates seeking a crucial political position at a moment of the most serious economic uncertainty in two generations, the credence that the U.S. public is willing to give to a relative unknown quantity, businessman H. Ross Perot, is indicative of a search for reassurance in the magnificent (in terms of personal wealth) and the grandiose. Early indications make clear that Mr. Perot is autocratic; that he engages in polarized thinking and tactics; and that he is intolerant. But the surrounding context of disappointment and uncertainty in which the U.S. electorate finds itself forms a context in which these attributes may not at all comprise a liability. What is most disconcerting about Mr. Perot's impact on the electoral process is the wish that he answers: for a decisive and speedy economic recovery reached in an ideological vacuum, without the agonizing processes of political debate and electoral decision. The most frightening aspect of Mr. Perot's undeclared candidacy is the voluntary ignorance in which the public has kept itself regarding its central character.

*The Man without Qualities* surely leaves us with a sense of the symbiotic, tortured, but nonetheless essential interrelation between the psychopathology of the modern self and intellectual work. Sensitivities and capabilities that are the *sine qua non* of intellectual and artistic achievement may make us unbearable as people; achieving comprehensive integration, on the other hand, as Rainer Maria Rilke mused in his *Letters*,[10] might signal the death of this creativity, might deprive it of its internal exigency. It is to Kohut's credit that in his scenarios of psychotherapeutic healing, advanced stages of working through are accompanied by a release of artistic talent and energy.

As is already evident in Kant's lucid and informed investigations of esthetics, the esthetic enterprise approaches a certain borderline or margin in demonstrating that human knowledge and capability are not limited by the constraints of an empirical world. Although there are examples deriving from throughout the history of culture, twentieth-century literature and art went to particular extremes in surveying and exploring this esthetic borderline. Does this mean that clinically, all writers and intellectuals are hopeless narcissists, to be dismissed on moral or sociological grounds? Emphatically not. Ulrich, the model intellectual in *The Man without Qualities*, confronts in virtually all directions around him narcissistic resistances to and devaluations of his work and character, without, under constant adversity, engaging in compensatory hauteur and self-aggrandizement of his own, save in close, private collaboration with his "sister." Figuring the intellectual as a narcissist constitutes an age-old reproach against our endeavors that is already achieving unprecedented prominence in the U.S. presidential election of 1992.

The economy of narcissistic disturbances does have, however, light to shed on the atmosphere and mood of intellectual and academic institutions, on the production of intellectual work (intellectual transference and working through), and on the interplay between institutional ideals and regnant conditions. If there is any ring of authenticity to Theodor Adorno's characterization of intellectuals as "competing supplicants,"[12] a striking contrast prevails between the *jouissance* of intellectual work, whose pleasure has been vaunted throughout the history of culture, and the unhappiness often pervading intellectual institutions, whether ascribed to external or internal conditions, to indifference and lack of support on the one hand, or to excessive competitiveness on the other. It will do no good whatsoever for me, a career intellectual, or anyone to introduce a rhetoric of pathological narcissism as yet another brand of ammunition to be deployed along the trenches of the intellectual wars, as an "n-word" to be hurled back and forth in efforts of mutual discreditation, in the manner of the Derridean "battle of proper names."[13]

On a broad and hopefully productive level, it should be noted that "the subjective experience of emptiness," while the tenor and location for a variety of narcissistic defenses, is an absolutely vital precondition and motivation for intellectual work. Intellectual satiety or fullness is analogous to the freedom that the butchers of the Paris *abbatoirs,* according to Georges Bataille, experience from aggression.[14] Without emptiness there is no intellectual hunger or thirst, no compulsion to register the rifts and dissonances within the self in some form of cultural notation. Kohut and Miller acknowledge and write illuminatingly about the narcissistic wounds at the basis of psychoanalysts' choice of profession.[11] By the same token, a certain subjective emptiness underlies the quest for an external language of one's experience and the impulse to externalize that experience, often in its most painful register, in language. This emptiness, this receptivity to language, may indeed have certain dysfunctional clinical implications, as Kohut, Kernberg, Miller, Masterson, and others have found. In the intellectual field, however, it is fundamental. It is there. It is a fundamental element in Being-there. The issue is never whether "the subjective experience of emptiness" is "present" or formative to intellectual endeavors and institutions, but to what degree the mature intellectual self needs to revert to this emptiness and its defenses; whether an education in letters and other cultural codes constitutes a "filling" to this emptiness, results in a "working draft" of a reasonably mature and integral intellectual self; or whether it encourages a confinement within the provisoriness of subjective emptiness.

"Strong personalities," although rooted in their own narcissistic histories, play a particularly decisive role in an endeavor predicated on the *relative* emptiness, the transitorial status of the student, and the ostensibly formal emptiness of the professor. Students learn from their professors' grandiosities; their teachers' orientations and polarizations as to what constitutes "good" or "worthy" work become models for their own. A significant element of professors' pedagogical responsibility, in Kohut's terms, carried over from the tribulations of childhood, is to *sustain* their students' idealizations, to whatever tests they are put.

Receptivity is the goodness making good students "good." But what is the distinction between receptivity and subjective emptiness? Teachings and readings ostensibly "fill in" this emptiness. But what is the point at which a measure of fullness or "contents" is attained by this emptiness, which in pedagogical terms we valorize? The tests and stages of academic life supposedly record and implement the transition from idealized emptiness to functional fullness. But do they?

Ideas gain power and currency in the intellectual marketplace in part owing to the grandiosity with which they are announced, dramatized, and advertised. The dynamics of grandiosity structures the "history" as it does the actualities of politics. Grandiose claims are what get "schools of thought," approaches, and methods "off the ground." They also stir up considerable ruckus and revive the wounds of those who, for a variety of reasons, don't subscribe to them, who may feel defensively compelled to repudiate them on the grounds of arrogance if not substance. Or the non-adherents may feel justified to "tone down" the dramatic assertions of the New School, to cook up the equivalant of "American style spaghetti dinner." The history of intellectual movements, I am asserting, follows a pattern of *declaration* through grandiose acting out, an accompanying polarization of values, and the dismissal of counter-approaches; and *reception* through conversion, repudiation, and rejection, or polarization or "toning down." Intellectual workers' needs, I am asserting, to feel superior to endeavors conducted in other sectors of the oceanic marketplace of ideas, often far supersede the ostensible themes and issues at hand as the impetus and shapers of intellectual projects.

As the preceding discussion has hopefully made evident, intellectual working through often first arises in an individual's development as a compensation for, a supplement to, basic narcissistic wounds. The flight into letters, images, or any singularity-bearing cultural code is predominantly a solo one. The partially objective and partially delusional privacy with which it is experienced constitutes one of its most powerful allures. Artistic and intellectual work is often first experienced as a very personal medium of mastery. In the aftermath of such an initiation, the intellectual worker's absorption into vast organizational and educational enterprises after completing a highly individualized training and after producing specialized presentation pieces (although these are mediated by current convention); indeed, the intellectual's dependence on vast bodies of individuals surely introduces a note of somber realism and limit into what had started as a voyage of exploration and personal transcendence. In this process of intellectual socialization, paralleling that taking place during the formative years of childhood, the writer or critic or artist experiences the commodification of the work whose motivation to some extent incorporated the illusion of its singularity. The very professions and institutions ostensibly promoting the values of inspiration and individual personal *Bildung* thus bring about, through their organizational needs, the deflation of these very values. They reinstitute the subjective experience of emptiness that much intellectual work was motivated to ornament, disguise, work through, or abolish.

It is in the context of the reemergence of the fundamental narcissistic wounds in the socialized sphere of intellectual and artistic activity that such a frenetic market goes on in the currency of important ideas and strong personalities. Backed by what Kohut would call a healthy exhibitionism, the discourse of deconstruction, founded on Modernism's realization of a linguistic dynamics underlying systems of knowledge and subjectivity, linked a varied group of literary-critical strategies to a powerful conceptual operating system with philosophical, linguistic, and social-scientific underpinnings. Both in the absence of an ongoing tradition of this kind of work (in the United States, at least) and in the genuine power of its elucidations, deconstruction succeeded in raising the quality and intensity of literary criticism. It augmented the standard "acceptable" critical performance with a dimension of methodological expertise and self-awareness. Rigorous deconstruction is hard work, demanding conceptual precision, readerly imagination, and scholarly familiarity with the history of the artifact's interpretation and reception. Deconstruction accorded its own contributions with a full awareness of their importance and quality. Its primary setbacks consisted in the ruffled feelings it caused its nonaffiliates, and the dynamics here are debatable. Did deconstruction, in the awareness of its own complexities and the pleasure of dealing with them *cause* injured feelings? Or, in this dynamic, were certain pumps already primed for disappointment at the vitality of deconstruction, within a vast public panorama in which the most private and intense work eventually loses its individuality and intensity?

The fluctuations of the intellectual marketplace correspond to a complex dance around the phenomenon of grandiosity. A new operating system announces itself, the ante is upped, and a host of thematically or theoretically-oriented counterapproaches arise, in order to qualify, possibly tone down, the new paradigm. Grandiosity in the assertion of an approach is never entirely deflated; it oscillates, rather, between professional and local levels, just as politics, in an age of the global village, hovers between "superpower" and national ideology.

The central debate in the academic marketplace at the current moment is between "theoretical," that is, language-oriented, and interest-oriented models. The former retain their wonder at the priority of linguistic process rediscovered early in the twentieth century and never lose sight of a fundamental intractability in the deployment of language, which any interpretative act must somehow take into account. Interest-oriented approaches, on the other hand, have grown impatient at a moment of intense, global socioeconomic crisis, with a conceptual neutrality in theoretical interpretations that would bracket the historical, epistemological, national, racial, and gender-determined constraints upon the subject. There is a sense of urgency in current New Historical and Cultural Studies[15] approaches, lest the disenfranchisement of traditionally excluded social groups continue past a certain breaking point whose dimensions are material as well as cultural.

There is enormous room for flex and positioning within this debate. Ironically, certain of the interest-oriented approaches putting deconstruction to its most rigorous current test owe the most to the radicality of deconstructive questioning. Once again, attention to grandiosity is as much the "way out" of this impasse as it might have been the way into it. Those critical positions emerging from patient and tolerant debate will surely outlast timebound broadsides, even if they are more complicated and less splashy. It is precisely within a critical space that has articulate with the greatest available philosophical rigor, the condition its own possibility and error, that we will be able to articulate most compellingly the historical, racial, national, and gender and class-determined constraints on subjects and subjectivity.

The esthetic and critical sensibilities demand, do not merely tolerate, the receptivity and eccentricity appearing, according to certain criteria, as weakness of character and narcissistic self-absorption. The empathy that for so many of us comprises the only way *through* our various narcissistic woundings, is also one of the qualities at the basis of critical discernment. The profession of this delicacy, both in the assertive and professional senses, twists sensibility around against itself, confronts the intellectual working through whose occasion is a painful void with the emptiness of public indifference, even when this takes the form of warm appreciation.

Robert Musil's decision to opt out of serious institutional commitments was one of the watersheds in his relatively early life. Through one of his surrogates, Ulrich von _____ , Musil illustrates the dynamics of the intellectual life, in its dangerous as well as admirable qualities. At the same time, he prepares his readership for the transition from classical modern psychoanalytic theory to the postmodern domain of the personality disorders.

The "I" of criticism is a perceptive "eye" on its times. Even when its ostensible subject matter is historically or geographically occult, the framework through which the critical I sees is structured by its moment. The critic is, then, vulnerable on a number of flanks: in the ur-wound or emptiness that is the basis of his/her sensibility; to the dissonance between the mutually negating signals that s/he picks up; to the speed with which "critical stimuli" mount up, merge, and displace one another; to joining the very chaos whose energy is the exigency of writing.


So what is it like to have been a subject at the end of the twentieth century? I can't answer this better than any other, but I was there. All of the simple answers to things, the myths: the nuclear family, the image of a harmonious, tolerant society, went the same way as the traditional European culture that might have existed before the Second World War; and we were left in the same ambivalent position that haunted, in the sense of possessed, Benjamin. To bemoan the loss of what had always been a mythical simplicity and to rejoice in the open field and unexplored possibilities. We increasingly benefitted from and had our lives qualified by a technology whose perfection consisted in the invisibility of its motivation, mechanics, and subsequent implications. And the politics around us seemed to take on the invisibility, De Lillo's *White Noise*, that operated our typing and calculating machines.

We were continually making up for lost structures, improvising new ones that would do for our purposes, and resisting those that emanated from the outside in the form of political, sexual, and corporeal constraints. This cost us a lot of energy, at the same time it liberated what energy was left for a consideration of the very parameters of structure. There was a lot of sweetness in this exploration, tastes and experiences and intellectual probings that would not have been possible in a more repressive order, but it was still not the aura of "love at last sight"[16] whose disappearance Benjamin could bemoan in the Paris of Baudelaire. We fashioned a register on which we could arrange the unheralded variety and heterogeneity of our experiences, but the nature of this register was precisely that it had holes, caesuras, the kinds of gaps that for Kafka defined the very nature of the Chinese Great Wall.

By some idiosyncratic combination of historical determinism and choice, we set ourselves on a course of immanent, fatal, but perhaps unavoidable fragmentation and inconsistency. The impact of this course, as evidenced in the psychological clinic, became the pretext for contemporary object-relations theory. We are the subject it studies; and our writing is the borderline that we secrete as the antidote to the conditions of inconsistency that has wounded our constitution and that we have intellectually and culturally celebrated. I close with the figure of Benjamin. Surely his own efforts at rescuing sensibility from oblivion and positing precise formulations on the transitions from older modes of industrial, esthetic, and economic production to newer ones were frail in the face of the historical conditions he faced. Yet he grounded the critical enterprise in the quest for and restoration of integration whose literary and psychoanalytical correlatives have been sketched out in the above pages.

# NOTES

## CHAPTER 2: ON CHARACTER

1. For the loss of "aura," the disappearance of personal involvement in production, the erasure of the signature of handiwork in manufacturing and craft, see Walter Benjamin, "On Some Motifs in Baudelaire" and "The Work of Art in the Age of Mechanical Reproduction," in *Illuminations,* ed. and intro. Hannah Arendt (New York: Schocken Books, 1969), 155–200, 217–51.

2. The personal landscape of Freud's exemplary patients is itself noteworthy. A case in point is the Wolf Man's domestic coterie when he was a small child. The following citation notes a discrepancy in his character that occurred when his parents were in fact away. Note the massiveness of the support system, nevertheless:

> But once, when his parents had come back from their summer holiday, they found him transformed. He had become discontented, irritable and violent, took offense on every possible occasion, and then flew into a rage and screamed like a savage. . . . This happened the summer while the English governess was with them. She turned out to be an eccentric and quarrelsome person, and, moreover, to be addicted to drink. The boy's mother was inclined to ascribe the alteration in his character to the influence of the Englishwoman. . . . His sharp-sighted grandmother, who had spent the summer with the children, was of the opinion that the boy's irritability had been provoked by the dissentions between the Englishwoman and the nurse. (*S.E.,* 18:15)

The marked change in behavior occasioned by the parent's shared absence is at least as significant from an object-relations point of view as from the Freudian. Yet around the parents in this passage are no less than three characters: the grandmother, the English governess, and the nurse. This is the kind of supersaturated psychological space in the Freudian mileu to which I am referring. It cannot be accidental that the illnesses occurring in this environment, at least in the phase of Freud's career centered around hysteria, are conditions of repression. From *Studies on Hysteria* on, access to repressed material or "incompatible ideas" is the "royal road" to psychoanalytical cure or symptomatic relief. As Freud describes repression in *The Interpretation of Dreams*:

The two psychical systems, the censorship upon the passage from one of them to the other, the inhibition and overlaying of one activity by the other, the relations of both of them to consciousness—or whatever more correct interpretation of the observed facts may take their place—all of these form part of the normal structure of our mental instrument, and dreams show us one of the paths leading to an understanding of its structure. . . . *What is suppressed continues to exist in normal people as well as abnormal, and remains capable of psychical functioning*. . . . In waking life the suppressed material in the mind is prevented from finding expression and is cut off from internal perception . . . but during the night, under the sway of an impetus towards the construction of compromises, this suppressed material finds methods and means of forcing its way into consciousness. . . .

*The interpretation of dreams is the royal road to a knowledge of the unconscious activities of the mind. (S.E., 5:607–08)*

The extended families in which many of the most memorable of the early subjects of psychoanalysis find themselves are the sociological organizations enforcing the repression characterizing the conditions that Freud was able to diagnose and treat first.

A classical statement of the repressive structure of the disorders that first aroused Freud's interpretative interest is to be found in his case study, of Miss Lucy R. from *Studies on Hysteria*:

Now I already knew from the analysis of similar cases that before hysteria can be acquired for the first time one essential condition must be fulfilled: an idea must be *intentionally repressed from consciousness* and excluded from associative modification. In my view this intentional repression is also the basis for the conversion, whether total or partial, of the sum of excitation. The sum of excitation, being cut off from psychical association, finds its way all the more easily along the path to a somatic innervation. The basis for repression itself can only be a feeling of unpleasure. . . . The repressed idea takes its revenge, however, by becoming pathogenic.

I accordingly inferred form Miss Lucy R.'s having succumbed to hysterical conversion at the moment in question that among the determinants of the trauma there must have been one which she had sought intentionally to leave in obscurity and had made efforts to forget. (*S.E.*, 2:116–17)

Citations of Freud in this footnote and throughout the book derive from Sigmund Freud, *The Standard Edition of the Complete Psychological Works of Sigmund Freud* (London: The Hogarth Press, 1953–74), henceforth abbreviated *S.E.*

3.    The retrospective overview of the early case histories that Freud achieves at the end of *Studies on Hysteria*, in his "Psychotherapy of

Hysteria," furnishes at least one major formulation of the inherent curative effect of the "breakthrough" to the repressed material:

> What means do we have at our disposal for overcoming this continual resistance? Few, but they include almost all those by which one man can ordinarily exert a psychical influence, especially one that has been in force for a long time, can only be resolved slowly and by degrees, and we must wait patiently. In the next place, we may reckon on the intellectual interest which the patient begins to feel after working for a short time. By explaining things to him, by giving him information about the marvelous world of psychical processes into which we ourselves only gained insight by such analyses, we make him himself into a collaborator, induce him to regard himself with the objective interest of an investigator, and thus push back his resistance. . . . For it is well to recognize this clearly: the patient gets free of the hysterical symptom by reproducing the pathogenic impressions that caused it and by giving utterance to them with an expression of affect, and thus the therapeutic task *consists solely in inducing him to do so*; when once this task has been accomplished there is nothing left for the physician to correct or remove. (*S.E.*, 2:282–83)

4.   One of many ways of describing Derrida's historical contribution is to say that he located on philosophical grounds a linguistically-based understanding of subjectivity, reality, and Being whose radical formulation had already begun with Nietzsche. When I read the "high structuarlist" contributions of Barthes and Lévi-Strauss, I strongly sense that they, starting out with the linguistic assumptions of Saussure and certain major Freudian constructs, are trying to instrument this language-based view of reality. The notion of structure to which such critics subscribe during the 1950s and 1960s is halfway between subjectivity and Being, on the one hand, and language on the other. Foucault invokes a notion of historical progression, albeit a highly enlightened one, in his effort to approach a language-based model of reality with constructs somehow both *of* language and more substantial than it. His understanding of history may be summarized as follows: what people think and know at any given moment consists in the possibilities afforded by the language they use. His *episteme* come very close to era-bound models of what Derrida will call metaphysics. Derrida, whatever hesitations he may have about these efforts, subscribes wholeheartedly to the overall enterprise of qualifying constructs of subjectivity, Being, reality, and history by means of the dynamics and play of language. His critical analyses are less based on linguistic or psychoanalytical constructs, though, than on resonant notions issuing from the history of philosophy. Barthes, Lévi-Strauss, and Foucault—along with Artaud, Bataille, and Blanchot—are among the reasons why an audience exists for his conceptual questioning of the

mainstays of subjectivity—presence, immanence—when he undertakes these interrogations, for example, in relation to Plato, Kant, Hegel, Nietzsche, Husserl, and Heidegger. See Roland Barthes, *Mythologies*, trans. Annette Lavers (New York: Hill and Wang, 1986), 9–12, 109–27; *Writing Degree Zero and Elements of Semiology*, trans. Annette Lavers and Colin Smith (Boston: Beacon Press, 1968), *Elements*, 13–17, 23–30, 35–44, 58–68; Claude Lévi-Strauss, *Structural Anthropology*, trans. Claire Jacobson and Brooke Grundfest Schoepf (New York: Basic Books, 1963), 31–38, 46–51, 206–19, 229–30; Michel Foucault, *The Order of Things* (New York: Vintage, 1963), xv–xxiv, 217–26, 303–28; Jacques Derrida, *Speech and Phenomena*, trans. David B. Allison (Evanston: Northwestern University Press, 1973), 78–82, 102–04, 138–43, 148–56; *Margins of Philosophy*, trans. Alan Bass (Chicago: University of Chicago Press, 1982), 126–34.

5.    Janet Malcolm, for example, in her *New Yorker* articles on the Jeffrey MacDonald murder case, referred to Kernberg's approach to personality disorders as a confrontation with the problem of evil. Her understanding of the parallelism between the exhibitionisms of the journalistic and psychoanalytical "subjects" is also indicative of what I will later call "the fatal dialectic between the neuroses and the personality disorders." Her articles have been reprinted in Janet Malcolm, *The Journalist and the Murderer* (New York: Vintage, 1990), 69, 71–78.

6.    These authors, Balzac, Goncharov, and Conrad, with respect to the formal experimentation and disfiguration that we associate with Laurence Sterne and the radical modernists (e.g., Stein and Joyce) write conventional-seeming novels; yet they strain the possibilities for characterization within the parameters of the conventional novel. Balzac does this through the vast expansion of a fictive world in the segments of *The Human Comedy*; also, in the absurdities of pacing and spatial movement in such a novel as *The Sentimental Education*; Conrad establishes strikingly detailed and believable settings for his tales, but then places them at the mercy of characters such as Lord Jim and Nostromo who are defined, precisely, by their ambiguity and impenetrability; Goncharov absorbs so many of the fictive resources of *Oblamov* within the *character* of Oblamov that there is nothing left for the development, conflict, and resolution that we ordinarily associate with novels. These authors and others, in a tradition stretching from *Don Quixote* to *Finnegans Wake*, "kill" the novel, if not with kindness then with the violation of mimetic conventions related to event and character. I am endebted to Piotr Parlej for an understanding of *Don Quixote's* mimetic treachery; to Richard Macksey for making me aware of *Oblomov's* characterological tyranny.

7. See, for example, Kafka's "Investigations of a Dog," "The Burrow," and "Josephine the Singer, or the Mouse Folk," in Franz Kafka, *The Complete Stories*, ed. Nahum N. Glatzer (New York: Schocken Books, 1976), 278–316, 325–76; "Malone Dies, " in *Three Novels by Samuel Beckett* (New York: Grove Press, 1965), 179–87; Italo Calvino, "The Chase" and "The Night Driver," in *t zero*, trans. William Weaver (New York: Harcourt Brace Jovanovich, 1976), 112–36; *If on a winter's night a traveller*, trans. William Weaver (New York: Harcourt Brace Jovanovich, 1979), 3–9, 253–60.

8. Neil Hertz has managed to explore major psychoanalytical issues in keeping with the "cutting edge" of theoretical sophistication while preserving a genuine interest in the clinical dimension of psychoanalysis. His two primary contributions are a notion of surrogation that allows us to discuss characterization in a way that is cognizant of the most persistent distortions of the classical theory of representation; and an understanding more profound than anything suggested in these pages of the groundings of psychoanalysis in the Romantic deliberations on the sublime. Both of these significant elaborations are evident in *The End of the Line* (New York: Columbia University Press, 1985), 40–41, 44–60, 75–96, 103–21, 217–39. Another significant addition to the literature of psychoanalytical criticism is J. Brooks Bouson, *The Empathic Reader: A Study of the Narcissistic Character and the Drama of the Self* (Amherst: University of Massachusetts Press, 1989). This is the first full-length study I know of to explore literary interpretation from a psychology of the self point of view. An introduction to this psychology frames valuable readings of Lessing, Dostoyevsky, Conrad, Kafka, Woolf, and Atwood.

## CHAPTER 3:
## CHARACTERIZATION IN *THE ANTIGONE* AND *OTHELLO*

1. See Michel Foucault, *The Archaeology of Knowledge and the Discourse on Language*, trans. A.M. Sheridan Smith (New York: Pantheon Books, 1972), 3–30, 178–211. Also, *The Order of Things, op. cit.*

2. For an extremely important New Historical account of Renaissance subjectivity, see Stephen Greenblatt, *Renaissance Self-Fashioning* (Chicago: Univeristy of Chicago Press, 1980).

3. G.W.F. Hegel, *Hegel's Phenomenology of Spirit*, trans. A.V. Miller (Oxford: Oxford University Press, 1977), 271.

4. I am endebted to John Peradotto, Raymond Chair of Classics at the State University of New York at Buffalo, for an illuminating discussion (and translation) of the names in *Antigone*.

5. For the purposes of my discussion, I have drawn on Gilbert Murray's rhymed translation of the play. Sophocles, *The Antigone*, trans. Gilbert Murray (London: George Allen and Unwin, 1967). In citing this text, I henceforth abbreviate it *A*.

6. G.W.F. Hegel, *Hegel's Phenomenology of Spirit, op. cit.,* 288.

7. Jacques Lacan, *Seminar Seven*. This text, on the ethics of psychoanalysis, with *Antigone* as its primary illustration has as of this writing appeared in France. Its English translation is forthcoming from Lacan's American publishers.

8. For Jacques Derrida's conceptual and linguistic plays on the significance of the hymen as a philosophical trope, see "Double Session," in *Dissemination*, trans. Barbara Johnson (Chicago: University of Chicago Press, 1981), 201, 206, 209–10, 212–15, 220–24, 229–30, 253, 261, 285.

9. A most useful overview of the transition from Freud's "drive/structure model" to the field of object-relations theory is to be found in Jay R. Greenberg and Stephen A. Mitchell, *Object Relations in Psychoanalytical Theory* (Cambridge: Harvard University Press, 1983), 16–25, 30–37, 43–49, 90–108. For an exemplary instance of the "drive/structure" model, see Sigmund Freud, "Instincts and their Vicissitudes (1915)," in the *Standard Edition, op. cit.,* 14:121–31. Greenberg and Mitchell provide useful recapitulations of contributions in this direction made, among others, by Harry Stack Sullivan, Melanie Klein, R.W.D. Fairbairn, D.W. Winnicott, Margaret Mahler, and Edith Jacobson. Crucial to this development is the shift in field toward interpersonal relations made by Harry Stack Sullivan. See his *Conceptions of Modern Psychiatry* (New York: W.W. Norton, 1953), 10–19, 89–105, 117–27, 175–77, 190–207, 219–25. Peter Buckley's collection, *Essential Papers on Object Relations* (New York: New York University Press, 1986), is an invaluable collection of primary contributions to this overall development. I henceforth abbreviate it *EPOOR*. Of considerable significance in this regard are Melanie Klein's reconstruction of a highly polarized experiential field in infantile experience, one sharply divided between "good"and "bad" objects; W.R.D. Fairbairn's translation of the classical Freudian stages of psychosexual development into object-relation terms; John Bowlby's departure from Freudian schemata in exploring primary relationships on their own terms; and D.W. Winnicott's investigations into the *Being* of childhood experience and his understanding of the fundamentally substitutive and supplemental nature

of object-relations. See Melanie Klein, "A Contribution to the Psycho-genesis of Manic-Depressive States," *EPOOR*, 40–51, 59–65, 68–70; W.R.D. Fairbairn, "A Revised Psychopathology of the Psychoses and Psychoneuroses," *EPOOR*, 74–82, 86–96; "The Repression and the Return of Bad Objects (with Special Reference to the 'War Neuroses'), *EPOOR*, 102–10, 118–23; John Bowlby, "The Nature of the Child's Tie to his Mother," *EPOOR*, 153–67, 172–77, 185–97; D.W. Winnicott, "The Theory of the Parent-Infant Relationship," *EPOOR*, 233–53; "Transitional Objects and Transitional Phenomena," *EPOOR*, 254–60, 264–71.

10. On this point, Derrida's dialectically complex qualifications regarding origins in general and the origin of languages in particular are indispensable. See *Of Grammatology*, trans. and intro. Gayatry Chakravorty Spivak (Baltimore: The Johns Hopkins University Press, 1976), 270–80, 302–16. In the clinical discipline of child language development, there has been considerable controversy over the absolute or relative origins of language utilization in children. There is general agreement that at the beginning of the second half of the second year, children experience a considerable enlargement of their capabilities: single word utterances elongate themselves into multiple word utterances; experiments in intension and extension begin; vocabulary begins to expand at an impressive rate for many years to come. This developmental stage corresponds, temporarily at least, with the Lacanian *stade du miroir*. Psychological researchers have worked hard at determining such issues as whether syntax (grammar) or semantics (meaning) is the primary motivator in language acquisition; whether universals or contextual and cultural factors predominate in determining its results. See, amid a burgeoning literature on this topic: Noam Chomsky, *Reflections on Language* (New York: Pantheon Books, 1975), 3–35; Roger Brown, *First Language: The Early Stages* (Cambridge: Harvard University Press, 1973); Jerome Bruner, *Child's Talk* (New York: W.W. Norton, 1983), 23–42; Susan Carey, "Semantic Development: The State of the Art," in E. Wanner and L. Gleitman, eds, *Language Acquisition: The State of the Art* (New York: Cambridge University Press, 1982), 347–89; Eve Clark, "The Principle of Contrast: A Constraint on Language Acquisition," in B. MacWhinney, ed. *Mechanisms of Language Acquisition* (Hillsdale, N.J.: Erlbaum, 1987), 1–33; Katherine Nelson and Joan Lucariello, "The Development of Meaning in First Words," in M. Barrett, ed. *Children's Single-Word Speech* (Chichester, England: Johan Wiley and Sons, 1985), 59–86; Katherine Nelson, "Individual Difference in Language Development: Implications for Development and Language," *Developmental Psychology*, 17 (1981), 170–87; Michael Maratsos, "The Child's Construc-

tion of Grammatical Categories," in E. Wanner and L. Gleitman, eds., *Language Acquisition, op. cit.,* 240–66; Steven Pinker, "The Bootstrapping Problem in Language Acquisition," in B. MacWhinney, ed., *Mechanisms of Language Development, op. cit.,* 399–431; Michael Maratsos, "Crosslinguistic Analysis, Universals, and Language Acquisition," in F. Kessel, ed., *The Development of Language and Language Researchers: Essays in Honor of Roger Brown* (Hillsdale, N.J.: Erlbaum, 1988), 121–52; Catherine E. Snow, "Conversations with Children," in P. Fletcher and M. Garman eds., *Language Acquisition* (New York: Cambridge University Press, 1986), 69–89; and, Elinor Ochs and Bambi B. Schiefflin, "Language Acquisition and Socialization: Three Developmental Stories and their Implications," in R. Shweder and R. LeVine, eds., *Culture Theory* (New York: Cambridge University Press, 1984), 276–320. I am endebted to Professor Joan Lucariello of the Department of Psychology at the New School for Social Research for an illuminating introduction to the theoretical issues and readings in this field.

11. Otto Kernberg, "Structural Derivatives of Object Relations," *EPOOR, op. cit.,* 350–84.

12. See Immanuel Kant, *Critique of Judgment,* trans. J.H. Bernard (New York: Macmillan, 1951), 38–39, 44–45, 117, 140–43, 176 (henceforth abbreviated *CJ*); Friedrich Schlegel, *Friedrich Schlegel's Lucinde and the Fragments,* trans. and intro. Peter Firchow (Minneapolis: University of Minnesota Press, 1971), 146–47, 234–36; Søren Kierkegaard, "Diary of the Seducer," in *Either/Or,* trans. David F. Swenson and Lillian Marvin Swenson (Princeton: Princeton University Press, 1971), 1:326, 335, 341, 396, 432.

13. See Immanuel Kant, *Critique of Judgment, op. cit,* 90–91; Mary Wollenstonecraft Shelley, *Frankenstein* (New York: Penguin, 1987), 69–70, 81, 135–36, 138–42; P.B. Shelley, *The Complete Poetical Works of Percy Bysshe Shelley,* ed. Thomas Hutchinson (London: Oxford University Press, 1965), 532–35; Jack Stillinger, ed., *Selected Poems and Prefaces by William Wordsworth* (Boston: Houghton Mifflin, 1965), 201–03, 262–71, 356–61.

14. See Sigmund Freud, "Psycho-analytical Notes on an Autobiographical Account of a Case of Paranoia (Dementia Paranoides)"—otherwise known as the Schreber case—*Standard Edition, op. cit.,* 12:19–30, 48–55. For a number of highly suggestive Lacanian approaches to this case history, see David B. Allison et.al., ed. *Psychosis and Sexual Identity: Toward a Post-Analytic View of the Schreber Case* (Albany: State University of New York Press, 1988).

15. See, for example, Samuel Taylor Coleridge, *Biographia Literaria* (New York: E.P. Dutton, 1975), 10–12, 18–19, 51, 175–80, 194, 229.

16.  Franz Kafka, *Amerika*, trans. Willa and Edwin Muir (New York: Schocken Books, 1974), 18.

17.  Citations refer to William Shakespeare, *Othello*, ed. Louis B. Wright and Virginia A. LaMar, The Folger Library Shakespeare (New York: Washington Square Press, 1957).

18.  American Psychiatric Association, *Diagnostic and Statistical Manual of Mental Disorders (Third Edition—Revised): DSM-III-R* (Washington D.C.: American Psychiatric Association, 1987), xxii-xxvi, 15–24.

19.  Otto Fenichel, *The Psychoanalytical Theory of Neurosis* (New York: W.W. Norton, 1945), 3–32, 168–210, 463–540; Silvano Arieti, *Interpretation of Schizophrenia* (New York: Basic Books, 1974), 71–212.

20.  See Marcel Proust, *Swann's Way*, trans. C.K. Scott Moncrieff (New York: Random House, 1956), 242–45, 323–28, 359–60, 389–400, 411–17, 445–53, 470–72, 479–83, 486–94; Joseph Conrad, *Lord Jim* (Boston: Houghton Mifflin, 1958), 33. 38–39, 61–65; Franz Kafka, *Amerika, op. cit.*, 208–71.

21.  For an excellent psychoanalytical interpretation of *Othello*, see Joel Fineman, "The Sound of O in *Othello*: The Real of the Tragedy of Desire," in *Psychoanalysis And . . .* , ed. Richard Feldstein and Henry Sussman (New York: Routledge, 1990), 33–48.

## CHAPTER 4: GRANDIOSITY AND THE ROMANTIC SUBLIME

1.  Aristotle, "Poetics," in *Poetics: Aristotle/On Style: Demetrius*, trans. Thomas Twining, Everyman's Library (New York: E.P. Dutton, 1934), 22.  For other relevant passages, see 14, 17, 24–25.

2.  Otto Kernberg, *Borderline Conditions and Pathological Narcissism* (New York: Jason Aronson, 1975), 235. I henceforth abbreviate this volume *BCPN*.

3.  See Noam Chomsky, *Cartesian Linguistics* (New York: Harper and Row, 1966), 31–51.

4.  Immanuel Kant, *Critique of Pure Reason*, trans. Norman Kemp Smith (New York: Macmillan, 1929), henceforth abbreviated *CPR*.

5.  See Jacques Derrida, *Of Grammatology, op. cit.*, pp. 144–57, 199, 223–29, 276–77, 283–87.

6.  For discussions of the problematic of language in Hegel, see Andrzej Warminski, "Pre-positional By-play," in *Glyph 3*, ed. Samuel Weber and Henry Sussman (Baltimore: Johns Hopkins University Press, 1978), 98–117; Henry Sussman, *The Hegelian Aftermath: Readings in*

*Hegel, Kierkegaard, Freud, Proust, and James* (Baltimore: Johns Hopkins University Press, 1982), 15–27, 49–62.

7.   Plato, *Phaedrus*, trans. R. Hackforth, in *The Collected Dialogues of Plato*, ed. Etith Hamilton and Huntington Cairns (Princeton: Princeton University Press, 1973), 484–506 (273a–260e).

8.   See Ludwig Wittgenstein, *The Blue and Brown Books* (New York: Harper and Row, 1965), 36–40, 52–53, 60–67.

9.   See Ludwig Wittgenstein, *Tractatus Logico-Philosophicus* (London: Routledge and Kegan Paul, 1961), 150–51.

10.   See Jacques Derrida, *The Truth in Painting*, trans. Geoff Bennington and Ian McLeod (Chicago: University of Chicago Press, 1987), 45–49, 61–73, 127–43.

11.   Herman Melville, *Moby-Dick*, Norton Critical Edition, ed. Harrison Hayford and Hershel Parker (New York: W.W. Norton, 1967), 2–11, 63–66, 116–28, 247–56, 342–44.

12.   See John T. Irwin, *American Hieroglyphs: The Symbol of the Egyptian Hieroglyphics in the American Renaissance* (New Haven: Yale University Press, 1980), 18–25, 31–35, 64–65.

13.   Percy Bysshe Shelley, "Mont Blanc" (1816), in *The Complete Poetical Works of Percy Bysshe Shelley* (London: Oxford University Press, 1965), 532–35.

14.   See Greenberg and Mitchell, *Object Relations in Psychoanalytic Theory, op. cit.*, 270–81.

15.   See such paintings by Caspar David Friedrich as "Woman in the Morning Sun" (before 1808), "The Traveller over the Sea of Mist" (c. 1818), "Morning in the Riesengebirge" (c. 1810/11), "Chalk Cliffs on Rügen" (c.1818), "The Monk by the Sea" (c. 1808/09), and "The Frozen Ocean" (1823/24), in Jörg Traeger, ed., *Caspar David Friedrich* (New York: Rizzoli, 1976). Also see such paintings by Turner as "The Hospice of the Great St. Bernard" (1806), "The Upper Fall of the Reitenbach" (1810), "Scene in the Welsh Mountains with an army on the march" (c. 1800), and "The Lake of Geneva" series (1842) in Andrew Wilton, *Turner and the Sublime* (Chicago: University of Chicago Press, 1980).

16.   See Jörg Traeger, ed., *Caspar David Friedrich, op. cit.*, 2, 88.

## CHAPTER 5: OBJECT-RELATIONS THEORY: OTTO KERNBERG

1.   Ferdinand de Saussure, *Course in General Linguistics*, trans. Wade Baskin (New York: Mc Graw-Hill, 1966), 71–73, 120.

2.   It is in this context that many of Jacques Lacan's additions to,

adjustments, and subversions of Freud may be read. See, for example, Juliet Mitchell and Jacqueline Rose, eds., *Feminine Sexuality: Jacques Lacan and the Ecole Freudienne* (New York: W.W. Norton, 1985). For a good elaboration of the cognitive implications of Freud's theories, see Matthew Hugh Erdelyi, *Psychoanalysis: Freud's Cognitive Psychology* (New York: W.H. Freeman, 1985).

3.  Henry Sussman, *The Hegelian Aftermath: Readings in Hegel, Kierkegaard, Freud, Proust, and James*, op.cit, 162–63, 171–77, 187–92.

4.  Henry Sussman, *The Hegelian Aftermath*, op. cit., 168–70.

5.  In addition to the Schreber case, *op. cit.*, see the following two crucial case histories: "Notes upon a Case of Obsessional Neurosis (1909)," *Standard Edition*, 10:151–250 (the "Rat Man" case); "From the History of an Infantile Neurosis (1918 [1914])," *Standard Edition*, 17:1-122 (the "Wolf Man" case).

6.  Sigmund Freud, "Instincts and their Vicissitudes (1915)" *Standard Edition*, 14:109–40.

7.  See, for example, Jacques Lacan, *Speech and Language in Psychoanalysis*, trans. and intro. Anthony Wilden (Baltimore: The Johns Hopkins University Press, 1968), pp. 19–27, 53–79.

8.  Jacques Lacan, "The agency of the letter in the unconscious or reason since Freud," in *Ecrits: A Selection*, trans. Alan Sheridan (New York: W.W. Norton, 1977), 146–75.

9.  Cf. Greenberg and Mitchell, *Object Relations in Psychoanalytical Theory*, op.cit.

10.  Cf. Sullivan, *Conceptions of Modern Psychiatry*, op. cit.

11.  Cf. Winnicott, in *Essential Papers on Object Relations*, op.cit. Also, Greenberg and Mitchell, *Object Relations in Psychoanalytic Theory*, op. cit., 188–209.

12.  Cf. Klein, in *EPOOR*, op. cit. Also, Greenberg and Mitchell, *Object Relations in Psychoanalytical Theory*, op. cit., 119–50.

13.  Cf. Kernberg, in *Essential Papers on Object Relations*, op. cit. Also, Greenberg and Mitchell, Object Relations in Psychoanalytic Theory 325–48.

14.  Jacques Lacan, "The mirror stage as formative of the function of the I," in *Ecrits: A Selection*, op. cit., 1–7; Klein, in *EPOOR*, op. cit., 48–51; Greenberg and Mitchell, *Object Relations in Psychoanalytic Theory*, op. cit., 270–81.

15.  Henry Sussman, "Psychoanalysis Modern and Post-Modern," in *Psychoanalysis And . . .* , op. cit., 148–50.

16.  With regard to the problematic of the gaze, see the four visual essays collected in Jacques Lacan, *The Four Fundamental Concepts of*

*Psychoanalysis*, trans. Alan Sheridan (New York: W.W. Norton, 1978), 67–122.

17. See Aaron Beck, *Cognitive Therapy and the Emotional Disorders* (New York: New American Library, 1976), 103, 105–16.

18. Cf. Beck, *op. cit.* Also see Lyn Y. Abramson, Martin Seligman, and J.D. Teasdale, "Learned Helplessness in Humans: Critique and Reformulation," *Journal of Abnormal Psychology*, 87 (1978), 49–74; Lauren B. Alloy and Lyn Y. Abramson, "Depressive Realism: Four Theoretical Perspectives," in Lauren B. Alloy, ed., *Cognitive Processes in Depression* (New York: Guilford Press, 1988), 225–28, 251–57; Paul H. Blaney, "Contemporary Theories of Depression: Critique and Comparison," *Journal of Abnormal Psychology*, 86 (1977), 203–23. I am most grateful to Professor Michael Raulin of the State University of New York at Buffalo for a splendid introduction to the above literature and to the field of Psychopathology.

19. The notion of a false self is elaborated by D.W. Winnicott, in "The Theory of the Parent-Infant Relationship," *op. cit.*, 242–44. James F. Masterson makes a good deal of this concept. See his *The Search for the Real Self: Unmasking the Personality Disorders of our Age* (New York: The Free Press, 1988), 1–37.

20. Greenberg and Mitchell, *Object Relations in Psychoanalytic Theory, op. cit.*, 9–20, 96–115.

21. For the debate concerning educationalism, see Otto Kernberg, "Further Contributions to the Treatment of Narcissistic Personalities," in Andrew P. Morrison, ed., *Essential Papers on Narcissism* (New York: New York University Press, 1986), 251–53, 264–69. Also See Heinz Kohut, *The Analysis of the Self, op. cit.*, 178; Otto Kernberg, *Severe Personality Disorders* (New Haven: Yale University Press, 1984), 182–89.

## CHAPTER 6: OBJECT-RELATIONS THEORY: HEINZ KOHUT

1. Some clinicians, for example, Frieda Fromm-Reichmann, Hilde Bruch, Heinz Kohut and his circle, write explicitly of how their mode of therapy operates. In the case of Freud, as critics have noted, the descriptions in the case histories are so graphic as to convey an explicit sense of what transpired during the sessions. In the case of others, including Sullivan and Lacan, it is clear how the subject matter under consideration might shift, but not how theoretical reformulation affects the delivery and mode of the therapy (the notorious Lacanian "seven-minute session" is an exception here). Clinicians with whom I have spoken readily acknowledge the impact that theoretical rethinking can have on their

work; nonclinical academicians who have not been actively involved in psychotherapy tend to exaggerate the correlation between the theoretical model and the therapeutic process. Clinicians tend to view theoretical orientation as one variable among a number of constants (e.g., rapport, compatibility) common to the major acknowledged schools of psychoanalytical procedure. See Frieda Fromm-Reichmann, *Principles of Intensive Psychotherapy* (Chicago: University of Chicago Press, 1960); Hilde Bruch, *Learning Psychotherapy* (Cambridge: Harvard University Press, 1974); Heinz Kohut, *How Does Analysis Cure?* (Chicago: University of Chicago Press, 1984), 80–115; Arnold Goldberg, ed., *The Psychology of the Self: A Casebook* (Madison, CT: International Universities Press, 1978); Charles Bernheimer and Claire Kahane, eds., *In Dora's Case: Freud-Hysteria-Feminism* (New York: Columbia University Press, 1985).

2.  Heinz Kohut, *The Analysis of the Self* (Madison, CT: International Universities Press, 1971), henceforth abbreviated *AS*.

3.  Sigmund Freud, "Studies on Hysteria," in the *Standard Edition*, 2:268–70, 288–96, 300; "The Interpretation of Dreams," 4:235–36; 5:530, 533, 617–21.

4.  Jacques Lacan, *The Four Fundamental Concepts of Psycho-Analysis, op. cit.*, 20, 24–25, 193, 204, 254–55.

5.  Cf. Beck, *Cognitive Therapy and the Emotional Disorders, op. cit.*, 104–07; *DSM-III-R, op. cit.*, 218–20, 230–31.

6.  Regardless of how one heeds Roy Schafer's call for a language of action in psychoanalysis, his questioning of such concepts as interiority, incorporation, the self, and identity comprises a major instance of deconstruction within the psychoanalytic field. Even where one retains certain operational definitions deriving from psychoanalysis's classical repository, one has been instructed and liberated through Schafer's logical and clinical rigor. See Roy Schafer, *A New Language for Psychoanalysis* (New Haven: Yale University Press, 1976), 117–18, 123–24, 155–60, 172–75, 259–62, 312, 350–51, 264–72.

7.  See Ludwig Wittgenstein, *The Blue and Brown Books, op. cit.*, 77–85, 91–101, 152–85; John Austin, *How to do Things with Words* (Cambridge: Harvard University Press, 1975), 1–52, 94–120; John R. Searle, *Speech Acts* (Cambridge: Cambridge University Press, 1969), 3–33, 57–71, 119–23, 162–74; Jacques Derrida, "Signature Event Contex," in *Glyph 1*, ed. Samuel Weber and Henry Sussman (Baltimore: The Johns Hopkins University Press, 1977), 172–97; John R. Searle, "A Reply to Derrida," in *Glyph 1, op. cit.*, 198–208; Jacques Derrida, *Limited Inc*, in *Glyph 2*, ed. Samuel Weber and Henry Sussman (Baltimore: The Johns Hopkins University Press, 1978), 162–254; Paul

de Man, *Allegories of Reading* (New Haven: Yale University Press, 1979), 270–73.

8.   Sigmund Freud, "On Narcissism," in the *Standard Edition, op. cit.*, 14:88–89, 98–101.

9.   See Sigmund Freud, "From the History of Infantile Neurosis," in the *Standard Edition, op. cit.*, 17:29–46; "Fräulein Elisabeth von R.," in "Studies on Hysteria," in the *Standard Edition, op. cit.*, 2:139–43.

10.   Franz Kafka, "The Country Doctor," in *The Complete Stories, op. cit.*, 225.

11.   Heinz Kohut, *The Analysis of the Self, op. cit.*, 300–7.

12.   Heinz Kohut, *The Analysis of the Self, op. cit.*, 45–47, 98–99, 300–1. For analytical theatricality, see Kohut, 210.

13.   See Martin Heidegger, "The Origin of the Work of Art," in *Poetry, Language, Thought*, trans. Albert Hofstadter, (New York: Harper & Row, 1971), 67–78.

14.   Robert Musil, *The Man without Qualities*, trans. Eithne Wilkins and Ernst Kaiser (London: Martin Secker and Warburg Ltd, 1954). This translation has been reissued under the imprimatur of a number of publishers on both sides of the Atlantic. My Volume 1 was published by Capricorn Books (New York, 1965). My reference to the narrator's formulation of the "temporary insanity" of sexual arousal comes from p. 332 of this volume. The second and third volumes I was able to secure were published in the Picador series (London: Pan Books, 1979). All citations in this study follow this translation and its various reprints. (The current Volume 1 available in the United States has been taken over by yet another publisher.)

15.   Walter Benjamin, *Illuminations, op. cit.*, 83–87, 155–60, 175–79, 188–94, 218–23.

## CHAPTER 7: OBJECT RELATIONS THEORY: ALICE MILLER

1.   Alice Miller, *The Drama of the Gifted Child*, trans. Ruth Ward (New York: Basic Books, 1990), henceforth abbreviated *DGC*.

2.   Alice Miller, *Thou Shalt Not be Aware: Society's Betrayal of the Child*, trans. Hildegarde and Hunter Hannum (New York: Meridian, 1986), henceforth abbreviated *TSN*.

3.   See Friedrich Nietzsche, *Beyond Good and Evil*, trans. Walter Kaufmann (New York: Random House, 1966), 13–19, 43–56, 100–3, 109–14; *On the Genealogy of Morals and Ecce Homo*, trans. Walter Kaufmann and R.J. Hollingdale (New York: Random House, 1969), 16–20, 35–56, 62–71, 88–94, 120–29.

4.   See Jeffrey Moussaieff Masson, *The Assault on Truth: Freud's Suppression of the Seduction Theory* (New York: HarperCollins, 1992), 3–54, 107–44, 189–200.

## CHAPTER 8: ROBERT MUSIL, *THE MAN WITHOUT QUALITIES*: SETTING

1.   See Henry Sussman, "Kafka and Modern Philosophy: Wittgenstein, Deconstruction, and the Cuisine of the Imaginary," in *Afterimages of Modernity* (Baltimore: The Johns Hopkins University Press, 1990), 58–60, 63–75, 81–94.

2.   For good general introductions to Musil, placing *The Man without Qualities* in the context of his other works, see Burton Pike, *Robert Musil: An Introduction to his Work* (Ithaca: Cornell University Press, 1961) and Fredrick G. Peters, *Robert Musil: Master of the Hovering Life* (New York: Columbia University Press, 1978); for a German treatment of the novel that, like my own, recognizes the importance of object-relations theory to its interpretation and that also senses the empathic-utopian tenor of the Third Volume, see Hans-Rudolf Schärer, *Narzissmus und Utopie* (Munich: Wilhelm Fink Verlag, 1990); for an introduction addressed specifically to the novel and its philosophical issues, see Philip Payne, *Robert Musil's 'The Man without Qualities': A Critical Study* (Cambridge: Cambridge University Press, 1988); for approaches to Musil emphasizing the dichotomies in his work—between intellect and emotion in the first case and fiction and reflexivity in the second, see Stephan Reinhardt, *Studien zur Antinomie von Intellekt und Gefühl* (Bonn: H. Bouvier, 1969) and Ulf Schramm, *Fiktion und Reflexion: Überlegungen zu Musil und Beckett* (Frankfurt: Suhrkamp, 1967); for an introduction by the English translators of Musil's meganovel, see Ernst Kaiser and Eithne Wilkins, *Robert Musil: Eine Einführung in das Werk* (Stuttgart: W. Kohlhammer, 1962); for an approach to "unconscious determination" at play in Musil's work by a fine theoretician and philosopher, see Peter Henninger, *Der Buchstabe und der Geist* (Frankfurt: Peter D. Lang, 1980); also see Dietrich Hochstätter, *Sprache des Möglichen* (Frankfurt: Athenaum, 1972); two important historical approaches are David. S. Luft, *Robert Musil and the Crisis of European Culture 1880–1942* (Berkeley: University of California Press, 1980), and Hannah Hickman, *Robert Musil and the Culture of Vienna* (London: Croom Helm, 1984); three valuable essay collections are Gudrun Brokoph-Mauch, ed. *Beiträge zur Musil-Kritik* (Bern: Peter Lang, 1983); Lothar Huber and John J. White, eds., *Musil in Focus*, Institute of Germanic Studies (London: University of London, 1982), and Josef

and Johann Strutz, eds., *Robert Musil—Literatur, Philosophie, und Psychologie*, Musil-Studien 12 (Munich: Wilhelm Fink, 1984). A valuable example of Peter Henninger's work in English is his "On Literature and Condensation," *Glyph 5*, ed. Samuel Weber and Henry Sussman (Baltimore: The Johns Hopkins University Press, 1979), 114–32. I also benefitted from an unpublished article by Professor Stanley Corngold of Princeton University, "Patterns of Justification in 'Young Törless.'"

3.   It was Hegel who provided the metaphor of the play of physical forces with its fullest philosophical elaboration. See G.W.F. Hegel, *Phenomenology of Mind, op. cit.*, 79–103. Also, Henry Sussman, *The Hegelian Aftermath, op. cit.*, 33–51.

4.   Cf. D.W. Winnicott, "The Theory of the Parent-Infant Relationship," in *EPOOR, op. cit.*, 246–52; "Transitional Objects and Transitional Phenomena," in *EPOOR*, 266–69.

5.   James Joyce, *Ulysses: The Corrected Text*, ed. Hans Walter Gabler (New York: Random House, 1986), 4–19.

6.   Marcel Proust, *Swann's Way, op. cit.*, 26–27, 142–43, 188–92, 205–12, 266–68, 274–82, 334–41, 490–92. I am indebted to Jason Erlich, a student in my Spring, 1991 Honors Seminar at SUNY/Buffalo, for clarifying the pathological "relationship" between Swann and Mme Verdurin.

7.   This type of temporal irony has long been associated with the genre of the historical novel. See Georg Lukacs, *The Historical Novel*, trans., Hannah and Stanley Mitchell (London: Merlin Press, 1982), 19–88; M.M. Bakhtin, *The Dialogic Imagination*, trans., Caryl Emerson and Michael Holquist (Austin: University of Texas Press, 1981), 84–91, 133–39, 167–87, 224–58.

8.   G.W.F. Hegel, *The Philosophy of History*, trans, J. Sibree (New York: Dover, 1956), 29–34, 103–07, 256–57.

9.   Friedrich Nietzsche, *Thus Spoke Zarathustra*, trans. R.J. Hollingdale (New York: Penguin, 1975), 54–56, 130–33, 184–86, 205–09, 257–61, 275–79, 326–36.

10.   Walter Benjamin, *Illuminations, op. cit.*, 255–58.

## CHAPTER 9: *THE MAN WITHOUT QUALITIES:* AN INTER"PERSONAL" READING

1.   Gilles Deleuze and Felix Guattari, *Kafka: pour une littérature mineure*, (Paris: Minuit, 1975), 12, 25, 29–50.

2.   Hans-Rudolf Schärer, *Narzissmus und Utopismus, op. cit.*, pp. 81–157.

3.  Heinz Hartmann, *Essays on Ego Psychology* (New York: International Universities Press, 1986), 34, 83–84, 107, 145–46, 164–65, 307, 328–29; Greenberg and Mitchell, *Object Relations in Psychoanalytical Theory, op. cit.*, 257–67.

4.  G.W.F. Hegel, *The Philosophy of History, op. cit.*; Henry Sussman, "An American History Lesson: Hegel and the Historiography of Superimposition," in *Theorizing American Literature*, ed. Bainard Cowan and Joseph Kronick (Baton Rouge: Lousiana State University Press, 1991).

5.  Heinz Kohut, *The Analysis of the Self, op. cit.*, 115, 122–25, 175, 250–52, 270–73.

6.  Henry Sussman, *Afterimages of Modernity, op. cit.*, 10–35.

7.  In *The Man without Qualities* as in object-relations theory, the subject is constituted through inconsistency, specifically through erratic fluctuations between overvaluation and devaluation, affectively, between contempt and shame. The self may be conceptualized, in both cases, as a palimpsest, a colloquy of grandiose and mature versions of the self that may be thought of as *drafts*. We have already suggested above the literary possibilities for the notion of introjections, the highly-charged language through which, according to Klein, Winnicott, and above all Kernberg very young children learn to store polarized images of themselves. For the persistence of shame, see Heinz Kohut, *The Analysis of the Self, op. cit.*, 180, 184, 230–32.

## CHAPTER 10: *THE MAN WITHOUT QUALITIES:* FRIENDSHIP AND PERSISTENT ENVY

1.  Heinz Kohut, "Forms and Transformations of Narcissism," in *EPOOR, op. cit.*, 67, 74–75, 77–79, 82–85.

2.  Harry Stack Sullivan, *Conceptions of Modern Psychiatry, op. cit.*, 37–43, 46, 50, 55–56.

3.  Heinz Kohut, *The Analysis of the Self, op. cit.*, 20–21, 57, 92, 139, 185, 198, 241–46.

4.  Sigmund Freud, "On Narcissism: An Introduction (1914)" in *Standard Edition, op. cit.*, 14:88–100.

5.  See Chapter 4, note 5 above.

6.  See Jacques Derrida, "Plato's Pharmacy," in *Dissemination, op. cit.*, 63–64, 70, 73–74, 77, 93, 97–103, 118, 130–39, 152–55.

7.  This question has also been taken up by Jacques Derrida in his work on Valéry. See "Qual Quelle: Valéry's Sources," in *Margins of Philosophy, op. cit.*, 273–306.

8.  See Kernberg, *BCPN, op. cit.*, 4–6, 24–25, 134–35, 256–57.

9  G.W. Pabst, dir., "Pandora's Box" (1928).

10.  Robert Musil, *Young Törless,* trans. Eithne Wilkins and Ernst Kaiser (New York: Pantheon Books, 1955), 47–51, 61, 97–102, 182.

11.  I think of Aubrey Beardsley's illustrations for Oscar Wilde's *Salome* (1894), and of such paintings by Gustav Klimt as "Pallas Athene" (1898), "Judith I" (1901), and "Judith II" (1909).

12.  D.W. Winnicott describes the optimal cohesiveness that can result for the infant from a nurturing environment as a "continuity of Being," in "The Theory of the Parent-Infant Relationship," in *EPOOR, op. cit.*, 248–51. Heinz Kohut speaks of bringing about an "integration" of the "split-off sector" of consciousness in psychotherapy. See *The Analysis of the Self, op. cit.*, 175–79, 183–86.

## CHAPTER 11: *THE MAN WITHOUT QUALITIES:* IDEALIZATION AND REPRESSION

1.  Henry Sussman, *High Resolution: Critical Theory and the Problem of Literacy* (New York: Oxford University Press, 1989), 3–14, 50–61.

## CHAPTER 12: *THE MAN WITHOUT QUALITIES:* EROTICISM AND CRITICAL DETACHMENT

1.  M.M. Bakhtin, *The Dialogic Imagination, op. cit.*, 3–5, 11–14, 26–40, 84–90, 353–66.

2.  Marcel Proust, "The Captive," in *Remembrance of Things Past*, trans. C.K. Scott Moncrief (New York: Random House, 1970), 2:559–64.

3.  Sir Arthur Eddington, *The Nature of the Physical World: The Gifford Lectures* (1929) (New York: Macmillan, 1929), xiv–xv, 1–2, 8–10, 13, 27–29, 33–36, 47–52, 61–62, 66–68, 70, 74.

## CHAPTER 13: *THE MAN WITHOUT QUALITIES:* AN EARLY "BORDERLINE CHARACTER"

1.  Gregory Bateson, *Steps toward an Ecology of Mind* (New York: Ballantine Books, 1972), 61–72, 201–27, 271–78.

2.  Otto Kernberg, *BCPN, op. cit.*, 29–39; *Severe Personality Disorders, op. cit.*, 10–26, 295–311.

## CHAPTER 14: *THE MAN WITHOUT QUALITIES:*
## SIBLING MIRRORING

1.  See Jacques Derrida, "Signatures," in *Margins of Philosophy, op. cit.*, 327–30.

2.  See Chapter 9, note 5 above.


## CHAPTER 15:
## BORDERLINITY AND CONTEMPORARY CULTURE:
## *THE SILENCE OF THE LAMBS*

1.  Roland Barthes, *Mythologies*, trans. Anette Lavers (New York: Hill and Wang, 1972), 114–21, 129, 131, 140, 155.

2.  Some of the most interesting and productive work being done in this vein is by Joan Copjek. See, for example, her "Vampires, Breast Feeding, and Anxiety," *October*, 58 (1991), 24–43; "The Grid and the Logic of Democracy," in *The Urban Text* (Cambridge, MA: MIT Press, 1991); "Unvermögender Other: Hysteria and Democracy in America," *New Formations*, 14 (1991). Also see Slavoj Žižek, *The Sublime Object of Ideology* (London: Verso, 1989), 55–129.

3.  Thomas Harris, *The Silence of the Lambs* (New York: St. Martins, 1989).

4.  The exegetical nuance in Lecter's name was pointed out to me by a colleague, Fred See, who kindly read the section on *The Silence of the Lambs,* and who made other helpful suggestions.

5.  See Roland Barthes, *Camera Lucida*, trans. Richard Howard (New York: Hill and Wang, 1981), 27, 32, 42–45, 55–59.

6.  See Slavoj Žižek, *Looking Awry: An Introduction to Jacques Lacan through Popular Culture* (Cambridge, MA: MIT Press, 1991), 26–39, 88–106.

7.  See, for example, Dorrit Cohn, "The Narrated Monologue: Definition of a Fictional Style," *Comparative Literature*, 18 (1966), 97–112.


## CHAPTER 16: CONCLUSION

1.  As extreme examples of this narrative emptiness which is at the same time a poignant "self"-expression, see Samuel Beckett, *Molloy, Malone Dies, The Unnameable: Three Novels by Samuel Beckett* (New York: Grove Press, 1965), 33–37, 40, 56–57, 68–74, 179–82, 260–64, 290–93, 304–10.

2. Albert Camus, "The Artist at Work," in *Exile and the Kingdom*, trans. Justin O'Brien (New York: Vintage, 1958), 154-58.

3. Roy Schafer, *A New Language for Psychoanalysis, op. cit.*, 135, 165–70.

4. See Sigmund Freud, "Psycho-Analytical Notes on an Autobiographical Account of a Case of Paranoia (Dementia Paranoides)" (1911), in *The Standard Edition, op. cit.*, 12:17–34, 39–43, 53–58; also David B. Allison et. al., ed., *Psychosis and Sexual Identity: Toward a Post-Analytic View of the Schreber Case, op. cit.*

5. Hannah Green, *I Never Promised You a Rose Garden* (New York: Signet, 1964), 12–16, 20–21, 51–57, 63, 101–02, 129–37.

6. Sydney Shanberg and Dith Pran, *The Killing Fields: The Facts behind the Film*, ed. Fenella Greenfield and Nicolas Locke (London: Weidenfeld and Nicholson, 1984).

7. See, for example, Silvano Arieti, *Interpretation of Schizophrenia* (New York: Basic Books, 1974), 74–78, 93, 102–07, 113, 121–23.

8. For the notion of soft structure, see Henry Sussman, *Afterimages of Modernity, op. cit.*, 179–81.

9. See Hannah Arendt, *The Origins of Totalitarianism* (New York: Harcourt, Brace, and World, 1966), 305–40; *Eichmann in Jerusalem* (New York: Viking, 1964), 29–35, 42–48, 65–67; Robert G.L. White, *The Psychopathic God: Adolf Hitler* (New York: Basic Books, 1977), 8–22, 36–38, 79–83, 87–89, 133–35, 219–22, 251–53, 335–43; William L. Shirer, *The Rise and Fall of the Third Reich* (New York: Simon and Schuster, 1960), 6–28, 80–90, 109–13.

10. See *Selected Letters of Rainer Maria Rilke*, trans. R.F.C. Hull (London: Macmillan & Co., 1946), 186–87 (to Lou Andreas-Salomé, December 28, 1911), 196–98 (to Emil Freiherr von Gebsattel, January 14, 1912).

11. Theodor Adorno, *Minima Moralia*, trans. E.F.N. Jephcott (London: Verso Editions, 1978), 28.

12. Jacques Derrida, *Of Grammatology, op. cit.*, 107–18.

13. For the productive power of aggression and self-destructiveness, see Georges Bataille, *Visions of Excess: Selected Writings, 1927–39*, ed. Allan Stoekl (Minneapolis: University of Minnesota Press, 1985), 66–71, 84–90, 92–102.

14. Heinz Kohut, *Analysis of the Self, op. cit.*, 276–81.

15. In search of some authoritative treatment of methodology in Cultural Studies, I consulted this heading in "Bison," the basic library inventory at the State University of New York at Buffalo. Under 250 entries, I saw nothing that appeared to serve this purpose. Instead, I found a wide variety of titles, many purporting to explore the cultural impact

of such interests as political power, sexuality, literacy, gender, and ethnic and racial affiliations. This finding is in keeping with the skepticism toward authority that the culture of Cultural Studies has fostered. It suggests at the same time that the term has arisen as much as a rallying cry as a category; that its contributions to some extent anticipate its theory and specifications. We should keep this *bricolage* in mind when we evaluate spirited debates between Cultural Studies and the movements it would reform, whether of the radical intellectual or stodgy varieties.

16. Walter Benjamin, *Illuminations, op. cit.,* 169.

# INDEX